WITHDRAWN

AVON PUBLIC LIBRARY
BOX 977 / 200 BENCHMARK RD.
AVON, CO 81620

A VILLAGE
WITH
MY NAME

A VILLAGE
WITH
MY NAME

A Family History of China's
Opening to the World

Scott Tong

The University of Chicago Press
Chicago and London

The University of Chicago Press, Chicago 60637
The University of Chicago Press, Ltd., London
© 2017 by Scott Tong

All rights reserved. No part of this book may be used
or reproduced in any manner whatsoever without
written permission, except in the case of brief
quotations in critical articles and reviews. For more
information, contact the University of Chicago
Press, 1427 E. 60th St., Chicago, IL 60637.

Published 2017
Printed in the United States of America

26 25 24 23 22 21 20 19 18 17   1 2 3 4 5

ISBN-13: 978-0-226-33886-6 (cloth)
ISBN-13: 978-0-226-33905-4 (e-book)
DOI: 10.7208/chicago/9780226339054.001.0001

Library of Congress Cataloging-in-Publication Data

Names: Tong, Scott, author.
Title: A village with my name : a family history of
    China's opening to the world / Scott Tong.
Description: Chicago : The University of Chicago
    Press, 2017. | Includes index.
Identifiers: LCCN 2017017823| ISBN 9780226338866
    (cloth : alk. paper) | ISBN 9780226339054 (e-book)
Subjects: LCSH: Tong family. | Families—China—
    History—20th century. | Chinese American
    families—History—20th century. | China—
    History—20th century.
Classification: LCC CT1827.5.T66 T66 2017 | DDC
    305.8951073—dc23 LC record available at https://
    lccn.loc.gov/2017017823

♾ This paper meets the requirements of ANSI/NISO
Z39.48–1992 (Permanence of Paper).

Contents

The Characters

Mildred Zhao (also Chao, Djao)—grandmother
Lily Sun Hsu—aunt
Constantine Sun (also Eddie Sun)—uncle
Anna Sun (Tong)—mother (also Sun Ailian)
    Welthy Honsinger Fisher—Mildred's teacher and correspondent
    Anna Melissa Graves—Mildred's teacher and correspondent
Sun Maozi—distant cousin in the Sun village
Sun Peipei—distant cousin in Shanghai
Cai Su—distant uncle in Shanghai

Preface

In the last weeks before returning to the states after a three-and-a-half-year work assignment in Shanghai, I became determined to make one last stop. To be specific, I wanted to visit a bank. Actually, to be more specific, I really only wanted to see its ceiling. This was an odd quest. Given the opportunity to report on the world's most dynamic and confusing economy for the public radio business show *Marketplace*, I'd taken far more exciting rides across China.

Typically they involved Chinese people rather than Chinese things. Two men in villages outside Xian in the remote western province of Shaanxi explained on tape how they'd been kidnapped and sold as slaves to brickmaking-kiln bosses—for less than a hundred dollars each. Mothers of children with lead poisoning from an illegal smelting furnace described the facility's smokestack: it was so low the belched pollutants simply fell to the ground and leached into the soil and groundwater. A convicted baby seller mapped out for me his trafficking network, which included the orphanage where my own daughter lived. Still, I hankered for this ceiling.

It had been added to my to-do list before moving back to the Washington, DC, suburbs, by my *Marketplace* bureau colleague Cecilia Chen. She'd heard me complain: I'd produced so many breaking news stories about Right-Now China—snapshots in time—that I shortchanged myself of the relevant history to contextualize what I'd been seeing. Sometimes you have to flip back in the album to try to understand the pictures you're seeing now. And flip slowly. So much of mainland life amounts to an arms race: beat the competition, bargain for the best price, stuff more knowledge into your kid than what the neighbor's has, hustle into the elevator and jab DOOR CLOSE before the next person can nose her way in. "If you're in a car waiting at a red light, you have to start driving *before* it turns green," my Shanghai friend John Lu advised me the first time we met. "Otherwise you never make it through." Without realizing it, I'd joined this race myself, and I needed to stop running and look around.

This building is likely familiar to you if you've visited Shanghai. It's the signature dome on the Bund, the historic skyline along the west bank of the Huangpu River. You can't miss it from the famous Pearl Tower, or one of the trophy skyscrapers across the river in Pudong. For my money, the best view of the domed structure comes from the deck of a budget river ferry, which at forty cents a person at the time was the best family deal in town. The building once housed the Hongkong and Shanghai Bank, and now belongs to a Chinese state bank.

On a baking summer day in 2010, I emerged from the Line 2 subway at Nanjing East Road and walked through the oldest part of town. Its narrow streets and world-beating traffic always bring to mind Lower Manhattan. At the waterfront, I took a right and minutes later entered the bank. Heeding Cecilia's advice, I walked with purpose to the center of the ornate marble lobby and looked up.

Before I could even reach for my camera, a security guard sidled up. "No pictures." Okay. And then I saw them: brilliant mosaic frescoes, each forming one side of an octagon surrounding the dome. Every tiled mural dates back to the 1920s and is an artistic rendering of a skyline from somewhere in the world. Each stands for a bank branch from a past golden age of globalization a century ago: Shanghai, Hong Kong, Tokyo, Calcutta, New York, London, Bangkok, and Paris. The Eight Seas, I said to myself. In the foreground of each city landscape is a protective Western god or goddess; the Statue of Liberty stands guard before the Manhattan skyline, for instance. Further up, in the center of the dome, is a mosaic of sun and moon goddesses, all with Caucasian faces—a Western-style masterpiece that might belong in Rome or Istanbul rather than Shanghai.

This captivated me, and then it puzzled me. These images hearken back to Shanghai's bad old days of colonial oppression and humiliation, at least in the party's telling of history (which, for most mainlanders, remains the only version). They represent a time when white men in gunboats shot their way into China and snatched up the best sections of port cities to build mansions, trading houses, bars, and racetracks. This is a shameful past, in a culture with no market for shame. How had this all survived Mao Zedong's closed-door, xenophobic regime of the 1950s and '60s, so adept at photoshopping China's past? Why was the art still up there? Before I could linger on this question, the guard returned to nudge me on my way. Transaction over.

I'd later learn the preservation story behind these frescoes. In the 1950s, after the party took over the building—and the country— to house the headquarters of the new Shanghai city government, the dome artwork was plastered over. But it was not destroyed. In one telling of the story, comrades sought to chisel off the mosaic tiles, but an enterprising architect suggested it'd be easier to just cover them. The masterpiece remained hidden underneath for four decades, until its discovery by renovators in the 1990s. Under new ownership, the Eight Seas were polished off and redisplayed for a new reform era. It had become okay for China to look outward again.

Globalization drifts in and out of fashion, often quickly and without warning. As I write this in early 2017, we are living in quite a moment here. The modern connected age of open borders and markets is being vilified in ways I've not seen in my adult life. Raising drawbridges appears on the ballot wherever I look, and in the States, the handy new epithet is "globalist." Where this all leads is impossible to know, and in any event I'm not in the predicting business (there are books and investment advisors for that kind of thing). But one thing is clear: much of the angst, ambivalence, and outright hostility toward today's interlinked world has to do with China.

Without question, the mainland has benefited from global inter-connections, paradoxically because its workers have been poor for so long and thus willing to work for what you and I consider peanuts. It seems to have happened quickly. China frequently is cast as a newcomer powerhouse to the top division, emerging out of nowhere. You know the framing of Instant China: Mao dies in the mid-1970s, Deng Xiaoping takes over soon after, and the story starts there. Anything relevant is After Deng, AD.

Instant China makes for snappy, compelling stories. If you're reading this, there's a reasonable chance that you, like me, have parachuted into the mainland for a few days and heard a memorable life story of a cabbie, bond trader, or grubby dumpling seller. That person's fortunes turned dramatically after Deng's policy reforms, known as "reform and opening," or *gaige kaifang*. Well-intended mainlanders can *gaige kaifang* you into submission: *Gaige kaifang* delivered economic and geographic mobility. It allowed for private property, for nobodies to open vegetable stalls and electronic work-shops. *Gaige kaifang* brought meat to the table. The implication is, whatever preceded *gaige kaifang* was a lengthy period of numbing suffering that amounts to China's Old Testament: famines, pesti-lence, floods, wars, colonialism, political witch-hunts, bound feet, and hyperinflation. The fall before the *gaige kaifang* redemption.

It's a very clean story I myself told at times on the radio. My first big profile story in 2005 was of a poor, barely literate farmer in the western province of Sichuan. Mr. Xu, a sinewy man with a deep outdoor laborer's tan and a crewcut, hailed from the village of Guang'an, the home of Deng Xiaoping. He sought his fortunes in the metropolis of Chongqing, finding grunt work as a porter; he roped people's goods and boxes to a bamboo stick slung across his shoulders, carrying them to the appointed destination for a nego-tiated fee. Part human, part mule. He slept in a drafty group house in a shantytown, on the bottom level of a barracks-style bunk bed for twenty. I joined him on a return trip home to his village. Sud-denly, Mr. Xu transformed into Big Man on Campus, the self-made tale of a village boy who went to the big city and made good. Mr. Xu used his savings to build the tallest house in the village. Stopping at a neighbor's house for lunch, he caught me admiring a gigantic wok in the kitchen, perhaps four feet across. Mr. Xu pointed at it and declared: "Mine's bigger."

This telling serves multiple constituencies. For the ruling Communist Party in desperate search of legitimacy, it undergirds the essential founding myth that an economic miracle occurred on its watch. For international reporters, it provides a clean narrative to make sense of a big, chaotic place. But I am not so sure now. It's like taking a snapshot of a flower with a closeup fish-eye lens, blurring the background. The picture is devoid of context.

There is a phrase that captures this context-less view of China, a phrase I've appropriated from a global banker and author named Graham Jeal: skyscraper syndrome. Wowed by a masculine high-rise, trophy bullet train, nineteen-course feast, or airport auto-flush toilet, an observer looks at China and vacates rational thought. He or she moves on to a series of regrettable business or personal decisions, and returns home convinced the mainland has taken a controlling stake in the universe. China is, well, different. Eventually for those who stay, the fog begins to lift. The toilets in the trophy high-rises aren't fixed quite right. The buildings stay vacant, and the workers inside underperform. A more nuanced picture starts to come into view.

At this moment in time, it's worth looking at China and its place in the world with fresh eyes. *A Village with My Name* is my own pursuit of a useful historical perspective, a project that began after I returned to the United States in 2010. It's a tricky undertaking, given there is so much history to consider. "The Chinese people have five thousand years of history," one of my first Mandarin teachers lectured to me in 1980—a line that has been repeated to me five thousand times since. But how can a new story about China be so very old? How relevant is all that mind-numbing history of emperors and dynasties to today? Where did today's China *really* come from?

My suggestion here—which, to be honest, reflects the thinking of many intellectual historians—is that critical roots go back to a prior heyday of globalization: the century before World War I. Going back at least to the nineteenth century, self-interested Chinese (and foreign) nationals took the seeds of modernity and sprinkled them on mainland soil. As it turns out, some of these first movers are on my family tree. If you know anything about China's recent past, you know that only some people were rewarded for looking outward. Others paid a heavy price when political winds changed and a newly xenophobic China slammed its doors to the world.

The upshot of that decision was to delay progress. Fundamentally, China's is a story of coming late to modernity. Many Chinese have told me: *We came late to the industrial revolution, late to the digital revolution. We are not going to miss the next one.*

This book exists in three parts. Part 1 is what I call the Great Opening. My paternal great-grandfather Tong Zhenyong was an early member of the scholar class to get out of the backwater Tong ancestral village along the Grand Canal. He made his way to Tokyo, studying politics and economics, dabbling in politics with radical Chinese revolutionaries, and marrying a Japanese wife (this apparently came as a great surprise to his Chinese wife upon his return). Maternal grandmother Mildred Zhao attended a boarding school in Nowhere, China, run by American missionary women. There she first dreamed of studying in the United States. She had her feet unbound, learned English and piano, and rose to become lead accompanist to the Nanchang Glee Club. American books and plays and ideas were all around her, until the political winds shifted.

Part 2 is the Great Interruption. Foreign connections became frowned upon, and Mildred and her husband, my grandfather Carleton Sun, were accused by cousins as "dressing too Western." Mildred fled when the Communists came. Carleton was arrested. Uncle Tong Bao on the other side of my family is a tale of two stories in one. Abandoned by his father and brother (my father) in wartime, he suffered for the anti-Communist political sins of his father, and then redeemed himself in the reform era, thanks to a top-shelf university education and a gig at a Black & Decker power tool plant.

Part 3: the Great Resumption. Uncle Tong Bao's son, my first cousin Tong Chengkan, works at a General Motors assembly plant and proudly drives a Buick, though in modern Shanghai he fears he can never afford a home. Or a spouse. The reform era has sparked an economic arms race, and so much money sloshing around in the system has tempted well-connected officials to bend the rules and take a cut, no matter the human implications. My wife and I adopted our daughter, Guo Shanzhen, from an orphanage we later learned was near the center of an international baby-selling trade—American dollars chasing Chinese baby girls. This book seeks to take a long view of how China opened up to the outside world, told through the lives of five people across five generations on my family tree.

At the outset of this project, I did what reporters do reflexively: hunt for books and experts. I read the Chinese history tomes on my shelf that I'd pledged to read in Shanghai but never got around to. I looked up scholars in Wuhan, Pittsburgh, and Ann Arbor.

Quickly, I stumbled onto a history fight, a debate this history minor from a long time ago should have remembered. To simplify ridiculously, there are two competing ways to understand change over time: the dominant "rupture" camp focuses on big turning points: the French Revolution and Enlightenment. The steam engine. Presidents and generals. *Gaige kaifang*.

In the opposing corner sit scholars who see change through gradual evolution. They are adherents of "continuity." As they see it, the Big Men in Time like Newton and Copernicus and Galileo cashed in on key moments, but their revolutions were built on earlier, incremental advances from the Middle Ages. Change builds on change. Things go further back. In the case of China, the argument is that the Communist era was less a beginning than an interruption in a longer process of opening up. What emerges from the continuity school is an under-told story of China: of a civilization and a people linked to an earlier, discredited age of globalization.

There was one big challenge in this project that surprised me. Yes, this pursuit crashed into censorship and maddening bureaucracy. Police officers and officials adept at stonewalling made head-scratching statements like "Personnel files are not for individuals to see (only employers can see)." But by far the bigger and unexpected barrier was self-censorship. The sources in my family were keen on not cooperating, and often avoided the most salient and personal questions. It's understandable. China is a society built on status and avoiding shame. You can line-dry your undershorts in a busy alley, but family dirty laundry stays discreetly inside. "We're ashamed of what we did during the Cultural Revolution," Aunt Qi Menglan told me over dinner at her modest apartment in Shanghai.

Picture an uncomfortable child on stage. When my youngest son, Daniel, was three, his preschool class at the Rainbow Bridge International School in western Shanghai performed a holiday dance to some Disney song (about animals, I think). The music began, and his young classmates—Elsa from Switzerland, Priya from India, Julius of Germany—marched, clapped, rolled over, and sang, side by side and somewhat in sync. Daniel disengaged. He retreated two steps from the formation, turned his back squarely to the audience, and bowed his head as if his chin were Velcroed to his chest. My family is a little like that.

In the end, though, the people I consulted for this project were gracious enough—or perhaps they simply relented. *A Village with My Name* is long-form journalism that borrows from leading scholars in history and economics. It draws from a reporter's notebook and audio recorder, preserved diaries and letters, a vast set of interviews, a multiyear reporting tour of China, return trips with my parents to their ancestral villages, government archives, old family letters, and a lifetime of dinner-table conversations with relatives.

Upon exiting the old Hongkong and Shanghai Bank, I paused at the waterfront as I always like to do, to observe the barges trolling up and down the Huangpu. For so many generations, the Bund stood as an outpost for opportunists—legitimate and shady—from every direction: opium sellers from London, property developers from Baghdad, bankers from Ningbo, barbers from Hangzhou, Jewish refugees from Germany, prostitutes from Russia, missionaries from Syracuse. I have conducted a bit of my own business here. At the north end of the Bund I drank lattes with a market researcher who likes to Google himself daily. Cathy and I rang in the New Year at a deafening waterfront bar with too many expats. I attended the grand opening of the Peninsula Hotel, microphone in hand. To the south end, I chased behind our older son, Evan, then a nine-year-old dirty-blond kid in wheeled Heelys sneakers, encircled by gawking tourists. I attended book talks at the Shanghai International Literary Festival, and dined with a journalist colleague visiting from back home in Washington—the late, great Gwen Ifill.

Staring at the river prompted a new thought in my head, the way only water can: Did Grandfather Carleton and Grandmother Mildred ever see that same bank ceiling? This was their town too, from a past golden age of the bourgeoisie. But by 1950 China had turned inward, and my grandparents were deemed enemies with foreign connections, even by members of their own families. Their experiences became historically incorrect, silenced and obscured along with millions of others'. But their stories, like the frescoes, are still there, just beneath the surface and waiting to be uncovered. If you find yourself on the wrong side of history, no one tells yours—except perhaps your grandson.

PART ONE | The Great Opening

| Chapter One | SECRETS OF THE TONG VILLAGE |

Next time, you eat at *my* house.
—Third cousin Tong Daren

My dad looks over and shakes his head, the way a doctor does after whispering *cancer*. We've squandered the better part of this steamy day pursuing a place that may no longer even exist: the ancestral Tong family village. Hours ago we set out in a rental car that came with a driver—a slim man named Mr. Xu and his silver Honda Odyssey minivan—with two clues: a very general location of the hamlet, somewhere in a vast stretch of soybean and rice fields in northern Jiangsu province five hours north of civilization Shanghai; and an obsolete name of the village dating to pre-Communist days.

We've been away awhile. The last Tong on our limb of the family tree was born in the village in 1880. Soon after, our direct ancestors began venturing out, during an age of discovery for China in the modern industrial era—its nineteenth-century enlightenment. They'd end up in faraway places: Tokyo, Nanjing, Nanchang, Taipei, Minneapolis, Poughkeepsie. And now Shanghai, where I was assigned as bureau chief for the American public radio business and economics program *Marketplace*. The cliché metaphor for China's economic transformation, most often attributed to the late reformer Deng Xiaoping, is "crossing the river by feeling for the stones." Now, Dad and I are trying to return back across the water.

Mr. Xu's Odyssey has driven in a series of big circles, returning once and again to the same nondescript stretch of China's Grand Canal. It just keeps looking the same. More than a thousand miles from Beijing in the north to Hangzhou to the south, this waterway outruns both the Suez and Panama waterways. On this day, it seems even longer than that.

The place we are looking for was once called Fu Ma Ying. The old name of the village went obsolete in 1949, when the Communists took the mainland and proceeded to rewrite history, street names and town names. At the local registry in the nearest city, Huai'an, no one had ever heard of the place, or of any Tongs in the area. At a nearby police station, officers said little and offered less. So we resorted to pestering strangers—pedestrians, cabbies, food peddlers—for some sign of Fu Ma Ying. Quickly, the inquiries took on a predictable sequence: an initial moment of hope, a diversion from the main topic, and finally the phrase *bu tai qing chu*. It's not very clear.

At a bus stop by the canal, I approach a middle-aged man with a crew cut and a face weathered by a life of farming. Before he can talk his way out, I pounce quickly. This much I've learned as a reporter in China: when you spot your prey, you cannot hesitate. "Hi, we're looking for a place called Fu Ma Ying," I say. "Heard of it?"

"Fu. Ma. Ying." The man repeats the words out loud. And then, as if it would provide further illumination, says them again but three times as loud. "*Fu. Ma. Ying.* Why are you going there?"

"It's our *lao jia.*" Old home.

"Ahh! *Lao jia!*" He moves in with a half smile, as if I've earned a few Confucian filial points for seeking out family roots. "Do you still have relatives there?"

"Don't know. That's why we're looking. Fu Ma Ying is the old name."

Pause. "Where are you from?"

"Shanghai. I was born in America. Can't you tell by my accent? Now I work here in China."

"Are you married?"

I know where this is going. "Yes."

"Children?"

"Three."

"Three! You must be rich."

There is an assumed equivalence here between children and wealth, which I must admit makes some economic sense: the more you have, the more you have. Okay. The thing is, the rule only applies to people making purely rational, long-term decisions.

"Not so much."

Crew-Cut Man moves on to the next topic. "Shanghai *tai ji, tai luan*." Shanghai is too crowded, chaotic. "They're snobs, looking down on us country folk."

"Yes, they are." For this I have no argument.

"Are you traveling by yourself?"

"No, my father's with me, in the car. He also lives in America. So, Fu Ma Ying? Can you help me find it?"

Another pause.

"Bu tai qing chu."

I move on. I've lived in greater China off and on for more than a dozen years. I have taken years of Mandarin lessons. I can recite a Tang dynasty poem. Occasionally I drink bubble tea. But my understanding of China ends at *bu tai qing chu*.

In a literal sense, the phrase does mean "not very clear." But it has a linguistic flexibility. Each time I grasp a new context for *bu tai qing chu*, it turns up in a new way. It means at least these things: *I can't help you. I will not help you. I don't want to tell you. I'll get in trouble. You don't deserve to know. I'm moving on now.* A great paradox of China is, people make declaratory statements with absolute certainty, yet at crucial moments reach into their pockets and pull out *bu tai qing chu*.

This roundabout exchange has eaten up twenty minutes I'll never get back, but this is how things work. Chinese civilization goes back five thousand years, the saying goes. My people have time.

I would later learn Fu Ma Ying was a place of military intrigue, going back to the Ming dynasty in the fifteenth century. According to historian Shih-shan Henry Tsai in his book *Perpetual Happiness*, an army leader named Mei Yin lived there with his wife, the princess daughter of a renowned emperor and Ming Dynasty founder, Zhu Yuanzhang. At some point, things got complicated. The emperor died, his fourth son usurped the throne, and the new guy in charge deemed Mei Yin in Fu Ma Ying a threat. Mei Yin died mysteriously soon after, in what his obituary calls a drowning "suicide." China has its share of mysterious accidents.

My father and I have limited time to find the place. He's flown out from his home in Oregon, with my mother, for a three-week stint with us. We have budgeted this weekend to look for the village. For him, this is a filial act. He fled the mainland during wartime at the age of ten, exactly sixty years ago, and his return to the *lao jia* amounts to a pilgrimage of respect to where the Tongs began. Still, I suspect this pursuit matters less to him than me. For Dad, this is something to do once: go to the place, cross it off the Confucian bucket list, and tell his friends about it. I can understand that.

I, however, am developing an obsession with this quest, and it's unclear why. To organize my own thoughts as we drive—and drive . . . I start scribbling words in my reporter's notebook. "First mover," I write. This phrase comes straight out of Father Spitzer's freshman theology class at Georgetown: the Problem of God (Aquinas: Every single thing must be moved by something else, but at some point there had to be an original First Mover, or God). Every migration story starts with person one leaving a place for another place. That person in the village was Great-Grandfather Tong Zhenyong. This much I know. But how did he get out? When? Why? A lot of Chinese Americans have written eloquently about their families' immigrant experiences, but often those are tales of second or third movers. I care about the first: Tong Zhenyong's story.

Then I write the Chinese phrase I've heard my mainland relatives utter over and over: *haiwai guanxi*. Overseas relations. This is the punishable offense that doomed so many in the 1950s–'60s era of strongman Mao Zedong. For his association with an anti-Communist father living in Taiwan, Uncle Tong Bao was sent down to the countryside for a full decade. His mother was publicly tortured and shamed for the same reason. In the twisted symmetry of the Communist Party, when one person goes abroad and becomes a de facto political enemy, several of that person's relatives back home incur a disproportionate cost. How did that play out in the village, for those left behind?

I write "stubborn." When I was young, my parents wore that word out describing this pesky younger brother who once threw a tantrum by lying down in the center of a busy Taipei street (long story). Simply put, I'm digging into the past because so many in my family want to bury it. My maternal grandfather's name has barely been mentioned in my lifetime because of his now-shameful politics during World War II. He died alone in a faraway prison labor camp, almost entirely forgotten by family members trying to survive and protect themselves. There's an old imperial saying that when a person commits a serious crime, punishment extends to nine generations of his family. So it's best to "draw a clear boundary line of separation" from offenders and never mention them. The upshot in my family is that certain stories get actively forgotten, wiped from the historical record. But not if I can help it.

Two barges putter by on the canal, with the innards of industrial modernity on their backs: rice, wheat, cement, coal, sand, logs, pipes. The vessels move at different speeds, like China itself. More than half the population is racing ahead, in cities, to join the global, digital, service-economy future; the rest toil in places like the Tong village—if it still exists—growing the same grains and vegetables their ancestors did.

The canal itself was, like China's Great Wall, built out of imperial self-interest. In the sixth century, the Sui dynasty emperor in the north ordered a canal to the south to provide access to two things: taxes and food. The waterway did not take form without cost or misery, and surely people in and around the Tong village paid a price. Half the conscripted laborers are assumed to have died on the job. Summer temperatures in this area peak at 105 degrees, and in winter the water can freeze over.

Once built, the canal carried revenue collectors southbound to China's fertile region, to take a share of grain from each family. On the way back, barges also carried produce, rice, and salt. Domestic water transport helped create a vast, efficient marketplace; rice sold for a remarkably similar price all across China in the early 1700s. In a way, the canal serves to connect the Chinese people, rather than separate them—the great anti-wall of China.

By the time my great-grandfather was born in the late nineteenth century, the canal was long in decline. Like the Erie Canal back home, these old waterways lost out to superior technology: steamships allowed bigger, faster vessels to travel the ocean and supersede canal trade. The new "iron horse" of railroads replaced horse-drawn canal boats. In China the problem was also maintenance. Dredging of the rivers and canals fell off in the late nineteenth century, as the Qing dynasty began to crumble politically and fiscally.

If this forlorn part of northern Jiangsu ever had a heyday, I don't know when it was. Across China, people from the area known as Subei are looked down on, and have historically occupied low rungs of society. My mainland-born friend John Lu, an ad executive, put it succinctly when I first met him and told him about my *lao jia*. "No one," he said, "has any reason to go there."

My father asks Mr. Xu to drive us back to our hotel, an acknowledgment of defeat—at least, for now. There's still time for a miracle. In this moment of fantasy, a classic '80s movie scene pops into my head, from one of the Indiana Jones films. You've seen it: the protagonist played by Harrison Ford finds himself stumped in a library, searching for a hidden tomb. Then, in a moment of illumination, he hustles up a circular stairway to gain a new perspective and sees it. X marks the spot.

"Do we know any Tong relatives still living in the village?" I ask my dad.

"I don't think so." He's never been there either. In a way, he's more of an outsider than I am. My father left the mainland in 1949, fleeing the People's Liberation Army. By now, I'd spent three years in Shanghai with my wife, Cathy, and our three young children. The kids attended Rainbow Bridge International School on the grounds of the Shanghai Zoo. Their favorite meal was a thirty-cent noodle bowl down the street from our apartment. Cathy had taken Mandarin lessons twice a week.

My Nokia cellphone rings. It's Cecilia, my news assistant, from Shanghai. "I found info on Fu Ma Ying online." she says. I'd texted her two hours back, suggesting a last-ditch Internet search for the place. This was the pre-smartphone era, and in any event we'd found the Chinese web unhelpful for this kind of thing. It was hard to find good maps and directions, analog or digital. "It's near the town Jinhe, just north up the canal." Cecilia gives a few directions, Mr. Xu fires up the Odyssey, and Dad sits up and smiles. X marks the spot.

I'm not so sure. Perhaps we have simply found the right haystack. If experience is any guide, we may still have in our way villages and sub-villages, roads without names, and *bu tai qing chus*.

By the time we enter the town of Jinhe it's almost five in the evening. Mr. Xu drives up to a bespectacled forty-something man walking out of a store, puts down the window, and gets to the point. "Fu Ma Ying?"

"Fu Ma Ying," he repeats, and approaches. A good sign. Mr. Xu passes him a cigarette, a down payment for his time. The man doesn't know the exact spot but offers the services of a friend, makes a cellphone call, and crosses the street—presumably to find this friend. Again we wait. So I get out and step into a gritty general-goods store, the kind you see all across China.

I love these. The smell brings me back to living in Taiwan in the early '80s (my father was recruited from IBM in the States to work for the Taiwanese government, and then he left for the consumer technology firm Acer). The whiff in the air is not exactly fragrant, but it's familiar: a mix of past-expiration soap and mothballs. The items on the shelves here are remarkably similar to that time: bottled orange juice separated into its constituent liquids, chocolate bars that have begun to powderize, knockoff-brand ramen noodles, prawn-flavored chips, batteries hiding under dusty glass countertops.

But there is one thing that is different: the toothpaste. During my days in Taiwan, the dominant and wholly politically incorrect brand we brushed with was known as Darkie. The logo featured a black man in a top hat sporting bleach-white teeth. But now, having been acquired by Colgate-Palmolive, the brand goes by Darlie, and in the revised logo the man appears racially ambiguous. He's somewhat lighter. Yet for all the corporate updating, the Mandarin on the packaging remains *black person toothpaste*. Upon seeing that, I experience a confusing sort of nostalgia.

Exiting, I look over the three blocks of shops that make up Jinhe. In America, a visitor might say this place's best days were behind it. In China, though, it's the opposite. Things are picking up here. Years ago, these stores had just two choices of chocolate instead of twenty. They didn't have plug-in freezers to stock ice cream bars. There were no sidewalk merchants hawking next-generation rooftop solar thermal panels for people to enjoy hot baths.

The bespectacled Jinhe guy returns to the car with his friend, named Mr. Zhu, who wears the round face and gray slacks of an office man. But something is wrong. Mr. Zhu has no cigarette in his mouth. He hesitates as we fire questions his way. "Do you know Fu Ma Ying? Can you point us there?" I wonder if he's assessing the situation for what's in it for him: perhaps a free meal, a potential business deal, maybe a kickback from any purchases he can recommend to us. I suspect he's waiting for some kind of offer. Then, to my surprise, Mr. Zhu fishes out his phone and things happen quickly. He calls a local village head and arranges for him to meet us; this would be our third middleman, and I have no idea how close we are. Mr. Zhu hops into the minivan next to me, and we drive on.

"Where are you coming from?" he asks.

"Shanghai."

"Too crowded. Too chaotic."

I nod and pivot the conversation. "What do you grow here?" We've left the town and turned right into a vast stretch of farmland.

"*Dadou, shui dao.*" Soybeans, rice. I nod and process *shui dao*. In English it's "rice," but Mandarin has different terms for the stages of a grain's life. Planted in the field, it's *shui dao*. After harvest and de-husking, it sells in stores as *mi*. Sticky rice is *nuo mi*. And once you cook it, it becomes *fan*, which to further confuse things also refers to an entire meal. There is a linguistic precision at work, similar to the way Americans have separate words for wheat, flour, dough, batter, bread, bagel, brioche.

The "road" we're driving on has turned into one-lane paved path, about the width of a bike trail back home. It has the added drama of five-foot-deep irrigation ditches on either side. As Mr. Xu drives, I try not to consider the odds of a car coming the other way, except that's all I can think about. About a mile down, we stop at a house on the left to pick up the village head. Surely he knows Fu Ma Ying.

"No, but I know someone who does," he says as he climbs in too. He points us down the road as I survey this circus car of five. Our driver, the village head, and Mr. Zhu are all standard height, skinny, nondescript. You'd walk past them.

But the man who suddenly steps in front of the moving mini-van, daring it to stop, is different. He stands taller and rounder. He sports a well-executed comb-over and has an overt self-confidence—the confidence and penetrating stare of a member of the Communist Party. He wears a beige zip-up polyester jacket, and I can't help but look for a Members Only logo. He is the area party secretary.

The man gets in. Party secretaries, even in remote places like these, are singularly important persons in a favor-based society. And he knows it. He says nothing and expresses nothing, yet transforms the mood of the minivan the way a priest might. We are all a little nervous. The party secretary directs us to a road where the gravel ends, yielding to a narrow brick walkway only navigable on foot. We get out and walk. To our left, newly planted poplar trees line the walk, and on the right a brownish creek creeps along more slowly than we do. A cluster of unremarkable gray concrete houses comes into view. No one has to say it: this is the Tong village.

This makes for an underwhelming homecoming. The path is populated by pink plastic trash bags and cigarette butts, but there is no sound, save for the occasional cluck of an unseen chicken. The main smell emanates from the creek, which appears to serve as clothes-washing basin, kitchen sink, and sewer. The Tong village seems more notable for what it doesn't have: roads, a central gathering spot, an organizational plan, anything to buy or sell. John Lu was right—there is no good reason to come here. I ask myself, *Is this all there is?*

And yet I pick up the pace, as we have found this place after all.

Fu Ma Ying, the Tong village, our *lao jia*, it is still standing. This lit-
tered ground to me isn't exactly hallowed, but how do I put this . . .
It's one thing to know where you were born; it's quite another to
walk in the place you are from. Generations of Tongs past have
walked this path before. I have to say, this reaction surprises even
me, someone so un-Chinese in so many ways.

A dozen people suddenly gather. In China, faster than anywhere
else I've seen, a crowd can materialize instantly at the sight of
something new: a fight, a car crash, a free product sample. These
people are almost all elderly; squinting, crooked, sun-beaten.
Hands clasped behind their backs, they stare intently and wait
for someone to start talking. This much I know: it's not for me
to talk first in the presence of an elder (my dad) and a political
leader (the party secretary in the faux Members Only jacket). So I
smile and search the faces for the trademark feature so many of us
Tong males have: unruly bushy eyebrows, suggestive of the thick-
browed Communist revolutionary Zhou Enlai. Or perhaps Michael
Dukakis. I do not see the brows.

"*Ni hao*," my dad begins. "Hello. May I ask your name, please? My
name is Tong Hu." I look down. Like me, he wastes a lot of words
getting to the point. People who have lived in Taiwan speak with
a Mandarin verbiage cluttered with polite, extraneous words that
make for inefficiency on the mainland.

A seventy-something man in a black wool driving cap steps forward. He is taller than everyone here. "We are all Tongs here, of
course! This is the Tong family village. For every hundred of us here,
ninety-nine are named Tong."

Naturally. We should have known this. Everyone here is from the
same root family, and this is not the kind of place to attract outsiders. Dad explains he's visiting from the States and moves on to his
own life story. He talks with his face and his hands, with a youthful curiosity that seems out of place here. Then he introduces me,
with a phrase I've never quite gotten used to all these years. "This
is my number-two son."

The villagers engage in a local dialect we struggle to follow. This
much I pick up from all directions: *We know your family. Your aunt,
the one from Taiwan, she visited a few years ago.*

That information would have come in handy earlier in the day.

I remember her. She wore red. What year was that?

Your grandfather is buried a couple miles away. What's America like? Is it nicer? Of course it is—why are you asking him that? Did you eat?

I start recording video on my camera to document the episode. Through the viewfinder, I see Dad talking to the tall man with great energy. Everyone seems to talk at once. At the edge of the frame, our driver, Mr. Xu, wears a satisfied grin of mission accomplished. Two of the local guys we've picked up smoke cigarettes on the perimeter. The party secretary stands alone, wearing an awkward pose. He has wedged his right hand into the zipper opening of his jacket, as if he's wearing a sling. Or reaching for an inside pocket. Or reciting some pledge of Chinese allegiance that doesn't exist.

As I record and listen in, new clues about my great-grandfather emerge. He hailed from an educated family here in the village, married and had three daughters, and then went off to Japan to study. He returned with a Japanese wife, something not uncommon for the time. And yet, I wonder how that went down.

A stooped old man approaches me, and I hit *stop*. He's likely in his late seventies and at this moment appears to be the smallest man in China. He wears a navy-blue jacket that reminds me of the traditional Sun Yat-sen suits from the past generation, and has a long face of curious determination. It's clear he has something he wants to say. Through an inefficient dialect exchange, I learn he is my third cousin, the closest relative I have remaining here. His name is Tong Daren.

"Do you remember anyone in our immediate family?" I ask. "My great-grandfather?"

"Of course." Tong Daren nods vigorously.

"What did he look like?"

"Broad chest. Tall. Much taller than you."

Tong Daren leads me in a new direction, to the small courtyard where he lives. His house is one of the smallest here, with separate structures for the living quarters, kitchen, and outhouse. The main house has rectangular cutouts for windows that have not yet been inserted, so that hot, humid air blows through in the summer, as do freezing winds in winter. The floor is an unfinished slab. No lights are on, and I just make out a small bed in the corner. Tong Daren is one of the poorest people here.

"Do you have children?" I ask.

"Two daughters," Tong Daren says with a pinch of regret. No sons. I'm reminded of the type of dead-end farming life so many have in China. Tong Daren lives on a tiny plot of land he's not allowed to sell or put up as collateral for a loan. There's no way he can produce any crop at scale and make a reasonable profit. So he exists here, eats the few vegetables he grows, raises a couple chickens for eggs, and waits for his daughters to send money back from their city jobs.

Tong Daren appears very anxious to speak, but first we have to engage in the requisite small talk: I take a seat, drink some tea his wife offers, and compliment the tea. Now it's his turn: *How old are you? What's your monthly salary? Why did the United States invade Iraq? How much does a chicken cost in America?* By now we are indeed warmed up, and he begins.

"We were affected," Tong Daren says, using the catchall euphemism for personal suffering at the hands of the state. If you were tortured, executed, imprisoned, or exiled, you were "affected." At some point, he helped care for my great-grandfather. The problem was, my great-grandfather's son—my grandfather named Tong Tong—had a history of siding with the anti-Communist Nationalist Guomindang (also Kuomintang) party. This was the US-supported side that lost the Chinese civil war. The purges of the 1950s and '60s targeted "class enemies": landlords, counterrevolutionaries, capitalists, spies, traitors, intellectuals—and those deemed associated with them. Tong Daren practiced no politics, yet paid a political price simply because he was related to my grandfather.

"Did you have to wear that high hat?" I ask, referring to the dunce caps that shamed individuals were required to wear, with handwritten words indicating traitor status.

"Of course. We were marched from village to village wearing them." The phrase "of course," *ken ding*, is by far the phrase I've heard most often in China, bar none. Above all, you are to speak with absolute certainty.

"And the name-tag boards around your neck?" These served the same function, to shame publicly. Tong Daren looks around and nods slowly. Forty years on, shame remains a powerful force.

My father appears on the path and beckons me over to meet someone else. I stand up to apologize for leaving early, and Tong Daren gives a feeble wave. "We'll talk later," he says.

"Scott, did you hear this?" Dad asks, interrupting my thought. The crowd encircling him is talking about my great-grandfather during World War II, something about being a village hero. When the Japanese soldiers came to attack and pillage the village, he went out and greeted them. Several people start talking at once. Each has a version of the story that goes something like this: Great-Grandpa spoke to the troops in Japanese. He trotted out his Japanese concubine. He fed them poached eggs. And somehow, he talked or begged them out of attacking, saving the village and its people from destruction.

I squint. This doesn't add up. In World War II, Japanese troops occupied Shanghai just to the south, and to the west, Nanjing (also Nanking), the site of unspeakable war crimes: beheadings, bayonet stabbings, killing contests, men buried alive, nuns and grandmothers gang-raped.

"Are you sure, Dad?" Hardly anyone in the village would have been alive in the late 1930s or so. I've heard lots of tales in China told with absolute certainty—*ken ding* this, *ken ding* that—with dodgy evidence. My father shrugs. "That's what they say." Even if it were true, there's surely more to this story. There always is. The China of this period is not one of happy endings. My own family's history is unremarkable in that it rhymes with so many others on the mainland—of people left behind, arrested, jailed, betrayed, abandoned, exiled. A number starved to death in the famine. One died in a labor camp in the northwest "Siberia" of China. Modern Chinese history can be a numbing metronome of suffering, with the striking exception of the prosperity today.

It's dark now, too late to talk more. Dad and I depart, but not before agreeing to return tomorrow with our families—my mom, Cathy, and the kids—for lunch at the home of the tall man with the hat. He turns out to be a former elder here. We say yes a little too quickly for me, without considering his motivations. In China, I've learned that a meal is never just a meal. They say in the Middle East that the first thing you learn is the meaning of silence. In China, it's the meaning of lunch.

On the way back, we drop all the middlemen off, including the party secretary, whose hand is still in the pledge-of-allegiance pose. He says nothing as he gets out, and I have a hunch we'll see him again.

"What's in the village?" my older son, Evan, asks. We are all in the Odyssey the next morning, seven Tongs en route to Fu Ma Ying.

"It's a place where everyone's last name is the same as ours," I say.

"That's it?" That's all I have for him. Evan is nine.

I look over at Cathy, quietly hoping for one of those unplanned China surprises we've experienced on many family trips: a post-harvest fire to burn crop waste, a basket of ducklings for sale, a baby kitten in the rice fields, a climbing tree that isn't off-limits the way it is in Shanghai. We come upon the village, and down by the creek a middle-aged woman looks up and waves. She has a dark, round face, short hair, an old red apron, and the familiar slight heft of a mainland woman who has spent a life outdoors. She smiles instantly, the way city folks tend not to, as she washes a pot of green raw vegetables in the creek water. I suspect these will end up on the table of our special lunch.

The villagers are ready for us. Two dozen greet us at once, led by the tall man in the hat from yesterday. He leads Dad and me to a round table in his home, which is far nicer than cousin Tong Daren's. It has actual windows, interior lights, and painted walls. After a round of tea and small talk, we sit on wooden stools to talk about Great-Grandfather Tong. He studied in Tokyo as an exchange student, one of the first men to venture out. I do a little math, putting him in Japan around the turn of the twentieth century, when some of the first Chinese students ventured abroad.

This suggests Great-Grandfather Tong was a reasonably big deal—at least, in this little place. Leaving for Japan back then was the equivalent of going from the farm in Kansas to New York City.

In Asia at the time, Tokyo served as the essential hub of modernity, the transmitter in Asia of what historians consider the second industrial revolution: electricity for lighting, petroleum for cars, steel for train tracks and buildings. By then, the Qing dynasty was on its last legs, and the Chinese had fallen far behind what many of them pejoratively called the "dwarf pirates" of Japan. My great-grandfather returned as a lawyer, practiced in Nanjing, and went back to the village at the end of his life. He was treated well, the hat man says.

"In the winter they stuffed his bed mattress with hay to keep him warm. When he died we buried him at a scenic spot at Pine Bamboo Village. It's about two kilometers away. I can take you there." Dad takes notes, and I venture outside.

"Where are the kids?" Evan asks. Out of perhaps one hundred families, we spot one boy toddler and one girl around five. That's it. Any person of working age has gone out to work, and their school-age children are with them or attending boarding schools. Four-year-old Daniel, our youngest, runs over with an urgent need for a bathroom. "He just needs to pee?" one woman villager asks rather directly, making it clear no outhouse is required. She points us to an open field where Daniel conducts his business.

Back at the host's house, about fourteen people crowd around a small wooden table for lunch. I spot a few familiar faces from yesterday, including the party secretary with the same jacket, plus the current village elders. There are no women, except for my mother and Cathy, though the entire meal has been prepared by women. Far too much food is served. Several local chickens and ducks have been sacrificed for this meal. Generous cuts of pork are stir-fried with locally grown vegetables, plus side dishes of tofu, eggs, and mushrooms. Lunch lasts a very long time, and soon after we have to beg off and return to Shanghai.

That's when I realize one person who is notably missing: third cousin Tong Daren. This snub can't be an accident. Our closest relative in the Tong village for some reason has no status in this place. Something has happened here.

On our way out, Tong Daren intercepts me for a word. I ask him why he didn't attend the lunch.

"Next time," he says, "you eat at *my* house."

Once again I have to interrupt him and leave. He watches quietly as I scoot up the path to join a group photo. Before ducking into the Odyssey, I turn back and see someone approaching my father for a final word. It is the party secretary. I listen in.

"We welcome you back any time," he says. Then he lowers his voice one level: "Next time, you might consider investing here."

Of course. I should have seen this coming. This man is best placed to make deals happen here, and take a personal cut along the way. I can't imagine why anyone would invest in this forgotten place, but surely the party secretary can think of some bridge to nowhere.

I take my seat, put Daniel on my lap, and keep thinking about third cousin Tong Daren's parting words. Like many Chinese family events, these occasions often take on the feel of a choreographed show, separate and distinct from reality. Next time, I will indeed head to his house.

Chapter Two	REVENGE OF THE PEASANTS FROM TONG EAST

Everything the man told you is a lie.
—Tong Yuhua

Two years later in the village, Tong Daren is dying fast. He has esophageal cancer, which has rendered him too weak to say much the next time I visit, in 2011. So his wife does most of the communicating, blaming his cancer on chemically polluted soil and water. In truth, she doesn't really know. The source could be runoff from chemical fertilizer, or waste sludge from nearby petrochemical and wood-processing factories. Or, as many cancers are, of unknown origin.

Still, as she and other villagers tell it, this specific cancer strikes here at a suspiciously high rate. There's a local poem about this part of northern Jiangsu:

Wash rice and greens in the 1950s.
Wash clothes and water fields in the 1960s.
Water goes bad in the 1970s.
Fish die out in the 1980s, and cancer occurs in the 1990s.

I already know this will be my last chance to see Tong Daren. He balances on the edge of his bed, short legs dangling over a concrete slab floor full of chips and holes. He looks around at walls with nothing except a dated coat of off-white paint that's stained and peeling. Several times Tong Daren opens his mouth to begin talking, then closes it instead. I imagine he is budgeting his words and breaths. It dawns on me that I will never get firsthand his version of village history—I'm too late.

Finally, he speaks.

"I'll treat you for dinner at a restaurant in the town, with my family." Too frail to host me as promised, he is providing an equivalent gesture.

"No, you're too weak." I say. "Stay home and rest."

He blinks in a way that tells me I've misunderstood. He opens and closes his mouth again. "No, I'm not going to the restaurant," he says. "I'm just paying." Only his daughters and their families will be at the dinner with me. Before I can protest, he holds up a stop-sign palm indicating there will be no discussion of this. He and I sit in silence, looking out his window without a window, at vegetable fields that have fed countless generations here. Neither of us needs to mention the critical difference between him and me: my side got out of this place long ago, and his did not.

If there's one determinant that separates China's winners from its losers, it's whether a person gets off the farm. Staying in the village means working a tiny plot of land for meager revenue. The economics simply don't work, compared with moving to a town or city, producing more and thus earning more. This is the basic motivation for the largest urban migration in human history, a dynamic not unlike the American farm-to-city movement a century ago. China's story is just that much bigger, compressed into a single generation. The longer a person like Tong Daren stays back, the further behind he and his family fall.

There is another striking contrast here: a tale of two cancers. Two decades ago, I was diagnosed with a soft-tissue cancer at Georgetown University Hospital: broken collarbone (basketball collision), angiosarcoma, shoulder replacement. Blue Cross Blue Shield picked up four-fifths of the cost. Tong Daren, like most in the Chinese countryside, has barely any insurance coverage and no money for chemotherapy. So his tumor simply grew and grew, and blocked his esophagus almost entirely. One person in the village told me Tong Daren's father starved to death during the great famine of 1960. He will go the same way.

"You've had a hard life," is all I can say. At these moments my Mandarin fails me. It's hard enough to express survival guilt in your native tongue. I state the obvious, that the historical burdens he had to bear are the result of my side of the family, but quickly he puts up another hand. "*Mei banfa*," he says. Nothing you can do.

A motor scooter appears, screeching to a halt. Tong Daren's older daughter, Tong Yuqin, swings by to meet me for the first time; she was traveling the first time I came around, with my father. Tong Yuqin and her younger sister grew up in this forlorn house but got married, had kids, and bought townhouses in the closest town, ten minutes away. Now in their thirties, they are finally moving up the ladder to lives with indoor plumbing and washing machines, broadband Internet and children addicted to screens.

"What should I call you?" Tong Yuhua asks. This is the first order of business, to establish our official relationship with each other. It's critical to know the status of the person you're talking to, and address your counterpart accordingly. I happen to be several years older, but in this calculation, age is irrelevant. What matters is whether I am of a higher or lower generation. Someone has to be above or below, and there are no ties. Tong Yuqin tilts her head to ponder this, as I observe how small she is by American standards. She's maybe a size-4 petite, perhaps a 2, with a round pale face that gives off the impression of innocence. Still, she describes herself as "fatter" than her younger sister.

"I should call you *xiaosu*." She has figured it out. Tong Yuqin's father Tong Daren and I are on the same generation on the family tree; our great-grandfathers were brothers. So I'm "equal" to Tong Daren, though he's thirty years older, and thus "above" his daughters. That makes me their uncle. But there's more: in Chinese there are many words for "uncle":

Your mother's older brother is a *jiujiu*.
Your mother's younger brother is also *jiujiu*.
Your father's older brother is a *bobo*.
Your father's younger brother is a *susu*.

Since I'm younger than Tong Yuqing's father, I'm a *susu*. But then—just to add another level of crazy—which *susu*? I have an older brother in Northern California, so we're both *susus* to her. So as a younger brother, I am her "small uncle," or the *xiao susu*. Or, for short, *xiaosu*.

It's complicated, but Tong Yuqin does the genealogy math faster than it just took you to read it. Now it's my turn to call her something appropriate, and she knows I'm still calculating, so she bails me out. "Just call me Tong Yuqin."

She explains she has two children, the older one a twelve-year-old girl with braces. That's it, a girl with braces, compared with her voluminous description of her baby boy: Smart. Talkative. Cute. Fat (which is good in this context). Chinese urbanites often proclaim not to care about the sex of their children, that they're all the same. But not here. When I ask Tong Yuqin if she prefers boys, she answers without hesitation. "Of course."

"But what about the one-child policy?" I ask (this conversation is taking place before the relaxation of the nationwide policy in 2015). Many rural parts have long allowed two children, but Jiangsu province has a reputation for strict enforcement.

"We know someone," she says, without giving specifics. Translation: bribe.

"What is the fine here for a second child?"

"Fifty thousand renminbi." In US currency, $7,000—a full year's income for an unskilled worker in a place like this.

The key to successful sex selection is having a pregnancy ultrasound test to detect the sex of the fetus. The procedure is nominally illegal, though it's easy to get around it. "Did you get an ultrasound? How?"

She shoots me a you-must-be-new-here look. "*Zou houmen.*" Took the back door. She doesn't seem so innocent to me now. Another motor scooter pulls up, with two more young women. Tong Daren's younger daughter, Tong Yuhua, has narrow, angular features and darker skin, and quickly I realize she is the direct one. She does not play the what-do-I-call-you game. And she does not introduce her companion, a teenager in a floral sundress that seems out of place in this dirty village.

"She just came to look at what you look like," Tong Yuhua says. *Kan ni shen me yang.*

I start telling the daughters about our previous visit to the village, mentioning the tall man in the hat who was our main contact. Tong Yuhua cuts me off: "Everything that man in the hat told you is a lie. He was a party secretary before. We hate him."

This takes some time to unwind. But Tong Yuhua is calling into question everything I'd learned here about my great-grandfather: that he returned to the village as an elderly man after the great famine; that villagers took in this successful scholar who ventured out to the big cities of the world and made good; that they stuffed his mattress with hay to keep him warm in the winter; that he was buried in a dignified spot of land nearby.

She shakes her head, as if to say I have been duped, and begins giving her family's version of the story. The Tong village has been divided for decades into two competing halves: Tong East and Tong West. Our families—mine and hers—all hail from the west side, the part closer to the canal and the outside world. Historically, Tong West turned out more scholars and government officials, people who made it out. Tong East, though, was a land of peasants.

"On the other side, they had no culture," Tong Daren's sister later told me with a sneer. "They came to our side to work for us."

What's most surprising is that Tong Daren, the frail and tiny old man with cancer, grew up in a well-off family of scholars. But everything flipped when the Communists took power in 1949. Tong East represented the Communist Party's agrarian power base, so people there who joined the party were quickly catapulted into positions of power. They became party secretaries, with authority to allot food rations and carry out political witch hunts against enemies of the revolution. During the period of "land reform" in the 1950s, they shamed and punished members of Tong West for their connections to landlords, the bourgeoisie, and other "bad elements." The first became the last and the last became the first.

Tong Daren's personal fate changed when a letter arrived in the village in the 1950s. "It was addressed to my father's great-uncle," Tong Yuhua says. "But party leaders in Tong East intercepted it."

The writer of the letter was an anti-Communist Tong who had fled in 1949: my grandfather.

"When the letter came, people knew my father had relatives in Taiwan," she says. "My father was scared to open the letter. He didn't want to accept it." Instead, party leaders from Tong East took the letter and held it as incriminating evidence. Years later, during the famine of the late 1950s, Tong Daren's family received fewer grain rations than others in the village, far below subsistence level.

"Is that how his father died?" I ask.

She nods. "He was fifty-eight."

Cadres confiscated Tong Daren's family land and gave it to poor peasants, who also swiped anything of value in his house: furniture, utensils, farm equipment. During the Cultural Revolution of the 1960s—and China's McCarthyite hunt for real and imagined enemies within—party leaders marched Tong Daren into public "struggle sessions" in nearby villages with a metal sign around his neck. It read: *haiwai guanxi*. Overseas relations. He was beaten and forced to kowtow.

And he was never given opportunities to succeed. "My father is good at math and the abacus," Tong Yuqing, the older daughter, says. But when businessmen came to hire villagers for accounting or construction work, he never got an offer. "He suffered his whole life," her sister chimes in. "I don't think he'll make it to Chinese New Year. I look at him and cry."

As for the tall man with the hat, his name is Tong Guangde, and he hails from the rival territory of Tong East. "He was party secretary before and punished my father the most," Tong Yuhua says. "That's why we hate him." I was told the Hat Man gave Tong Daren a small plot of bumpy, low-quality land (perhaps this occurred during the distribution period in the 1980s). As the village man in charge, Hat Man barred Tong Daren from burying his parents in caskets and forced their cremation, an act of filial disgrace. Also in the early '80s, when Tong Daren's wife was pregnant with her second child and at home on bedrest, Tong Yuhua says Hat Man "grabbed her out of the house and pulled her by her hair to the family planning enforcement official." The plan was to force her to undergo an abortion, but she was deemed too weak for the procedure. "Otherwise," Tong Yuhua says, "I wouldn't have been born." Still, Tong Guangde extracted a fine and pocketed a portion of it, she suspects. "He's more capitalist than a capitalist."

She goes on: about five years before my father and I found the village in 2009, one of my aunts from Taiwan came, and the man in the hat hosted her for a meal just as he'd hosted us. "He never told us she came," Tong Yuhua says. Here, sophisticated visitors from far away aren't treated as relatives returning home, but rather as financial opportunities. They may bring business deals, investments, or donations. "They treated her like a bag of money.

"The good news is, my father will die with his children and grandchildren next to him. Tong Guangde—his children never come to see him. He deserves to die alone."

That night at dinner, eight people—five grownups, three kids—gather around a large round table at a restaurant described as the best in town. To my eye, it seems the only one in town.

"Students today, they're much dumber than before," says Tong Yuhua, the feisty younger daughter who is a grade school teacher nearby. "In the classroom, I explain an idea to them, I write it on the board, and they just sit there." She shovels in a clump of rice. "Like vegetables." I tell myself this place might be freshened up with more snarky younger sisters like her. But younger sisters are rare in villages like this. Even in places that allow two children, a woman pregnant with a second girl often terminates the pregnancy. Tong Yuhua's class of fifty-six children is made up of thirty-eight boys and eighteen girls.

As a teenager, Tong Yuhua ventured out of the village to work in textile mills in the Yangtze River delta cities of Suzhou and Shanghai. She saved enough money in two years to afford university. And upon graduation she returned home to marry a man from a nearby village. "I could have taken a job in Huai'an city," she says. "Would have doubled my salary. But it's too black," by which she means corrupt. In Huai'an city, as she tells the story, too many parents show up in school to give teachers red envelopes—bribes to ensure their children get the right attention and the right grades. And for now, Huai'an city is too far from her ailing father. "Maybe after he dies we'll move to the city."

The main dishes begin to arrive, including local delicacies that I'd feared. Small rivers surround the Tong village, so it's a sure thing underwater creatures will be on offer. "Lobsters!" A waitress dumps a giant plate of small, red, steamed river "lobsters," which are actually spicy crayfish. I've eaten these in Shanghai before: pluck off the tail, suck out the meat, and toss aside the remaining carcass before grabbing another.

Then the snakes come.

"These are not real snakes, just river snakes," says Tong Yuqin's husband, a friendly man with a crew cut. The other spouse, Tong Yuhua's husband, does not engage me at all. The only thing he says to me during this meal is "Eat more rice." Perhaps to him I'm a rich outsider who has come to look down on the people still here. Before I can say anything, three specimens land on my plate, at which point all activity at the table stops. Everyone is watching the *xiaosu* from America.

"How do I eat this?" I ask.

"There's a bone in the middle, the spine," Tong Yuqin's husband instructs. "Take a bite, eat the meat, and spit out the bone." I do as instructed, partly expecting the flavor of *unagi*, the Japanese eel. But Jiangsu river snake is less meaty and more mushy. I force down a few bites, spin the round lazy Susan to try to divert attention somewhere else, and lift my glass for a toast to wash it down. We are drinking the Chinese brand Great Wall red wine, mixed with Sprite. "That's how we drink wine here," Tong Yuqin's husband explains.

I raise my glass to him, and he nods before we drink. The women do not drink. Silently, I toast my ill cousin Tong Daren and then nudge the river snakes to the edge of my plate.

Tong Yuqin's husband drives me to my hotel in a neighboring town, in a Chinese-brand mini pickup truck. The roads are narrow, and it's very dark out, without street lights. But he turns his head directly at me as he drives. Like many in the countryside, he quit school as a young teen and went out for work. He's done construction jobs across China and the world: in Datong in northern Shanxi province ("too cold"), rural Japan ("they treat us well there,") a building construction project in Saudi Arabia ("no beer"), housing construction in West Africa ("they're lazy"). A modern-day "coolie," one might say in an unguarded moment. Domestic jobs pay the equivalent of $700 US a month—far less than most overseas gigs. Like most blue-collar couples in China, he and his wife go where the work is, separating them for months or years at a time. She's been a garment factory worker in central Asia and a nanny in southern China, hundreds of miles away. For now, he's returned home in between gigs, to help raise the family's baby boy and to be close to his dying father-in-law. But expenses are piling up. One more family member means more food, more pricey infant formula. "My daughter's braces, they cost three thousand renminbi," he says—around $400.

"I thought about going to South Sudan next to drive a construction truck," he says, still looking at me as he turns right. But the shady middleman asked workers to surrender their passports for the duration of the job. "I didn't trust them. Too risky." Then he peppers me with money questions about America. *Can you find me a dishwashing job at a Chinese restaurant there? Is it true they subsidize second children in America? How much is a plane ticket to China? A bottle of beer? A pack of Marlboro smokes, the non-knockoff ones? Does your house look like ours? Do you eat steak for dinner every night? Does the US government fight foreign wars to stoke the American economy? Do you own a car? How much?*

I need a brief break, and look around. More than a century ago, my great-grandfather Tong likely traveled these same roads, perhaps asking these same kinds of questions about the outside world. But then, as now, this much was clear: staying behind in the village was a guaranteed way to be left behind.

Chapter Three	FOREIGN EXCHANGE
	Student Life, Tokyo Wife

Don't urinate in public. Speak quietly at night. Swap your shoes for slippers indoors. Don't ask people their ages.

From our home in Virginia outside Washington, I occasionally ride my bike into work if the conditions are right: there has to be enough time, and the temperature must exceed 40 degrees Fahrenheit. It is a glorious ride to start the day, along a bike path that that is tree lined and quiet. The other morning my lone companion in the first fifteen minutes was a male deer. Sometimes, though, the whole experience backfires. Those are the days I get passed by the wrong people—people who should be going slower than I.

Middle-aged dads are not supposed to care about such things. And yet, certain riders have inferior equipment, or they look much older or less healthy. They don't *look* like they should be sailing past. "On your left." This is what they typically say, a phrase that on a bad day can set me off. It is meant as a courtesy, but instead reminds me of my creeping pace. *On your left*. On certain days I consider making a counter-pass, as if that will return the world to its proper order. One morning as I thought about this, I gave my own insecurity a name: I have on-your-left syndrome.

So too, I believe, do many Chinese people. In a society that runs on hierarchy far more than the United States, there is an individual and collective fear of being left behind in the world. This has, after all, happened in the twentieth century. The preferred position in any relationship is to be the "big brother," or *da ge*. If you spend any time in real China, you will learn the primacy of *da ge* status. On one reporting trip to the border town of Ruili, just across from Myanmar, a Chinese seller of smuggled jade explained to me why all the trucks stuffed with smuggled goods flow in the direction of China. "Because we are the *da ge*," he said, with a slight puff of chest.

The *da ge* conversation is long time coming. China's economy was once on par with Western Europe in the fifteenth century— some say even the seventeenth century—until it stagnated. By the late 1800s, the tiny island nation of Japan overtook the mainland as Asia's *da ge*. This was a moment of pure humiliation for the Chinese, as Japan prior to that had idled on the periphery of imperial China. The Japanese in 1868 chose to open up to the modern technology and science of the West, ushering in what was known as the Meiji Restoration. In came steel train tracks and telegraphs, coal mines and factories, shipyards and guns.

In 1895, Japan shocked the world by defeating the Chinese navy. Under the treaty that followed, the Japanese took the island of Taiwan, and the Liaodong Peninsula in the northeast. A decade later brought an even more unlikely military rout: Japan annihilated Russia's navy. For the first time since the Middle Ages, a non-European power had defeated a European country. Germany's kaiser declared it the most important naval battle in a century. US President Theodore Roosevelt called the victory "the greatest phenomenon the world has ever seen."

Japan had overturned the historic order of Asia and became its hub of modernity. Reform-minded Chinese students began flocking to Tokyo, to study, to develop professional skills, to plot revolution. It was the place to be. One of those students was named Tong Zhenyong—my great-grandfather.

He was born in 1880 in the Tong village. Way down the canal in Shanghai, residents read books by Edison's lightbulb and rang one another up on Bell's telephone. But for Tong Zhenyong, that life was a million miles away. What he had going for him were his grades and, apparently, his looks. *Mei nanzi*, pretty boy, is the phrase

Great-Grandfather's niece uses when I visit her in the village and barrage her with questions. *Why did he leave? What did he look like? What were his habits? His loves?* She is now in her eighties but still lucid, particularly when talking about his personal life.

In her telling, Tong Zhenyong married at least two times, perhaps as many as four. He did not take to the chief vice for men in the village: gambling. Instead, he liked to take walks down the village path, and spit. "Kind of a small *pu pu*," the niece mimics. "Not very loud." The way she describes it, this seemed an act of habit rather than pulmonary necessity. He married a woman from Tong West and had three daughters right around the time of a new social practice imported from abroad: natural, unbound feet for daughters. For centuries, girls with bound feet were deemed sophisticated, their tiny feet forcing them to walk in a way considered attractive in the day. The shuffling developed strong hip, thigh, and buttock muscles.

I still remember the first time I saw an old woman with small feet. In Taiwan in the early 1980s, my mother pointed her out—an old woman at a Chinese New Year mahjong party. As tiny as her body was, her miniature cloth shoes could have fit a doll.

My great-grandfather rejected foot binding, but it was gradual. For his first daughter, he hired a traditional foot binder for a process that went something like this: the binder soaked the girl's feet and clipped her toenails. Then he took the four small toes—all but the big toe—and forcibly curled them under the bottom of the foot, breaking the bones and the arch. All this shrank the foot, and to keep it that way, the foot binder wound a bandage tightly to keep the foot from growing. Periodically, the bandages were unwound, bones were rebroken and the foot was rewrapped.

Foreigners in China considered it beyond barbaric. Here are the words of the English missionary John Macgowan, from his modestly entitled book *How England Saved China*: "One morning there came a succession of screams, sharp, shrill, and piercing, that rose distinctly above the babel of sounds that penetrated to us from our neighbours across the wall. . . . When I asked my wife what was the meaning of these distressing cries, she explained that some woman was binding her daughter's feet, and the agony was so great that the child was screaming to relieve the pain from which she was suffering."

Macgowan founded an anti-foot-binding society soon after the Taiping Rebellion (1850–64) against the imperial court. Taiping leader Hong Xiuquan had studied under an American Baptist missionary, and his rebels promoted gender equity. Their strongholds included parts of southern China where foot binding was not practiced. The rebellion failed, but the foot-binding issue remained.

In Beijing, the reformer and public intellectual Kang Youwei made the case that foot binding held back women's productivity. It symbolized a weak China that had lost its, well, footing. Shortly after, in 1902, the empress issued an edict to ban the practice.

By then, Tong Zhenyong's second daughter was born. When she was young, her feet were bound too, until he intervened to have them unwrapped. He saw her feet grow partially, but not fully. The youngest daughter had full-size feet, which struck his niece as ugly and uncivilized.

"When we walked into their house, her feet were the first to greet us," she says with a head shake. To be sure, the new cohort of big-footed girls was not universally celebrated. To some, they served as a reminder of coarse, barbarian women of foreign lands—"Cinderella's sisters," in the words of one historian.

———

When Tong Zhenyong was in his midtwenties, the empress in Beijing began overturning the entire educational system. She phased out the imperial civil service exam. The ground shook. For more than a thousand years, this test was the main vehicle for males to get ahead. Simply put, top performers got top-level government jobs. This three-day ordeal assessed a young man's understanding of classic Confucian writings, and his ability to articulate it through long essays. It also tested his calligraphy. In its prime, the testing system won praise as a merit-based tool to discover China's best and brightest.

By the end of the nineteenth century, though, it became widely dismissed as an anachronism. To critics, the created a corrupt club of aristocrats: it was offered only to men; it stressed outdated texts and classical writing over science and math. Perhaps the one area it fostered creativity and innovation was in the cheating. Students hid mini cheat sheets in their palms, sewed important texts inside their sleeves, and sometimes arranged for academic hired guns to take the test for them. Sometimes they took the more direct route of bribing test proctors.

The imperial court first tried to make mild changes to the test. According to Benjamin Elman's *A Cultural History of Civil Examinations in Late Imperial China*, one turn-of-the-century exam was divided into two sections, one old school and the other forward looking.

SECTION 1

The military policies of Guanzi (725–645 BC)

The policies of Han Wendi (179–156 BC) toward Southern Vietnam

Imperial use of laws

Evaluation procedures for officials

The proposals of Liu Guangzu (1142–1222) for stabilizing the Southern
    Song dynasty

SECTION 2

The Western stress on travel as a part of studying

The Japanese use of Western models for educational institutions

The banking policies of various countries

The police and laws

The industrial basis of wealth and power

But in the end, the whole test was scratched, creating a social vacuum. Imagine the impact of ditching the SAT and ACT and the GPA system, as well as the nation's entire university system. In this confusion, there was one thing in early twentieth-century China that still held value: a degree from overseas. It paid to be an exchange student.

Which is what Tong Zhenyong did. A number of his peers went to Europe, home to Immanuel Kant of Germany, Thomas Aquinas from Italy, and John Locke and Charles Darwin of England. A smaller portion chose America, then the land of capitalist tycoons John D. Rockefeller and John Pierpont Morgan. But most chose

Japan for practical reasons—it was closer and cheaper. The written language overlapped with Chinese, and the food was not strange. By the time my great-grandfather sailed, some ten thousand Chinese students were setting off to Japan every year, making up one of the first large-scale exchange-student programs in the world.

I had no idea if I could find any information about my great-grandfather's time there. When did he go? Was he picked for this? What did he do there? There is no guidebook for chasing a long-deceased ancestor born in the same year as Helen Keller and W. C. Fields. There is only trial and error.

I began with oral histories, interviewing a few relatives in the Tong ancestral village about him. My uncle in Shanghai—my father's half brother Tong Bao—shared some information he'd heard as a child: Tong Zhenyong studied at the elite private school Waseda University in Tokyo. He married a Japanese wife, a key piece of information conveniently withheld from his Chinese wife. The problem was, there were no photos of him, no documents corroborating any of this information. The wealth of online genealogy resources in America excludes Chinese surnames, except for immigrants. On today's Internet, Cathy and I constantly warn the junior Tongs that any info put out there is forever. But those who lived and died just two generations ago left without a trace.

A breakthrough came in 2013. That fall I took leave from my reporting job at *Marketplace* to be a journalism fellow at the University of Michigan. I knew Great-Grandfather attended private Waseda University, and on the advice of a Waseda grad at Michigan, I sent an e-mail query to the librarian there. Her reply:

Dear Scott Tong:

Thank you for your inquiry about visiting our library. We found your great-grandfather's name in the book you mentioned (p. 14, 7th line from the right). Attached please find the copy of the relevant pages.

Best regards,

Aya

She attached a scan of a 1906 registration list of Chinese exchange students. Page 14 reads:

Tong Zhenyong.
Alternative name: Tong Fengwu.
Age: 28. Jiangsu.
Scholarship type: Public
County: Baoying
Village: Fu Ma Ying

Fist bump. I forwarded to my father this first independent confirmation that Tong Zhenyong actually lived. It's one thing to hear about a great-grandfather over dinner in Shanghai, or in the village from distant relatives speaking with a bit too much certainty; it's another to see it on paper.

The Waseda document indicates he attended on some sort of public scholarship. But exactly how Tong Zhenyong got accepted remains unclear to me. I received conflicting answers on this question: some in the village said he actually took the imperial civil service test and did well enough to be sent to Japan by the central government. Others said the province sent him. Either way, I try to picture a tall, chubby Tong Zhenyong wandering the Waseda campus, spitting, *pu pu*, as he went along.

Those were heady times for a student from the sticks of Subei. Surely my then-redneck Chinese great-grandfather and his fellow students spun their heads at everything new to them in Tokyo: Western suits, rickshaws scooting down paths of gravel rather than mud, P.E. class, electric power lines, a library that lent books on the honor system, girls in class. Arriving in Japan for the first time, reform scholar Liang Qichao wrote upon arrival: "It is like seeing the sun after being confined to a dark room, or like a parched throat getting wine."

One scribbled in his journal about "thousands of electric lights" in Tokyo's famed Ueno Park, in contrast to his home village, where days ended when the sun went down. "Very favorable. The whole country was a garden."

The challenge was for these peasant Chinamen to fit in to a modern society. Liang Qichao lamented his people's "village mentality and not a national mentality." To encourage more dignified behavior, a Chinese Student Union in Tokyo in 1906 published a *Handbook for Students Abroad* with a tally of dos and don'ts.

Don't urinate in public.

Walk down the street on the right.

Offer up your streetcar seat to the elderly.

Speak quietly at night.

Wash your clothes often.

Swap your shoes for slippers indoors.

Don't ask people their ages.

The all-purpose handbook even provided earnest advice on how to swim. Still, Chinese students faced hostility from some of their Japanese hosts. One wrote in his journal, describing Japanese locals as "inwardly conceited but courteous to strangers." Tokyo kids chased after the Chinese university students, shouting *Chanchanbotsu*—pigtailed Chinaman. To them, the students' hair was both long and short in the wrong places: for generations, Chinese men shaved their foreheads and grew braided ponytails at the behest of the ethnic minority Manchu rulers. Tong Zhenyong cut off his queue when he got to Japan.

Many students viewed China's place in the world—and their own—through the lens of social Darwinism, a leading idea of the day. The British sociologist Herbert Spencer coined the term, taking evolutionary theory from biology and applying it to human societies. An early analysis of Spencer found its way into Chinese print in 1896.

"The weak invariably become the prey of the strong," Chinese scholar and translator Yan Fu wrote. "The stupid invariably become subservient to the clever." Chinese society, after thousands of years, faced an existential crisis. The lesson of extinct empires—the Persians, Turks, Irish, American Indians—was clear: adapt or die. One Chinese ambassador to Britain described countries that had incorporated modern culture and politics with the transliteration of a word he'd learned in London: *se wei lai yi si de*. Civilized. One point of sending students to Japan was to civilize China to save it.

The question was how. Some students opted in favor of revolution, joining secret societies such as the Tongmenghui, or Revolutionary Alliance. "Your great-grandfather joined the Tongmenghui in Japan," Uncle Tong Bao once told me at his house. He'd heard this from Great-Grandfather Tong Zhenyong's brother, who is now deceased. I couldn't find any documents to corroborate this, but later learned that the Tongmenghui as a secret society may not have regularly kept meeting minutes or membership lists.

The group hatched several revolutionary plots, seeking to "slay" and "exterminate" the ethnic minority Manchu, or Qing, dynasty, which had ruled since 1644. The Tongmenghui was founded by Sun Yat-sen, the man revered in both Taiwan and the mainland as the father of modern China. Today that seems an overstatement; at the time of the revolution, Sun was living in, of all places, Colorado. To be sure, he served as an effective fundraiser and organizer. Bankrolled by a US-educated Chinese entrepreneur who found a way to mass-produce noodles by machine, Sun brought several secret political groups together under the Tongmenghui umbrella.

The Tongmenghui failed several times to overthrow the dynasty, until its eleventh try in 1911. A mutiny at an arsenal in the central Chinese city of Wuchang sparked a chain of events leading to the end of imperial rule. By then, one Tong relative tells me, my great-grandfather had likely moved on from politics in Tokyo. Perhaps he had a case of risk-aversion: students found participating in the shadowy Tongmenghui could be expelled or, if discovered back home, executed.

It is the summer of 2014, and I am strolling on the campus of Waseda in Tokyo. The buildings are not the exact same ones my great-grandfather walked in. They were destroyed by fire bombings in World War II and have since been replaced by fancy glass structures. Still, there is one statue that remains from the old era, of school founder Ōkuma Shigenobu. He was a finance and prime minister, and an early advocate of Japan adopting Western science and culture.

Surely Tong Zhenyong was struck by the same observation I have now: Japan has a discernible sense of order. It's the same feeling I get when walking into a newly built house (our split-level is a 1958 vintage), where the towels in the guest bath hang just right. The armrests on the bullet train from the airport hang just right. During one reporting trip to the Japanese countryside, I visited a noodle house with the most amazing bathroom. Once I opened the door, the light automatically turned on. The toilet lid raised up, ready for action.

I'm on my way to an appointment at Waseda's main library. To get in, I'm required to submit my passport, my university ID, and a letter of introduction from the University of Michigan Asian Studies Department. Only then does the security officer hand me a card to pass through the entry turnstile and head to the basement. There, I spend the next hour sitting and waiting for an archivist to bring the book I've requested. For a moment I'm thankful my own great-grandchildren will discover my own paper trail in a more convenient way.

Eventually, a staffer presents a hardback book with the page from the e-mail attachment. This is the registration book bearing my great-grandfather's name, but there's more information on the next page: Tong Zhenyong studied political science and economics. The reading list for his class included Rousseau, Locke, and Adam Smith. A second book I've requested contains writings published by graduating Chinese students. I flip through and find that Tong Zhenyong wrote a poem in calligraphy brush. The message of the poem is one of self-determination reflecting the spirit of the time: Asia for the Asian people, led by Japan.

SAFEGUARD THE WHOLE YELLOW RACE
Pattern the political system after North America
Greater power than Western Europe
Safeguard peace in East Asia
Aid the independence of South Africa

The date: July 11, 1906. Each line in the poem makes sense to me, except the South Africa reference at the end. "Aid the independence"? Perhaps Tong Zhenyong was identifying with Chinese laborers in the mines there, or the Boers freeing themselves from colonial rule in 1907. Or perhaps, for literary symmetry, he simply had to insert the word "south." I photocopy it all and e-mail it back to the States that night. My father's sister—Aunt Pu in Fremont, California—e-mails back, proclaiming it "incredible." Their younger sister, Aunt Alice, also in Fremont, posts it on Facebook with the word "amazing." My dad calls it "gold."

To them, what's important is the ink-brush writing. You see, in a Chinese family, life stops abruptly at the sign of good calligraphy. You must pause for a moment of lavish praise for the artistic value—or at least, the perceived value—before moving on with your day. Honestly, I wish I'd developed this appreciation or this skill. In second grade, my mother tried to teach me calligraphy, explaining that every Chinese character has geometric balance. It's like a house. A character must stand on a strong base and not lean and fall over. Every line, curve, right angle, hook, or dot has to be stroked boldly, not too fast or too slow. Every so often, a character appears with a long tail—think of a capital *R* or *T*—that ends in a dramatic flourish. At the same time, an individual stroke cannot invade the personal space of the neighboring word. I tried this, failed—just as I had failed piano—and moved on to baseball.

Why did my great-grandfather write this poem about China and its place in the world? Perhaps he felt strongly about Asian solidarity, as Sun Yat-sen did. More likely, my father suggests, he was simply brownnosing. This could have been a mandatory assignment, presenting him an opportunity to please his Japanese teachers.

He did have one extracurricular activity we know about. The Waseda student manual warned visiting students against "dangerous lures and a host of temptations." Tong Zhenyong's temptation came in the form of a young Japanese woman named Arai Yamako. She would become his wife. "She was the daughter of a Japanese mayor," Uncle Tong Bao told me. "And she worked for Panasonic." I honestly wonder how they got together. She was an educated woman of privilege, while he was a village kid from poor China with a penchant for spitting with the *pu pu* sound.

They wed over her parents' objections, I've been told. And there was one thing Arai Yamako didn't know: Tong Zhenyong already had a wife back in the village in Jiangsu, and three daughters. If he were alive today to defend himself, he might argue that polygamy was widespread back then and did not become illegal in China until decades later. He might argue that his first wife failed to bear him a son.

Arai Yamako is my great-grandmother. Fortunately, a number of photos of her are still around. Most are standard, wallet-size black-and-white shots of her: long and serious face, closed mouth, high-bridged nose. Her eyebrows can generously be described as bold. Surely mine came from her. But there is one picture that looks strikingly different.

She is smiling in the shot. It's not the subtle grin of a person hiding a secret, but rather an open-mouth smile that seems quite unfit for her era. Even in today's Shanghai, I've taken pictures of mainland women with big smiles that they've later asked me to delete. *A bit too happy.* Arai Yamako is kneeling in a kimono with her hands together, as if she's reuniting with a sibling returning from war. She seems casually comfortable with who she is: a modern Japanese woman showing her teeth and marrying who she wants.

Intermarriages between Chinese exchange-student men and Japanese women in fact occurred on occasion. But most did not last. Often they dissolved when the Chinese husband graduated and returned home. Or the Japanese woman remained loyal to her homeland and stayed behind. Tong Zhenyong and Arai Yamako managed to stay together, however, and in the year of the 1911 Chinese revolution that overthrew imperial China, she bore a son— my grandfather. He was half Japanese, which makes me one-eighth Japanese.

Perhaps the most striking example of China's grudging acknowledgement, if not acceptance, of the Japanese model is that of supreme leader Deng Xiaoping. Early on in his reforms of the late 1970s, Deng visited Japan as the first Chinese leader to meet a Japanese emperor. Upon touring a Nissan plant, where each worker produced an astonishing ninety-four vehicles per year, Deng proclaimed, "We are a backward country and we need to learn from Japan."

You only have to look at the Chinese language today to understand how many modern ideas came via Japan. A remarkable number of words in Mandarin have been imported from Japan: Independence (*duli*). Women's rights (*nvquan*). Gender equality (*nannv pingdeng*). Science (*kexue*). Industry (*gongye*). Atom (*yuanzi*). International (*guoji*). History (*lishi*). Market (*shichang*). Invest (*touzi*).

Economics (*jinji*). Society (*shehui*). Telephone (*dianhua*). The list goes on.

After studying at Waseda, Tong Zhenyong chose a career of stability over politics. He became a lawyer. This will strike an American reader as mundane (I am typing this from our house in Arlington, where I count sixteen attorneys in a half-mile radius). But the modern legal profession was very new to China in the early twentieth century. Before that, independent, private legal counsel did not exist, aside from the foreign barristers and solicitors in Western-controlled treaty ports.

It would be nice to claim that Great-Grandfather's generation of lawyers ushered in a Chinese legal renaissance. They did not. You can ask anyone on the street if the basic rule of law exists today, and you will get an earful in return. You don't have to conduct a dramatic interview with a dissident in jail; just ask anyone who has tried to enforce a contract, or bought a bootleg version of Microsoft Windows on Nanjing Road. Legal bans tend to be more speedbumps than walls—temporary barriers. Without appropriate enforcement or an underlying moral code that once existed in Chinese society, it simply pays to cheat.

Every morning in the *Marketplace* bureau in Shanghai, our fax machine would spit out an unsolicited advertisement. It offered to sell official transaction receipts, handy for padding an expense report or invoice. Each receipt has a price. If you need evidence of a $100 "transaction," it may cost you $1. A receipt for a $500 "purchase" costs $5, and so on. Bending the rules remains the norm.

That doesn't mean China's legal system hasn't made important reforms this past century, due in part to scholars who imported modern concepts from abroad. The Qing dynasty established a Chinese Supreme Court in 1906. It created laws governing business transactions and marriages.

Some changes abolished grisly forms of criminal punishment. The old system included *lingchi*, death by a thousand cuts; *xiaoshou*, displaying head of the executed; and *lushi*, mutilating a prisoner's corpse. These practices gave way to fines, detention, imprisonment, and labor. The death penalty remained, though guilty persons were no longer executed before large crowds. They were strangled in private instead.

I found only small bits of information about my great-grandfather's legal practice. He was a member of an attorney association in Huaiyin, Jiangsu. He authored a painfully dry document: a translation of an international intellectual property conference. Yikes.

"It means he probably wasn't so famous or successful," my Shanghai cousin Tong Chengkan suggests. He's probably right. If Tong Zhenyong had become a top government official or a notable professional, there'd likely be more in the public record.

The more important point is the status that overseas study provided him. It made him a scholar from abroad. After Japan, Tong Zhenyong returned to the west side of the Tong Village and a rather complicated personal situation. He went back with three children and a Japanese wife, which by all accounts came as a great shock to his Chinese wife. All this time, she had been raising three of their daughters in China. Now here she was, challenged by a younger concubine. Things apparently did not go well for Arai Yamako either. She learned Mandarin—something that impressed villagers mention to this day—but her stepdaughters were rude to her, and villagers made anti-Japanese comments to her. Eventually she returned to Japan, to escape the comments and, as one uncle recalls, whispers of her husband's interest in yet another woman.

———

Back in the Tong village, my third cousin Tong Daren does not make it to the next Chinese New Year. He died a few months after my second visit with him. His older daughter, Tong Yuqin, tells me he that at the end, he went twelve days without eating or drinking. Still, she says, "he waited until the whole family came before taking his last breath." On a Thursday he declared, "I'm going." He died that Saturday.

I'm here to visit his grave, and his younger daughter, Tong Yuhua (the feisty one), pulls up in her motor scooter to take me there. Hers is a step-through electric model, which comes in handy, as she's wearing a pink sundress on this 95-degree summer day. She does not wear a helmet, nor does she offer me one. Ten minutes later, I spot the outdoor mini-cemetery built on a concrete slab. About twenty rows of identical-size gray headstones stand erect.

Near the back row, Tong Daren's image looks out from a standard headshot. He is not smiling. His trustworthy long face appears too naive, too un-savvy for today's dog-eat-dog China. His daughter brings a stack of blank red sheets of paper to burn, a countryside variation of a ritual I'd joined in the past: sacrificing pretend paper bills for the deceased to spend in the afterlife above. The big cities provide more upscale offerings to burn: printed bills that look like real currency, paper BMWs, faux Viagra pills, and flammable paper condoms (you never know what can come in handy up there).

"In America, do you do the same thing?" Tong Yuhua asks. It's a fair question, though I don't know where to start. It's a long answer; I'd rather focus on bidding farewell to a Tong who deserved a better life than he had. So I simply shake my head and set another red paper ablaze.

This is a quick trip, so I hustle to the bus stop to board a long-distance bus back to Shanghai. I'll have a couple days there to research before flying back to the States. The good news is, I'll be taking the bus ride with our old nanny from our years in Shanghai. We call her Ayi, or "Auntie." Ayi's village turns out to be just three miles from ours, which is the main reason we hired her in the first place. During our first week in China, my father came with us and happened to meet her in our building elevator. Somewhere between the eleventh floor and the lobby, he figured out the two of them came from the same part of northern Jiangsu. We hired her the next day. Ayi did everything for our three children. She walked them through the neighborhood, picked then up from the bus stop, took them daily to the playground and barbershop. She taught our youngest, Daniel (who was then two years old), how to rest outdoors by squatting with his bottom one inch above the ground. She also inadvertently got the kids to mimic her unfortunate Subei-accented Mandarin. Ayi is family.

By the time I board the bus, Ayi is already on, sitting in the very back row and waving me toward her. I make my way up the aisle slowly, and that's my mistake. The impatient driver takes off quickly, leaving me to wobble and stumble up the aisle with a backpack and rolling suitcase.

A hand flies out into the aisle, forcing me to halt abruptly. "*Rang yixia,*" an elderly voice rings out. Excuse me. A grandfather with a crew cut and a nice-to-meet-you smile has stopped me. Right beside him, a toddler boy is standing, and peeing. The urine creates somewhat of a fountain that arcs directly across the aisle. Had his grandfather not stopped me, I would have stepped right into the stream. I have no choice but to wait. And here is the oddest part: no one on the bus bats an eye as I stand and try to balance myself, waiting like a car at a railroad crossing. Eventually, the old man's tollgate hand rises up, and I continue on.

But there is another obstacle. Every seat is taken, except for two in the back row next to Ayi. To get there, I have to step over a migrant worker man holding a freshly killed chicken in a bag. His other hand steadies a bucket on the floor, which is filled with some nontransparent liquid that sloshes with each bump and sway. I wait for a steady moment and high-step over.

"Did you give them any money?" Ayi asks once I sit down. I look at her and blink. As a former hired nanny who still calls me "Mister Tong," she hardly speaks this directly. But this is important.

"No," I say. "I brought gifts, cosmetics from America." Brand-name facial moisturizers, vitamins, leather wallets. But this is an inadequate answer.

"You should have. They're your family, and very poor."

I tell her I'll try once we get to Shanghai, but am not sure Tong Daren's daughters will accept it. Giving money to friends in China often requires an awkward set of social dance steps performed by both giver and receiver. *No, I can't take it. Yes, I really want to give this, it's expected. Really, you don't have to. Yes I do, I have to.* But the critical part is reading a person's body language and tone. Sometimes no really means no, except when it actually means yes.

The return trip to Shanghai takes far longer than the five hours advertised, as the driver makes several side stops off the freeway to make unauthorized passenger pickups. In any event, this is a "black" gray economy bus, Ayi tells me, so there may be no company rules to break in the first place. Upon arriving, I call Tong Yuqin and offer to send her money. I have prepared myself for this conversation, knowing she will initially refuse.

"Sure. This is my bank account number," Tong Yuqin says. Ayi was right. I make arrangements to wire three thousand renminbi, or about $400. The village relationship, as best I can tell, is restored.

Chapter Four

THE NANJING GLEE CLUB AND A REVOLUTION FOR GIRLS

It was almost amusing the degree to which the Chinese wives "bossed their little Japanese husbands."
—Welthy Honsinger, missionary

Rousong is my chief comfort-food memory from childhood. If you wander through any Chinese grocery store on the planet, you will encounter an odd-looking pork product called *rousong*. It comes in plastic tubs large and small, and sometimes in bulk. Tan and fluffy, *rousong* is what cotton candy or fluffy wool might look like if they were meat. It may be the world's most processed food product. First, you take pork shoulder and stew it. Then strain it, pull it apart, shred it, dry it in an oven. Mash. Pummel. Wok fry. Eat it on a bun, or rolled into a rice ball or sushi maki, or atop tofu or rice cakes or toast. *Rousong* is quite possibly the best food in the world. It is also true that *rousong* is fatty and unattractive. And in English, it suffers from an unfortunate translation: pork floss (insert your own joke here).

I was born in Poughkeepsie, in New York's Hudson Valley, where everyone (including my father) worked for IBM. Every morning in our split-level home, I requested *rousong* for breakfast. It never ran out, which is curious because it was illegal at the time. In the early 1970s, *rousong* had not yet hit the shelves of Asian grocery stores in the States, and US customs laws banned the import of meat products. So how did we get it? I later learned my maternal grandmother in Hong Kong shipped it over and gamed the postal system. Here's how: she'd mail tins of tea leaves, taped shut with Scotch tape across the top. Even if a border official opened the tin, he or she would see only tea leaves—at least, on top. The densely packed *rousong* cargo hid underneath, like a thief in the trunk of a car.

Rousong was the center of my relationship with my maternal grandmother, which is another way of saying we didn't have one. I learned in the process of reporting this book that she was part of a groundbreaking generation of women pioneers. They joined the industrial workforce, marched in strikes alongside men, and went on to be doctors and suffragists. They built schools for the girls who came after. Until recently, I knew none of this, and none of the details as they pertained to my grandmother—because I met her only once.

In 1971, I was two when we flew over from the Hudson Valley to see Grandmother in Hong Kong. My mother referred to her as my *waipo,* which is the term for one's maternal grandmother. Waipo lived in a five-hundred-square-foot apartment in a modest section of Hong Kong's Kowloon territory. Modern parenting practice might argue against that kind of strenuous trip, but modern parenting practice is no match for filial obligations. It was my parents' job to bring us to see our grandparents—in Taiwan on my father's side and Hong Kong on my mother's. First we landed in Taipei, where sources say I threw a remarkable tantrum. I greeted a smiling male customs officer with an efficient kick to the shins. Then, after a couple weeks, off to Hong Kong.

This of course is all my mother's telling of a trip. Waipo—by then a widow for more than a decade—took us around to see Hong Kong harbor. She boarded the Star Ferry with us to cross the stinky harbor and bought us street food. That's pretty much everything I knew of her. Waipo died of a brain aneurysm when I was seven.

So what was she really like? For years, I could only default to the general Chinese grandmother image my Chinese American friends and I liked to mock as kids: a penny-thrift woman who lived in the kitchen and watched bad Hong Kong soap operas. She couldn't pronounce "three." Second-generation immigrant kids have third-world grandmothers.

By contrast, my wife, Cathy, had a long, close relationship with her own maternal grandmother before she passed. We know a lot about Grandma Jane: she was the daughter of a steel mill worker, with a hankering for black bean soup. She liked to dress up as a clown for kids' birthdays. She paid close attention to grandchildren who gained weight, or didn't dress sufficiently "smart." Even Cathy's great-grandmother lives on in our house, through a couple of pieces of antique furniture. When it's time for flashlight tag, the kids flip the top of Great-Grandmommy's secretary's desk and grab the batteries inside. Upstairs, Great-Grandmommy's cherry bookshelf is loaded down with books for parents of a certain age: *The Adventures of Tintin. Handbook for Coaching Youth Soccer. Everyone Poops.*

For my *waipo*, there is no bookshelf. Now that I have teenagers, I wonder about someday creating memories for my own grandchildren: maybe shuffling playing cards the way my dad taught me, or hitting a one-handed backhand, or pinching a pork dumpling the absolute correct way before ladling it into boiling water. Did it ever occur to Waipo that she might not be remembered?

It's not as if her children didn't try. My mother's sister, Aunt Lily, recalls a failed effort to save a set of old family photos. In March 1950, nearly a year after the Communists took control of Shanghai, my mother and her siblings fled for Hong Kong. They left with a heavy chest full of family papers, heirlooms, and photos, carrying the chest from one packed train to another. By the time they arrived at a cheap hotel in Guangzhou, near the Hong Kong border, the chest was gone. "Maybe it was stolen," Aunt Lily tries to recall. "Or just left behind" in the rush. One way or another, the mementos are gone.

That is, except for the contents of the accordion file.

Name: Miss Djao Dji-djen (Mildred Chao)
Age: 43
Occupation: elementary principal
Home: Hubei

Issue date: June 13, 1949

Date of birth: xx 1904

Travel destination: USA, via all necessary countries en route

This is the main page of her passport, which has survived. I'm looking at it in Houston, at the kitchen table of Aunt Lily. She's my grandmother's oldest child and my mother's big sister. On this brief visit (I'm attending an oil and gas conference for work), I have come straight out and asked Aunt Lily if she has any information about Waipo, for a book I am trying to write. She steps into her bedroom and produces a thick accordion file loaded with documents, and the passport of Mildred Chao (also Zhao).

Mildred was her English name. When she was born, hers was the tenth most common girl's name in the United States, trailing just behind Dorothy, Marie, and Florence. I did not know she was born in 1904, though it turns out she actually wasn't—Mildred lied about her age on occasion, including this one. She was in her midforties for the passport photo, revealing her dominant feature: a sharp widow's peak that has passed down to my mother and me. Mildred does not smile. She has the face of an introvert.

I reach again into the accordion file, this undiscovered toy box of the past—how come no one told me about this?—harvesting trifold aerogram letters, diary entries, even a handwritten shopping list. I'm most interested in a thick, yellowed sheet folded up for so many decades the corners have holes in them. Opening it up carefully, I notice a small black-and-white photo of Mildred, surrounded by dozens of tiny rectangles pieces meant to be torn off—like a bulletin-board ad for babysitting services. The pieces were meant to be surrendered when buying grains, meat, cloth, or oil. This is a ration coupon booklet. I mistakenly assume this came from the Communist era; this booklet, on closer inspection, dates back to the prior government of the Nationalist Guomindang Party.

"Take the file with you," Aunt Lily says. "But bring the letters back later."

Months later, I call my mother to discuss the discovery. She knows about the documents, as she and Aunt Lily have saved them ever since Grandmother Mildred died in 1976. "They're sad," she says. This is why she never mentioned the letters. "My parents argued a lot." Some of the letters were written by my grandfather during their family's separation in the early 1950s: Mildred and the children lived in Hong Kong while her husband, Carleton Sun, stayed back in Communist-occupied Shanghai to run the school they'd built decades earlier. The couple disagreed about money, where to raise three children, whose relatives mattered more, and most fundamentally, whether it was safe enough for him to stay on the mainland.

The letters are sad most of all because my mother knows how things ended for her father.

What is striking to me is that just about every letter in the folder comes from a US address: West 67th Street in New York City. Colorado State College in Greeley. Baltimore, Maryland. Franklin Springs, Georgia. One letterhead bears the logo of the United Council of Church Women. In all, there are more than a hundred pages. Almost every one of Grandmother Mildred's correspondents were American.

The two women who penned most of the letters to Mildred were her old teachers. More than a century ago in middle-of-nowhere Jiangxi province, she attended a Methodist missionary boarding school run by American women: the Stephen L. Baldwin School for Girls. Welthy Honsinger of Rome, New York, was principal. Anna Melissa Graves of Baltimore was a teacher.

But these were only the letters Mildred received. What about the ones she wrote? Remarkably, Honsinger and Graves kept all the letters from their lives, and with a bit of Googling I was able to track them down. Graves's collection lives at Swarthmore College outside Philadelphia, and Honsinger's is stored at Boston University. Combining the letters from those special collections with the accordion-file letters, I assembled a thick, perhaps three-hundred-page chronology of Mildred's life—at least, the life according her letters. It became an essential primary source for this book section.

It's better to be lucky than good. My father-in-law likes to say this on the golf course. Cobbling together my grandmother's lifetime of letters turns out to be a very unusual finding. The feminist historian Wang Zheng at the University of Michigan has told me most personal writings from back then have not survived to today. "Even if many educated women had kept diaries and written letters," she writes in her book *Women in the Chinese Enlightenment*, "the chances were slim that these personal documents had survived civil wars and the War of Resistance against Japan." Another China historian was more direct, dismissing the possibility of turning up some old treasure chest of family letters as "a historian's wet dream." Don't bet on it . . . unless you get lucky.

At first glance, the letters seem to amount to a pile of very bad advice. One, from Anna Graves during Japan's occupation of China during World War II, suggests the occupying soldiers were not so bad, perhaps even wimpy:

> I knew a missionary in Shantung [Shandong] who told me that the rate of intermarriage (and hence amalgamation) between Japanese soldiers and Chinese women was extraordinary (marriage, not simply sexual relations) and that it was almost amusing the degree to which the Chinese wives "bossed their little Japanese husbands."

This much I know: These "little Japanese husbands" murdered fifteen thousand Shandong civilians during the Pacific war. In the same letter, Graves turns bossy. She criticizes Mildred for abandoning China for Hong Kong during the Communist takeover, apparently attributing this unwise decision to menopause.

> My dear child you must be about 48, i.e., you must be passing through the period in a woman's life when she is least apt to be reasonable, most apt to be excitable, and less apt to be able to judge matters calmly. That is not women's fault.

For her part, Honsinger dispenses the absolute opposite advice: Leave. Get as far away from China as possible and travel to America: "You have chosen the right college in Colorado, and it will be wonderful if you can take some classes by correspondence, and finally get here for one year. . . . Your husband and you may have to be separated many years—who knows? But God knows the way he takes, and this may be a deepening of character for you."

Mildred Zhao was born in 1903, smack in the middle of a world-wide debate over the role of women. That year, a woman—Marie Curie—won the Nobel Physics Prize for the first time. In Britain, women marched for the right to vote. And in the United States this was the Progressive Era, when individual states were holding votes one by one on women's suffrage.

Across China, leading intellectuals questioned why their country had fallen to the status of Asia's "sick man." They challenged authority, history, tradition—particularly, three Confucian relationships underlying traditional society: father guides son, emperor rules subjects, husband controls wife. A woman's traditional job was inside the home: sewing, cooking, and designing gardens and home interiors. Her marriage was prearranged, and she did not attend school. "To be a woman means to submit," went one Confucian teaching at the time. "The wife's words should not travel beyond her own apartment."

Perhaps the most famous female Chinese counterculture voice in my grandmothers' day was writer and self-proclaimed revolutionary named Qiu Jin. "Arise! Arise! Chinese women, arise!" screamed one of her manifestos, *Stones of the Jingwei Bird*. Qiu Jin likened to slavery traditional society's treatment of females: cracking foot bones and binding their feet, keeping them inside the home, depriving them of the ability to read. "Chinese women will throw off their shackles and stand up with passion; they will all become heroines."

As a young women, Qiu eschewed sewing for archery and martial arts novels. In her twenties, she divorced her husband—an unheard of act in the day—and sailed to Japan, funding her education abroad by pawning her dowry jewelry. Often dressing in male clothing, she chopped her hair dramatically short. She exhorted young men and women to overthrow the Qing dynasty and helped train revolutionaries in Chinese cities. Qiu herself tried to assassinate a Qing governor in Zhejiang province, but failed. For that attempt, she was beheaded in 1909.

This debate over women's rights was filled with metaphors and slogans—good and bad. Freeing women from old Confucian culture would liberate China. Women were held down the way China had been restrained by Western colonial powers. Binding women's feet, well, bound China to an underperforming past. And the Chinese economy was going nowhere in the midst of an industrial revolution on the outside.

Consider these numbers from noted British economic historian Angus Maddison: In the fourteenth century, the typical Chinese person made a tad bit more than his or her Western European counterpart—annual income per person totaled $600 in China, compared with $560 in Europe. But then Europe grew and China stood still. China's income fell to two-thirds of the European standard by 1700, and then it cratered. By 1900, the median Chinese person earned $545 annually—in dollar terms, almost unchanged from six centuries prior—compared with $3,000 in Germany and more than $4,000 in England and the United States. Industrialization and its benefits were passing China by.

The Qing court's abolition of the civil service exam was its attempt to reverse this. The test was an avenue of mobility available only to males, and to its critics was outdated and backward looking. It focused on moral and political theory, rather than modern essentials of science and math. So the empress shut down this heir club for men. This phaseout of the test created a social power vacuum that opportunistic entrepreneurs, foreign-trained students and educated women sought to fill.

When Mildred was young, two critical decisions were made for her. The first was that she should receive a Western, missionary education. I presume, but don't know for sure, that her father made this call; he hailed from an elite family of scholar officials going back to imperial days. Thankfully, Mildred was an only child. If she'd had a brother, surely he would have gone to school instead. Second, Mildred had her bound feet unwrapped at a young age, allowing them to grow naturally for most of her life—Cinderella's Sisters style. By the time she enrolled in boarding school at the age of eight in 1911, my grandmother had joined a rare club of Chinese girls with the privilege to do two things their mothers never could: read and run.

The Yangtze River is China's Mississippi, its economic lifeline. To the north, the mammoth Yellow River is indeed the birthplace of Chinese civilization, but the Yangtze is the essential waterway, dotted by many of China's most important cities and transportation hubs. When it comes to freight transport, no other inland river in the world comes close. In the case of my family history, on both my parents' sides, I could tell an awful lot of the story by simply following the river downstream.

At the headwaters to the far west in Qinghai province, I'd point out that my maternal grandfather spent his last years at a prison labor camp there. Halfway down the mountains in the megacity of Chongqing is where my father was born during the Chinese civil war. If you float down further, to Wuhan, you pass both ancestral villages on my mother's side. Downstream in Changzhou is where my uncle Tong Bao grew up and hunted for frogs to eat during the great famine. And the delta city where the river dumps into the sea—Shanghai—is where my mother was born. And where my father boarded a dangerously overloaded boat to flee the mainland ahead of the Communists in 1949.

As best we know, Grandmother Mildred was born in the central Yangtze River city of Nanjing, a historic capital to dynasties and governments past. Her grandfather served as a government official there, relatives say. Then, when she was eleven, her parents took her upriver to attend boarding school. "It seems to me my mother and father took me there," my grandmother said in an audio interview that still exists on tape at Boston University.

This is how I imagine the trip went: During the steepest upstream portions of the trip westward, shirtless male workers onshore had to tug the boat up and over the rocks. At the port city of Jiujiang, or Nine Rivers, they boarded a second, smaller boat; turned left (south); and crossed a massive body of water known as Lake Poyang. Surely it was hot and sticky, as their destination city, Nanchang, today brags about being in the club of Chinese "furnace cities." For some reason, a number of Yangtze cities I've visited (Wuhan, Changsha, Chongqing, Nanjing) also seek to market themselves that way, as if the label confers a certain branding advantage.

On one broiling-furnace day in July 2014, I have come to Nanchang to try to find her old school. I've learned the Baldwin School has now become a public school in the city, the Number Ten Middle School. My father and I have just visited one of his uncles, and we are stopping at the school address on the way to the airport. We've asked the cabbie to stop and wait.

Back in 1911, this was a walled city ringed by a moat, with dogs and chickens roaming the interior. Now it looks like any midtier Chinese city: you can cruise the mall to buy a new smartphone before catching a movie in the IMAX theater. To me there is a certain sameness to cities like this: a river, a few bridges, a set of familiar chain stores, nondescript medium-rise buildings. It's not unlike a stretch of road back home that features the same exact chain stores and restaurants—Anywhere, USA.

"*Gan shen ma?*" What are you doing? a male voice rings out as I attempt to walk through the gatehouse and into the school. Most Chinese public institutions are not what you and I might regard as public. They hide behind guarded gates. A skinny man with a comb-over in his fifties stands to block me. He is simply doing his job. He wears a sweat-soaked security guard uniform with the pants rolled up to the knees. "Can't come in here."

I have a plan. In these moments, I've had luck playing my family history card, so I start in with my pitch: "I'm an overseas Chinese visiting from America. I'm coming to 'dig for my roots.' My grandmother once went to school here." The keys, I've learned by error and trial: Stay on message. Speak quickly. Keep talking until they relent.

He cuts me off. "You can't come in. No outside people."

"I'm just here for today, flying out in a couple hours," I appeal, pulling out my grandmother Mildred's 1949 passport. This is the next-level intervention, to present a historical document. It does nothing for him. "These are not my rules. They're school rules. If you don't have permission, you can't go in." In my head, I can hear the voice of my teen daughter: *Fail, Dad.*

I walk out to devise a workaround plan. My imagination is not the greatest, but I am a reporter and this is China, where everyday survival requires a plan B and C. Dad is still sitting in the cab up the street, and we don't have much time. I decide to try to identify a collaborator, someone who can at least go into the school and snap some pictures for me. That's what I'm really after—to compare the place today with the old vintage photos of the old Baldwin School. It is lunchtime at the Number Ten School, and students are filing in and out of the gatehouse. For the next ten minutes or so, I discreetly approach one middle-schooler after another, requesting this favor and delivering the same elevator pitch: grandson of China, traveling from America, digging for roots. They all walk on by without answering—except for one pair of students, a girl and a boy. "Would you take my iPhone in and take some pictures for me?"

The girl is in charge here and answers immediately. "Can't you go in yourself?" I like this dynamic. The student wears tortoiseshell glasses and a level of fearlessness.

I shrug my shoulder. "I can't. The guard in there stopped me."

"You're from America?" she asks. Non sequitur, no problem. "America where?"

"Washington, DC."

She nods. "Okay." In this rush, I fail to consider the risk of handing over my iPhone to a twelve-year-old whose name I don't even know, and just foist it on her. She asks: "What do you want me to take pictures of?"

I hadn't planned for this. "Anything you find interesting. Trees. Old buildings. Anything that might have been around a hundred years ago."

They disappear in, and I retreat up the street to avoid the sight line of the guard. But on this day it's pretty hard for me to blend in, with my fire-engine-red T-shirt that says "Washington Capitals" on the front and "BACKSTROM 19" on the back. Within a minute, she reappears.

"Battery's dead." So I pull out my low-end Android purchased just for this trip. It's a lousy phone with a lousy camera, but that's all I have at this point. My dad pops his head out of the car, and I motion for him to wait just a bit more. The girl runs back in five minutes, heaving victoriously, and shows me the snapshots: main entrance, signs, administration building, trees, garden. Perfect. "I ran out of time for the sports field," she says. I thank her profusely. "*Mei shi*," no worries, and she's gone.

The pictures make clear the old Baldwin School has retained a rare, park-like feel in the middle of a Chinese city. Many of the green, open-space areas in Chinese cities are spots once controlled by foreigners in nineteenth-century neocolonial days. Here, there is still a pavilion with traditional characters—pre-Communist—and an arched stone bridge sloping over a lily pond. Surely this is where female students in Baldwin uniforms sat and studied and wondered what New China might bring. Just before ducking into the cab, I notice a sign on the outside wall of the school, with a quote attributed to Deng Xiaoping. It would have been relevant during my grandmother's time there as well, perfectly capturing an ambitious China trying to find its place in the world: "Education must face modernity. Face the world. Face the future."

A hundred years ago, in roughly that same spot, a different sign stood on the wall. In English, it was a Gospel passage from the book of John: "Ye shall know the truth. And the truth shall set you free."

The woman who put up that verse: the towering school principal at Baldwin, Welthy Honsinger (later Welthy Honsinger Fisher). She would go on to become a lifelong mentor to Mildred Zhao. Their story is, to me, a fascinating collision of two separate stories—of women from opposite corners of the world, unsatisfied with the choices before them.

Honsinger's life in America began predicable enough. Born in Rome, New York, alongside the Erie Canal, she attended Syracuse University and taught at a local high school. Then she shocked her family, announcing that she was going to teach in China. In 1906, Honsinger attended a missionary recruiting talk at Carnegie Hall and, as she put it, "heard the call." She quit her job and left behind two things: a promising soprano opera singing career and an aggressive suitor named Tom.

Her family and friends expressed horror. "Why waste your abilities on the dirty heathen?" one coworker asked helpfully. Honsinger's half sister tried to dissuade her by taking her to New York City's

Chinatown. "Look around," the half sister gestured with her arm. "*These* are the people you'll be living with next year." But Honsinger sailed. Her timing could not have been worse, to be honest. Anti-Western sentiment had been brewing in China for decades, and in recent years came to a head. In a bloody uprising known as the Boxer Rebellion, rebels targeted foreigners and murdered countless missionaries. In Nanchang, her eventual destination, local children drowned rats they labeled "foreign devils."

Honsinger arrived at the Baldwin School and proceeded to rankle the American teachers already there. She demanded to live in the same quarters as a Chinese colleague, upsetting the established protocol. But she got her way. In the early days, Honsinger complained about her American colleagues as expat snobs, deriding them as spoiled women living in "Grand Rapids homes" and eating cured meat from Montgomery Ward back home.

I'm sure the veteran teachers at Baldwin viewed Honsinger as idealistic and naive. *Give her a little time and China will wear her down.* This was exactly the sentiment I got myself upon moving to China. "You cannot be too nice to them," one Chinese Malaysian expat who worked in the water business warned me during the first week. One father from our kids' international school observed that I appeared a little new and a little too friendly. "Which is too bad," he said, shaking his head, "because China turns you into an asshole." He moved on to his next assignment shortly after.

At the Baldwin School, the locals didn't take to Honsinger either. One domestic school worker described her feet "as big as boats." Students complained that Honsinger stank of mutton (she later gave up meat). But over time, she learned a bit of Mandarin and mastered the ice-breaking activity of eating watermelon seeds and spitting out the shells. Honsinger remained determined. In a missionary journal article, she wrote: "Here, little waifs, plucked up from the gutters ere the dogs should devour them, have been sheltered. . . . Here broken-hearted women have found a sympathetic ear. . . . Hobbling cripple girls with tiny feet have come and gone away healthy girls."

Honsinger may have had honorable intentions, but it must be said that the Chinese never welcomed the American Bible-toters with open arms. It's impossible to separate the missionary era from the broader semicolonial backdrop that began with China's defeat to Britain in the Opium War. The 1842 treaty that followed compelled China to open up key port cities that came to be known as "treaty ports." In came a motley assortment of opportunists: British traders, German brewers, Japanese industrialists, General Motors, Standard Oil, and American soul savers. Ever since the US Civil War and settlement of California, missionary groups had looked further west to expand their influence. Protestants first penetrated mainland China in the 1800s (Catholics started earlier), but their numbers exploded after an 1860 "unequal treaty" that flung open the doors further. Women did most of this work; six out of ten American missionaries serving overseas were female.

In the end, did the foreign missionaries help China? This is a long debate. Two very different historical narratives collide on this point. In the traditional Chinese Communist Party telling of history, these were the years of humiliation at the hands of the foreign devils. A billion people held down. This remains the ideological grand narrative today, that the Chinese spent a century under the thumb of outsiders before standing up and liberating themselves. The Chinese people built today's China. This underlies the hypernationalistic streak the world is seeing now, the new attitude of: we are now due.

An opposite view is that the foreigners delivered modernity. In the lingo, the Western "impact" brought a Chinese "response." As the argument goes, the benevolent colonialists went over to build hospitals and universities, modern cities and industry. They transformed an agrarian people weighed down by tradition. One can debate this endlessly, but somewhere in the middle is an emerging view: that the key players here are the Chinese people who actually engaged with the foreign barbarians—the students, the reformers, the brokers and middlemen, the Mildred Zhaos. These young Chinese adopted the leading ideas of the time and adapted them to Chinese society.

At the Baldwin School my grandmother and her classmates learned American-style calisthenics. They sang "American the Beautiful," "John Brown's Body," and Handel's "Hallelujah Chorus," and on stage they performed *A Christmas Carol*. English was the language of the classroom, and over time some students took on American names: Sally, Pearl, Grace. On the other hand, she always remained traditionally superstitious. Even though she was a Christian, Mildred Zhao also went to fortune tellers, my mother has told me, "paying people lots of money to write her fortune on a piece of paper."

In 1919, China exploded in a rage of nationalism. This is the year Mildred would have been a high school sophomore. In faraway Versailles, the talks to conclude World War I set off a collective anger among Chinese worldwide. In their view, the treaty should have returned the German-controlled ports in Shandong province to China, thus rewarding Chinese contributions to the Allies. Instead, negotiators stiffed Beijing and ceded the area to Japan. Riots and protests broke out across key Chinese cities beginning on May 4.

In Nanchang, two hundred students turned out to encourage a boycott of Japanese goods. The events that later became known as the May Fourth Movement were part of a broader collective rant against everything that held China back: foreign villains, traditional Confucian culture, feudalism, the suppression of women. The word thrown around was "new": New Culture Movement. *New Life* magazine. The intellectual journals of the day included *New Youth, New Tide, New Education, New Voice of Society*, and *New Woman*.

It must have been a confusing time for Mildred Zhao and her classmates. On one hand, the movement was an appeal to modernize; yet at the same time, foreigners were the enemy. It's as if the desire was for foreign things but not foreign people. Whose side was she on? In the end, she chose to look outward.

In the earliest letter I have from my grandmother, she writes of the violence and death around her. It is 1920, a time when China is a Balkanized mess run by regional warlords. Mildred Zhao has taken a train trip with her teacher Anna Graves to northern China, getting off to visit her parents living in a place called Paotingfu in what is today Hebei province. Graves continues on to Beijing (or

Peking) and then Tokyo, where news comes of a mutiny in Pao-tingfu. Mildred writes that everything is safe:

> My dear Miss Graves.
>   When I got your first letter from Peking, I was very glad to hear that you got to Tientsin and Peking safely.

She switches gears to the mutiny, a rebellion of a few soldiers against the warlord Wu Peifu. No big deal, Mildred writes, "just a short mutiny about a day." Her family inside the city wall is safe, though residents outside "were plundered by these soldiers. . . . The cholera has been very serious here this summer. Many people have died from it every day."

The handwritten letter is written in the old-school cursive where your pen does not leave the paper. It is so neat and tidy that today only a software program could replicate Mildred's practiced uniformity. It is that perfect. Then Mildred moves on to life at the school, mentioning names of her classmates and teachers.

> Phoebe will teach kindergarten. Miss Hsia moved to Soochow. Miss Honsinger has returned to China. Miss Baker wants me to translate newspapers into English. I just wrote Audree in France, where my cousin will go to study.

Then she asks her teacher's advice on studying overseas. Even at the age of seventeen, Mildred is thinking of going abroad.

> What do you think about this? Do you agree with this or not?
>   My parents and cousins give their best regards to you.
>
>   Your loving pupil,
>   Mildred Chao

It was a thrilling time to engage outside ideas and visitors. The American feminist Margaret Sanger went to the mainland to espouse new contraception techniques. Bertrand Russell, the British philosopher, visited and spoke of his work on mathematics and logic. Albert Einstein even stopped by, after finishing his work on relativity theory. "We are very lucky of having heard the playing of the world famous violinist, Miss Parlow, an Englishwoman," Mildred gushes in another letter. "It makes me crazy about good music."

Around the same time, another imported idea showed up in Shanghai, one that would affect Mildred greatly. A small group of political radicals met on the top floor of a girls' school in the city's French Concession. They formed a new organization they called the Chinese Communist Party. It was 1921.

For Mildred, the wheels would fall off a year later. She enrolled in China's first women's college, Ginling Women's College in Nanjing, a school started in 1915 by five American women educators supported by US mission groups. Today, it stands as one of several foreigner-founded universities still around today (though some exist under new names). Soon after beginning at Ginling, Mildred contracted malaria, forcing her to stop playing piano; then she caught influenza. Soon after, in 1923, she had what she called a mental health "brokedown," writing that she lost her self-control. "My parents were bitterly distressed on my illness especially, and they spent a great sum of money in the cure of my illness."

Ginling Women's College forced her to recover at home, so Mildred moved in with her parents. By then they worked at a silk-spinning plant in Wuhan, near her ancestral village. "I don't know how I can go on with my college education," she writes. "Probably I shall never have this hope in my life again." So Mildred sought help from her American teachers. She asked Anna Graves for career ideas—"do you like me to be a secretary?"—and for money to attend university abroad.

"I do hope that someday I can come to London to study in the School of Economics," she wrote to Graves, then in England. "I liked England better than I liked America, because England is much older and probably higher in her civilization, although her people are not agreeable enough than the Americans. I really feel very embarrass [sic] to ask your help like this, but I cannot keep it in since I want to go on in my studying very much."

"China Longevity Insurance Company reminds you, the next station is the Nanjing Massacre Memorial Hall," booms the automated voice on the public bus. My father and I are visiting Nanjing in the summer of 2013, and we are on our way to Ginling Women's College. My grandmother's old school has since been absorbed into Nanjing Normal University. An elderly woman rises to exit, shoving my father quickly into her seat before anyone else can claim it. "Sit," she instructs. "My stop is next."

It is another leafy campus, in another scorching Chinese furnace city. Not knowing where to start looking, Dad asks a student walking by if she can steer us to the Ginling Women's College part of the school.

"I am a Ginling student!" she exclaims, explaining that she's in a graduate program studying English.

"Then we can speak English," my dad says. "You can practice."

She looks down, with the pained smile of someone who has just stubbed her toe. No, she is too shy to try out her English on us, so we keep speaking Mandarin. This student is a bit heavyset, with wire-rimmed glasses and hair pulled back in a simple ponytail. She wears jeans and a green long-sleeve T-shirt that reads "VANIIY FAIR."

The original Ginling Women's College campus is stunning. It's a circular drive surrounding a main, classically styled Chinese building that looks straight out of the Ming dynasty. Here's the odd part: I later look up this building and learn it was designed by an American named Henry Murphy. It is a fascinating tale of cultural mixing from the time.

Murphy, who also designed the Yale-in-China campus in Hunan and Fudan University in Shanghai, described the Ginling style as "adaptive Chinese renaissance." The walls were built from the new technology known as reinforced concrete. There were modern lighting fixtures inside, as well as the latest indoor plumbing. But outside, it was entirely Chinese looking. Even this Chinese-looking building is a hybrid—a metaphorical Twinkie, as many would deride: Asian yellow on the outside, white on the inside.

Chinese cities again exploded with anti-foreigner rage in 1925. Mildred Zhao was teaching Chinese to students at a boarding school in Wuhan when she wrote Anna Graves. "I am afraid we are not allowed to write you about government affairs, otherwise I will tell you a little about China, for she is changing every day. Have you heard about the Shanghai incident of May Thirtieth?"

On May 30 in Shanghai, thousands of students and laborers demonstrated in front of the police station on Nanjing Road. They protested the arrest of six Chinese students venting against foreign imperialism. Some of the chanters screamed, "Kill the foreigners!" Just after ordering the crowd to scatter, a British law enforcement official ordered his Sikh and Chinese officers to shoot. They fired forty-four shots and killed eleven people. Protests erupted across China. Then in Canton (Guangzhou) a month later, British troops fired on demonstrating students, workers, military cadets, children, and Boy Scouts—killing fifty-two. A follow-up strike in Hong Kong lasted more than a year.

The politics that followed proved tragic to Mildred's family. Two political parties capitalized on the nationalistic sentiment across China. Membership in the newly born Communist Party skyrocketed, and the Nationalist Party of the brief 1911 revolution, the Guomindang, was revitalized as well. The two parties formed a marriage of convenience to take out powerful regional warlords and reunify a strong, new China. In July 1926, the joint forces began what became known as the Northern Expedition. After taking the Hunan city of Changsha, they moved toward Wuhan.

Controlling Wuhan was the ruthless warlord Wu Peifu. He was known for taking commanders who'd lost key positions and publicly beheading them. But Wu's armies had lost two of the three cities of Wuhan and held only the political capital, Wuchang. Inside the double walls of Wuchang was Mildred Zhao's family.

The attackers laid siege, cutting off all supplies to force or starve the people out. Newspaper articles suggest Wuchang was entirely blocked off by the ninth day. In one newspaper account, a woman named Liu Tai Ching of Shanghai was visiting Wuchang when the attack began. "I myself saw a family of three killed" by a bomb, Liu said. "Together, blackened and horribly wounded."

Families rationed their remaining food, watering down rice to make porridge. Three meals became two. One Episcopal church took in five hundred hungry people, and a Catholic hospital treated the malnourished. According to Liu, the price of scarce dry beans and turnips rose fivefold. Every dog was eaten.

Mildred Zhao's father, my maternal great-grandfather, did not survive. "National troops under the leadership of Chiang Kai Shek came to Hupeh from Kwantung," Mildred wrote to Anna Graves. "Wuchang was besieged. For forty days we were in a great horror inside the city wall. My father died on the thirty-second day."

I don't know exactly how he died, though many succumbed to starvation. One Irish missionary caught inside the walls of Wuchang, surnamed O'Donohugh, provided this description in William Barrett's book *The Red Lacquered Gate*: "In this city many thousands have died of starvation. The sights witnessed daily are revolting and deplorable. The helpless and the hopeless, the women with faces wan and haggard, the younger people with hands pressed against their stomachs shouting with hunger, all like walking corpses, moving about, heedless of bombs or bullets. Within the city there is no burial ground and the supply of coffins has long been exhausted. Along the street, corpses lie around any old place."

In a world dominated by males, Mildred's father—her chief advocate and financial patron—was gone. By the time her mother passed four years later, Mildred Zhao was twenty-seven years old.

Chapter Five

GENEALOGIES AND
CORRECTIONS
We Regret the Error

The problem with China is what you can't see: Morality. Underground aquifers.
Creativity.
—Wuhan driver

I never expected my mother to ever return to China to help me
track down her mother's story. Sure, I spent hours probing her
memories over the phone and in person in the States. But going
back to the mainland—that would replay too many memories that
are uniformly bad: war and death, barely outrunning the Communists, starting over in a Hong Kong squatter village, losing her
father at the age of eight. "I'm not ready," she often said.

There is an irony here. As much as I've been drawn to China
for opportunity and history, she has spent her adult life leaving
it behind. The state took away her family's property, and then her
father. But her adult life kept bringing her closer to the mainland.
In 1978, as China began to reconnect to the outside world, my
father's engineering job at IBM transferred us to Hong Kong for
two years. In 1980 we shipped off to Taiwan when he was recruited
to help start up the island's first science and technology development park. Later he was asked to lecture at business schools on the
mainland. Surprising to me, my mother joined him on one of these
trips. They met my father's younger brother, Tong Bao, who was left

behind on the mainland and later punished for the political sins of his father (my grandfather). "Every family has a story like this," he told her, recounting the famine, the exile, his mother's torture. "This is just ours."

This unlocked something inside her. As she describes it, she came to a sort of solidarity with so many others haunted by history. "My family is not the only victim," she told me. So she agreed to join me in 2013 on a sleuthing trip.

"Welcome to Hankou," a sixty-something man greets us at the train station of the Wuhan tri-city's most international city. His driver takes our bags rather forcefully but with good intentions. Our host, Liu Xuechao, is a distant cousin of my mother's. He has offered to take us to the Sun family village on her father's side, a couple hours outside Hankou (also Hankow).

"How was your hotel?" Liu Xuechao asks from the front seat. These initial meetings require a specific small talk that allows the host to speak and demonstrate authority. *How much did you pay for your room? You overpaid. Here, have a bottle of water—from Tibet, so it's not polluted. Have you visited the Yangtze riverfront? Chairman Mao once swam across it. Did you know Wuhan is considered the Chicago of China?*

The protocol demands we play along, at least for a few minutes. *Wow, Chairman Mao swam here—all the way across? Yes, surely that's a true story. The subway lines are impressive. As is your Citroën car. No, I did not know it was assembled here. I agree, Wuhan is the Zhijiage (Chicago) of China.*

The pride of Hankou is its comparison with Chicago, though I wonder why. After all, a "foreign devil" journalist coined the phrase. Perhaps it is Chicago's reputation as a vital inland city, a proud river-and-rail crossroads. More likely, it's Chicago's status as a brand-name city in the world, with bragging rights to one Chicago Bulls legend known here as Mai-ke-er Qiao-dan. I didn't hear much about Wuhan during my posting in China. A few auto industry friends came to visit parts facilities, but they referred to it as more as a backwater than a *Zhijiage*. It no longer has its past luster.

"Wuhan suffered under the Guomindang," retired historian Yuan Jicheng told me when we later visited him at Zhongnan University of Economics and Law. Investments were not made, and the city never returned to its industrial status of the 1920s and '30s. Today, its economy relies on stodgy, state-owned companies that make things like alcohol and cigarettes. To goose GDP numbers, Yuan said, the city digs up roads and paves them, and then repeats the process. "*Pianren* GDP," he said. Fool the People GDP.

We set off the next morning to the village of my maternal grandfather. Both our guide Liu Xuechao and my mom confess they aren't sure how they're related. "My mother didn't tell me much about the family," he says, taking a swig of Tibet Water, Unpolluted. "So she could protect me."

"Protect? How?" I ask.

"My grandfather was a landlord before liberation." If a child knew this and blabbed it around, this status could come out later and hurt the family. Best to keep incriminating information under wraps. Liu's grandfather tried to flee by boat to Taiwan to escape Communist retribution. "But they didn't let him in" to Taiwan, Liu says. "He didn't have the right papers." The grandfather returned and was later publicly beaten and shamed during the land reform campaigns. "So he committed suicide."

The car goes quiet for a moment. I've grown eerily accustomed to how comfortable people can be talking about tragedy. Quickly, though, Bureaucrat Uncle Liu fills the silence. "Now it's the government officials who are the rich ones," says this government official. "They're the new landlords. Drink some water."

The driver jumps in. "What do you think of China? Of Wuhan?"

"The party took my father away," my mother says. This is the first time I've heard her mention this in a public way. "But I look around here, and see the party has made people's lives better. Look at the buildings, the airports."

The driver does not take the compliment. "Those are just the things you can see: cars, skyscrapers, railroads. The problem with China is what you can't see." He looks at us squarely in the rearview mirror. "Morality. Underground aquifers. Creativity."

I jot it all down. He articulates this better than I can when trying to describe China's challenges. It's the things you can't see.

"What do the people think of the party?" my mom asks.

"Seventy to eighty percent of the people are dissatisfied," the driver says. That seems an awfully high number to me.

Bureaucrat Uncle Liu jumps in. "But we don't want another party in charge either. It's too *luan*." Too chaotic. Americans can have a romantic attachment to *luan*—a messy process of change, disruption, creative destruction, failing fast. Perhaps you crave these things if you have lived too long without any *luan*.

The highway turns into local paved road, and then gravel. We're following villages along a Yangtze tributary known as the Han River, with cotton and corn crops surrounding us. In all, this trip will take less than two hours. "Growing up, if I went to Wuhan from the village, it took twelve hours by boat," Liu says. "Now it's so fast. During the famine in 1959, I was just a child. I would steal rice from home during harvest, and then get on the boat and carry it to my family in the city."

We stop at the house of the one known relative still in the Sun village. My mother has always referred to this place as Mianyang, though now it's incorporated into the city of Xiantao. There's nothing visibly urban about this place. A white concrete outhouse features a hand-painted character *nv* for "women." We get out, duck under a few clotheslines, and step over a pile of broken bricks to approach.

It doesn't take long to see the disparity. Six houses are connected in a row, but they don't match. The units on the far left and right stand three stories high, topped with Spanish-style shingles. These are the wealthier families. In the middle are two older, single-floor houses that look dark and squat.

This is the house of Maozi, my mother's second cousin. "My father worked with yours," Maozi tells my mother as we walk in, "in the family honeybee business." I don't know all the details, but after World War II, their business involved a large population of bees on a boat that floated from one pollination site to another. After the Communist liberation, authorities arrested and jailed Maozi's father for working with my grandfather, whom the regime deemed a counterrevolutionary. "He died in prison. They said natural causes, but I'm not so sure." Maozi offers a cigarette to Bureaucrat Uncle Liu. "After he died, we received his ashes and his bedding mosquito net. It was stained with blood."

Maozi has a crew cut and is wearing a faded blue T-shirt and cotton shorts. One of his flip-flops has a broken strap, making it easier to see his thick, yellowed toenails. Everything about his body strikes me as weary except for his youthful eyes, which greet a female cousin with energy. He hands her a navy-blue hardback book, thicker than a dictionary (I'd later learn it contains 828 pages). The title reads: *Sun Clan Genealogy*. This is why we have come.

The genealogy was written in classical Chinese, a style that went out with the May Fourth modernization push in the early twentieth century. A rough analogue might be Latin, or perhaps King James English. No one in the room can read this very well. But one thing is clear upon flipping it open: this is not a simple family tree. Hundreds of pages of introductory sections precede the actual names. There is a history of the Sun clan travels (across China, then Jiangxi, then Hubei). There are rules to address different relatives (your father's paternal great-grandmother shall be referred to as *gao zeng zumu*). There's a set of clothing dos and don'ts for funerals (wear coarse hemp fabric without a hem, for three years). Respect the elderly. Do not steal. Violators are deleted from the Sun book of life.

I start to realize why people set genealogies on fire during political witch hunts. All these lineage connections can be used as incriminating evidence if powerful people deem one of your relatives a bad actor. Journalist Frank Ching writes about this in his own family history, *Ancestors*. One scholar in the family wrote a glowing history of the Ming Dynasty that its successor, the Qing, frowned upon. The new leaders sought to kill the writer, plus nine generations of kin, plus the book printer, plus book buyers. "Whole clans have been slaughtered because of the wrongdoings of only one member," Ching writes.

There's even an intro written by the most famous Sun in Chinese history—Dr. Sun Yat-sen, the founding father of modern China. There is no suggestion he had direct ties to my mother's clan. Rather, this passage seems more of a celebrity cameo. It's as if an American family surnamed Robinson asked Jackie Robinson to put in a word or two. Or perhaps Smokey.

"Here it is." My mom puts her finger on a page of her generation. It's her father's name.

Sun Guangde
Born Guangxu (Emperor) thirty-first year, third month, sixth day,
    twelfth hour
Attended Jiangxi Normal University
Date of death not known

Wife
Ms. Zhao
Birth and death not known
Bore one son

Guangde Son
Wendi
Also named Xiaodi
First moved to Hangzhou with father. In 1948 moved with mother
    to United States. Father died in mainland China. No further
    information.

I've never given my mother a fist bump, though this would have been the time. This has made the China trip hers, rather than just mine. She has spent a lifetime raising children, running a family and following my father and his jobs around the world—without an anchor. In a way, this is her anchor, and I can see it in her face.

But it doesn't last long. She moves her finger down the page and furrows her brow. "This information is wrong," she says. "All wrong." Her brother, listed here as Wendi, never moved to Hangzhou. Neither he nor his mother went to the States. This calls the whole publication's accuracy into question.

Maozi gently reminds her that the genealogy authors were not professional researchers, but family members who did the best they could. He offers her an opportunity: any corrections can go into the next—the twelfth—edition. It's like my day job: sometimes you just have to issue a correction or clarification.

I stand up, as my back is hurting from all the bending over, and wander out to the outhouse painted *nan*, men. This version is a simple hole in the ground. There is no toilet paper, though a paperback Chinese novel sits on the ledge—or to be accurate, half a book.

I tear out a couple pages, conclude my transaction, and return to the house.

"There are three things in history the party doesn't talk about," Bureaucrat Uncle Liu's driver says on the ride back. "The great famine. The Cultural Revolution. And Six-Four," a reference to the June 4, 1989, bloodshed in Tiananmen and elsewhere in China.

"What do *you* think of these three events?" My mom asks the obvious question in the air.

The driver pauses. "The party has made mistakes."

I ask the men about their memories from the famine, and they respond—as so many do—in a quantitative way.

"We only got two *jin* of cooking oil per month," Bureaucrat Uncle Liu says. Farmers here grew rice and delivered it to the government for money. "But money was useless. We had no ration coupons for more oil, so we couldn't buy any. We were living like North Korea."

Then Liu's mind wanders to the Korean War, when China sent so many soldiers to fight against the Americans in the early 1950s. "We lost so many soldiers to the Korean War. *Tamade gongchandang.*" Fucking Communist Party, says the retired Communist Party official. "Deng Xiaoping fixed it all."

It is time for lunch. We stop at a restaurant they know, even though I can barely see it from the road. On more than one occasion in China, I've dined at semiprivate spots known only to party members. After a narrow entrance, the restaurant opens up to a big outdoor courtyard, with large photos on the walls. It's like a Hard Rock Cafe of political superstars: Premier Wen Jiabao visiting the restaurant, a local party secretary and his entourage. The VIPs in the photos wear either suits or the alternate uniform: golf shirt, cotton pants, black leather belt and shoes.

"*Tamade gongchandang.*" Fucking Communist Party, the driver says. "All corrupt." A hostess they clearly know ushers us into a large, air-conditioned private room. Each table setting has chopsticks, napkin, spoon, bowl, and plate. And four cups.

"One is for tea," Bureaucrat Uncle Liu explains, pointing to the round, ceramic cup. Next to it, a wide-mouthed wineglass holds beer. "The third is for *baijiu,*" a mini wineglass for sorghum alcohol. And finally, a somewhat larger glass-handled container serves to pour *baijiu*. Like a sports bar back home, the drinks here matter more than the food.

Our hosts order twice as much as we can eat. Steamed bright-green lotus seeds and breaded pork ribs are the local Hubei specialties. I assume the sardine-size fish stir-fried with potato strings are from local waterways. Potatoes by most accounts entered China in the 1600s, by way of Portuguese traders, but the ones here grow locally, the driver explains. "Not polluted."

I try feebly to grab the check, for appearance's sake. Bureaucrat Uncle Liu responds with a talk-to-the-hand gesture, indicating things have already been settled. But as we walk out of this establishment for the politically privileged, I'm not sure if anyone has actually paid.

The Zhao and Sun villages of my maternal grandparents sit on either side of the Han River. The next day brings a second village visit, this time to the side of grandmother Mildred Zhao. For this we have no relative, no chauffeur. Instead, we take a ninety-minute long-distance bus ride—landlords Monday, peasants Tuesday.

The bus waits until it's filled with paying passengers before departing. As always seems the case on rides like this, a DVD movie plays on the screen in front. The audio is poor, but I can make out the obvious point of the film. It's to showcase beautiful woman with unrealistically fair skin. One damsel finds herself forced by lecherous, darker-skinned men to drink herself crooked at a banquet. Another appears on trial for something, and is found guilty. She cries. Two fair-skinned women serve to brighten up the jury, at which point my mother and I trade observations about China's skin-lightening market for lotions and creams: a billion pairs of cheeks.

Two young men from the local government's foreign affairs tourism bureau greet us in Hanchuan city. Indeed, they wear the golf-shirt-and-slacks uniform. I have come with low expectations. Several observers criticize these offices with "foreign affairs" in their names as thinly disguised fronts for graft and corruption: schmooze overseas Chinese and foreigners, talk them into investing, and lop off a personal cut.

Here, though, the workers get straight to our business. They talk briefly in their office, take us to a quick lunch (one cup per person), and we're off to the Zhao village. Today, the roads are paved, an indication the Zhao village might be better off than the Sun village. We pass a set of townhomes with a government message painted on the wall, for birth control:

> The nation's family planning for the countryside: To encourage families, we will provide assistance of 680 renminbi.

That's about $100. The "encouragement" was a reward for birth control. Another message indicates that Hanchuan families are allowed two children:

> Work hard to carry out the parenthood of 2.
> Ensure the 2 Plan works properly.
> Control migrant workers accordingly.
> Work hard to bring home the goals of science and technology.

I read the next sign aloud. "Love girls."

"Because it's a weakness of ours," one of the officials explains. "They still prefer boys in the countryside."

The Zhao village is a scene of chaos. A choir of cicadas serenades us as we walk into the house, and at first blush it seems to be entirely men here. Next door, a funeral of someone unrelated is under way, indicated by an inflatable blue gate at the door and music oozing out of a boom box.

As we enter, I can't understand any of the introductions. They're speaking in a local dialect. Wading through the bodies as if in a bar, my mother and I find stools to sit on, at which point a giant slice of watermelon appears in my hand. "Spit the seeds on the floor," someone says in Mandarin. Okay.

The Zhao family genealogy is different from the Sun version. Rather than a hardback book, it's six or seven flimsy paperback publications stacked on top of one another. Each is half an inch thick, cheaply bound—and easy to set on fire in case of political emergency. This edition will not last a century. One cousin settles next to my mother and the local official, flipping through. Others pass around the 1977 obituary of Grandmother Mildred Zhao we've brought.

"She looks like a capitalist," says one cousin with a blue golf shirt and side-parted, sculpted hair. It's neither an insult nor a compliment, just an observation.

The genealogy readers struggle with the classical Chinese, and most of the date references. Rather than Arabic numbers—or numbers at all—the dates of births and deaths are based on which emperor is on the throne. For instance, one person's entry shows he was born in Guangxu emperor Year 25.

"There might not be any information about your mother," the official warns, "because she was female." Plus, Mildred Zhao was not born in this village. We believe she was born in Nanjing. "If people go out, then there's no news here," Side-Part Cousin adds.

Then the official notices something is wrong with the time references. Mildred Zhao's uncles are listed as being born during the rule of Emperor Qianlong, who reigned in the 1700s. That was way off. Since she was born in 1903, her father's brothers lived in the mid-1800s, long after Qianlong died. But no worries, they say: there is always a next edition. In fact, Side-Part Cousin says Zhao family members are drafting it already, and raising funds to pay for it.

"If you want your name put in, it costs one hundred renminbi," he says. About $13.

"Can women's information go in?" my mother asks.

"Sure." So long as you pay. "Whatever you want. If you want to buy the whole genealogy, it will cost five hundred renminbi." Sixty-five dollars. I sit there and realize this is a good deal: $13 for published immortality.

Chapter Six | THE COMMUNIST MOLE IN THE SCHOOL

I was compelled to leave Hankow on account of the great flood.
—Mildred Zhao

Shanghai, upon first arrival, is almost impossible to place in a familiar context. Is it a Chinese city, or a global one? Who's in charge? There is something here for everyone: bankers, hucksters, beggars, British, multinationals, construction workers, prostitutes. At the historic Jing'an Temple on Nanjing Road, migrant factory workers from Anhui scurry across the street alongside Chinese men in Western suits working for Nestlé or Eveready. Buicks swerve by. A few blocks east, the latest Hollywood blockbuster is showing at the Grand Theater. If you can't find the theater, walk past the YMCA and you'll see it; if you get to the big department stores, you've gone too far.

The year is 1931. The visitor is Mildred Zhao.

She arrived during a golden age of capitalism in Shanghai. The city was the inaugural laboratory experiment in the treaty port system, first opening to foreign trade in 1843. This arrangement was built on what historian Marie-Claire Bergère calls a "double misunderstanding." The Mandarins in Beijing assumed that opening up a few treaty ports would be a one-shot deal to appease the barbarians' appetite, whereas the British treated it as the first crack in a doorway to later open wider. The place began, Bergère writes, as "a frontier town on the edge of empire."

The Great Flood of 1931 delivered Mildred Zhao to Shanghai from Wuhan. In China, floods are markers of time. The long history of China can be told in many ways: as a procession of dynasties, a hockey-stick chart of GDP, calories consumed, or the times rivers burst their banks. Between the Yellow and the Yangtze Rivers, there were major floods in 1870, 1887, 1911, 1931, 1935, 1938, 1948, 1951, 1954, 1975, 1998. Observers have attributed tragedies over time to bad dredging management, or signs that an emperor has lost the mandate of heaven to rule.

The 1931 deluge came after a record snowfall in the Tibetan Plateau. The spring thawing sent record flows rushing down to the east and the Pacific. Combining with twenty-four inches of monsoon rainfall in July, the ensuing flood overflowed the banks of the two rivers that converge in Wuhan: the Han and the Yangtze. Hankou fell under nearly five feet of water.

Mildred wrote in one letter: "I was compelled to leave Hankow on account of the great flood. Shanghai was the only refuge, because there were many friends there."

She gave no specifics. Perhaps she witnessed the riverfront rise an astonishing fifty-three feet above normal levels, higher even than the fifty-foot dikes. Maybe she lingered as the waters did, for half a year. This was not a rushing, high-speed disaster, but a slow-motion inundation of seventy thousand square miles. "This is an area approximately equal to the whole of England plus half of Scotland or to New York, New Jersey, and Connecticut combined," a report from the China Flood Relief Commission noted. It described the deluge as "the greatest flood on historical record."

Certainly she saw death. The flood commission estimated 140,000 drowned in the disaster. Separately, smallpox, cholera, and dysentery claimed another four million lives. The flooding destroyed crops nationwide, prompting starvation and food inflation. To survive, men sold their children for money, or sometimes their wives. Living bodies ate dead ones.

The numbers are mind shattering. The total casualties from this flood exceeded by fifteen times those of the Indonesian tsunami of

2004. The area flooded is triple that of America's most destructive flood, the Mississippi disaster of 1927.

Mildred Zhao went downstream as part of a mass evacuation. Half a million people—more than the entire population of Minneapolis or New Orleans at the time—were displaced. She was twenty-eight and alone. Her dreams of studying in America had long been stalled, and now she was simply trying to start over.

Shanghai was a city of second chances. During the bloody Taiping Rebellion of the mid-1800s, millions of Chinese sought haven in the city's international concessions. More came during the 1911 revolution. During their own revolution, Russians who defended the tsar against the Bolsheviks found themselves without a home, so many fled south. From 1926 to 1927, when regional warlords controlled much of the north around Beijing, intellectuals and writers escaped to Shanghai. During World War II, tens of thousands of Jews ejected from Nazi Europe went to the only place that would take them without visas: Shanghai. The city had not become a safety net for people by design; it was haven because local governance was so weak.

As so many newcomers did, Mildred Zhao sought out members of her tribe. In her case, it was teachers and classmates from the Stephen L. Baldwin School for Girls. She'd stayed in touch with so many over the years: Gladys Wang. Cheo Lan Ching. Tang Mo Chiao. Sylvia Fu. Some she mentioned in letters by first name only: Harriett, Ruth, Lydia, Phoebe.

One Baldwin alum taught at a university and found Mildred Zhao a job teaching world history and geography. From the campus, Mildred wrote a long catch-up letter to her old Baldwin teacher Anna Graves in Baltimore. By my math, this was her first letter in nine years.

August 12, 1934

My dear Miss Graves,

I do not know the reason for my laziness as sending you a letter telling about all my past. Excuses are unnecessary as you said in your last letter which came to me a few days ago; only one I must tell you that since the death of both my parents, I seldom write letters.

Examining the letter, I can see the Mildred's penmanship evolved over the years. It's less bold. Compared with a decade prior, each letter slants a little less and has shrunk down one font size. Her capital *P*s, once drawn with a dramatic loop, have evolved into a pragmatic stick–plus–half circle. If Mildred Zhao by now is dreaming less big, less ambitious, her handwriting suggests it.

The letterhead says "Great China University," and I realize I have been there. After the Communists took over China, Great China University became part of what's now East China Normal University. I've probably gone there twenty times, walking up the same campus steps my grandmother did. The campus is just across the Suzhou Creek from our old apartment complex.

On weekends I'd sometimes jog over a bridge and make my way over to the university's giant statue of Chairman Mao. He stands on a square base and rises up twenty feet high in a buttoned coat, hand raised high and waving as if he's Pocahontas bidding farewell to Captain John Smith. Then I'd turn around for home. Sometimes the kids and I rode bikes to East China Normal: typically our older son, Evan, would pedal in front on his own bike, and I'd follow with Daniel (then a preschooler) on the bike seat behind. On the way back, we'd buy a bottle of their favorite sports drink: the Japanese brand Scream.

A few times, I gave guest lectures at the university, mostly to visiting students from the States. I'd stand before them and tally everything I got wrong about China, and then take their questions. *No, an undervalued Chinese currency does not help Chinese consumers, it hurts them. Yes, the dollar has lost value against the renminbi—you can check my pay stub. Yes, we think we're being bugged. No, the people trying to track the* Marketplace *bureau do not seem very smart. No, the profits from an iPhone assembled in China do not stay in China; they go to Taiwan, Japan, and mostly Cupertino.*

I imagine my grandmother addressed some of the same issues of China and the world when she taught there in the 1930s. But there was one difference: I told stories about all the provinces and countries I'd already visited. She spoke of places she *wanted to see.*

In 1933 Mildred Zhao married. She recounted the events in a letter to Anna Graves in Maryland.

His name is Carleton Sun and is three years younger than I. His family and mine lived together while both our fathers were working in the same place in Nanchang about twenty years ago. Both fathers and mothers were friends and we two were small friends.

During the siege of Wuchang, Mildred and Carleton met again, and after her father died in the siege, "he helped us a lot and my mother loved him the more."

He was handsome. Carleton Sun appears in half a dozen black-and-white photos from the time, looking out from deep, confident eyes. His face was defined by high, symmetrical cheekbones. His hair parts on the side, in a way more suited for a television anchor than a grandfather. "He was a very good-looking man," my mother has said more than once.

Early on in his life, Carleton chose politics—or perhaps politics chose him. In the mid-1920s, China had fallen into a volatile mess of competing warlords and bandits, Nationalists, Communists, student protesters, and unions. During this messy time, Carleton was studying business at Wuchang Zhonghua University.

"This was during the Wuhan revolution," Carleton wrote in a letter to Fudan University administrators. "Students, in addition to studying, also participated in the revolution. At the time, I was ordered to participate in youth movements."

The movements targeted warlords and imperialists. Students and rioters ransacked the British concession in Hankow (today Hankou) city, tearing open sandbags tacked at the entrance and penetrating barbed-wire barricades. Panicked British citizens responded by hustling their wives and children onto riverboats bound for Shanghai. Before long, London abdicated its treaty port possessions in Hankow and nearby Jiujiang.

Carleton also had reason to oppose the budding Communist Party. Mildred writes: "He did not have a chance to finish college courses, for his family property was occupied by the Communists for nearly seven years."

I've spent a lot of time trying to understand this Communist property-taking. This is important, because my grandfather later on took a strongly anti-Communist position, and it turned out tragic for him. Around that time, the young Communist Party was actually struggling and had retreated to the countryside. They'd severed their Northern Expedition alliance with Chiang Kai-shek's Guomindang (the GMD betrayed the Communists with a bloody purge in Shanghai). One of the party's rural bases was by a lake Honghu near Wuhan. There, a Communist-allied bandit named He Long led campaigns to torch villages and execute landlords. More than one person has suggested it was He Long's men who took my grandfather's family land. Perhaps. But how could I confirm this?

My next step was, in retrospect, not very savvy. I asked a local Wuhan historian where to find documentation of this persecution at the hands of the Communists. He gave me one of those you-must-be-stupid looks. "Even if they exist, they won't show them to you," he said. Public evidence of Communist bandits pillaging villages and executing people was not something the party was going to make easy to find. "I can try to look for you," he said, suggesting he could leverage his connections to get documents through the back door. He never followed up with me.

Then I realized something: I had just waded inadvertently into a broader fight over historical documents in China. Since the state controls the narrative, it naturally limits information that can undercut that narrative. Many Chinese archives are available only to the powerful and well connected. As I researched this section of history, one entire historical archive, the number two national archive in Nanjing, was closed. Or at the very least, it was "only unavailable to those with the best *guanxi* relationships," one historian told me. The number two's official status was "closed for digitizing." But the rumor was that documents incriminating to top leaders had leaked out, so archive staffers had to go over everything carefully to prevent a recurrence.

Many historians I know fume about this, but none as eloquent as sinologist Jeremiah Jenne in Beijing. "I feel like getting some friends together to 'Ocean's Eleven' the number two archives," Jenne told me. This was a reference to a movie about a brilliant casino heist pulled off by George Clooney plus ten friends. Here, though, Clooney and Co. would never stand a chance against the Chinese bureaucrat librarians.

The digital speedometer on the bullet train hits three hundred kilometers per hour, or 186 miles per hour. I'm sitting in the aisle seat next to my mother, as we are now on our way to visit her cousin in the eastern city of Suzhou. Like an idiot, I blurt "Three hundred!" every time we hit that speed.

We're on our way to Suzhou to visit my mother's cousin she calls Sanjie (*sanjie* means "third sister"). Sanjie is my grandfather Carleton Sun's niece who spent a lot of time with him. After Sanjie's father died in his early twenties, Carleton supported her family and moved them to Shanghai.

"She joined the Communist Party," Mom says as the train slows, "so she cut herself off from our family. Drew a clear boundary line." This is a common phrase: *hua qing jie xian*, draw a clear boundary line. This was a Mao-era survival mechanism, to cut yourself off from anyone with an incriminating past: a spouse, a sibling, a child. Otherwise, if that person got caught, your mouth was attached to the same hook. At the time, Carleton Sun and his family had anti-Communist pasts, so Sanjie had to cut loose from them.

But time has a way of healing things. "Ai lian!" Sanjie walks out of her bedroom to greet my mother by her Chinese name. They don't hug, but instead do a handshake that turns into a handhold. Several others join us in the living room of her modest apartment: Sanjie's husband, daughter, and son-in-law.

On the way here, I've suggested that my mother not mention this book project—it tends to cause lips to tighten. It's one thing to sit and chat, and quite another to put information in the public domain. My mother deftly winds down the small talk and asks Sanjie her recollections of Carleton Sun,

"He came from a tradition of Western learning," Sanjie says, throwing out a term I need a little help with: *xi xue dong zhe*. Western learning spreading East. "He dressed Western. White suits and white shoes. He was very cultured."

This came as a surprise. My grandfather was by far the more culturally Chinese than his wife. Even though he loved to eat at the American restaurant at the Shanghai YMCA, he hardly spoke

English, whereas Mildred spoke it fluently and went to the opera. I suppose this was all a matter of degree. To Sanjie and her siblings, who were never exposed to Western things, Carleton and Mildred dressed Western—perhaps too Western.

Carleton's mother—my great-grandmother—it turns out, was quite a character. She stayed home with bound feet and a feisty demeanor. Sanjie says: "She peeked into strangers' doors during the Japanese occupation and was never scared of anyone." She owned a textile dye house that she later bequeathed to a younger relative. But he gambled and squandered the money.

Sanjie sits back. "So, one year at Chinese New Year, he returned home and she beat him."

Later, Sanjie disappears into her bedroom and brings out something for my mother. It is more than sixty years old: a decorative porcelain cup that sat in my mother's family apartment in Shanghai. They had left it behind when they fled ahead of the Communists in 1949.

I'm surprised she still has it. "Didn't this kind of thing get destroyed in the Cultural Revolution?" I ask. Surely keeping this cosmetic item would have invited accusations of punishable status: bourgeois, landlord, rich peasant, running dog of capitalism.

"No." She shares no further details. I have a feeling this octogenarian remains as wily as ever. To survive all these years of mainland tumult, as a member of the party, you develop a certain savvy of what information to share and what not to.

We move onto other topics, and Sanjie loosens up about Carleton. He loved kids. He would proclaim to a group of children: "Boys and girls, what do you want to eat today?" He loved to eat peanuts, whole peanuts, except for the tiny nub piece protruding from the tip—the seed. Otherwise, "peanuts will grow up and out through the top of your head," he told them. He gave each child ten peanuts for every spoonful of cod liver oil they downed. He could work a room.

The interaction with Sanjie and her family goes really well—until it turns combative over dinner. Nearly twenty extended family members gather for a restaurant banquet near the China–

Suzhou Singapore Industrial Park. We sit around a giant table, perfectly suited for grandstanding men to challenge other men. Particularly, men from America.

One of Sanjie's sons begins: "Do you eat genetically modified
foods? Americans eat lots of GMOs."

"Yes." I explain that GMO and non-GMO corn, at least in America, are stored together. You can't separate them out. And then I
regret going there.

"Europeans don't like them," he replies. "Neither do Chinese."

This is a familiar moment to any American who has spent five
minutes overseas—the moment he or she becomes an unwilling
proxy for everything good and ugly about the United States. Not
only must I engage in my second language, I also have to address
distorted facts. In China, so much news about the outside world
lacks context, or is presented in an outright anti-foreigner context. So I'm not just defending America, I'm defending Funhouse-
Distorted America.

Another son jumps in: "You know, China is becoming better
friends with the Middle East. This is a good opportunity, because
America abandoned this part of the world. It's because America
now has its own oil. It's all about the oil."

I can't resist this one, because I've reported a fair bit on this
exact question. "That's overstated. Americans still import a lot of
oil from the Middle East, several million barrels every day." And, I
add, Washington has historically spent billions to support stability in the whole region—to gather intelligence, to protect shipping
lanes, to defend Israel.

The son nods and gives me a few seconds to eat, which also gives
him time to circle and jab from a new direction. "Do Americans
care about Edward Snowden?"

"What do you mean?"

"Of course they do!" Often in this situation, a combatant will
pose a rhetorical question simply to give his own answer. I do know
there's a lot of news about Snowden in China, but in a different
context. Back home in the States, the focus of the Snowden leaks
is on the US government spying on its own people. But in China,

it's all about American hypocrisy: Washington accuses Beijing for hacking US databases, yet now the Ugly Americans are caught spying on other countries—including China. Gotcha.

Son 2 goes on: "Do Americans think the Snowden news is good? Or bad?"

I take a breath and try to explain the American government is actually not the same thing as the American people, the same way official Beijing does not equal real China. Then I make the case that even though these leaks are embarrassing for the US government, transparency is good. My job is not to protect the reputation of Washington. In fact, if I as a reporter expose something embarrassing about my own government, I win awards.

It's a good argument, except that it takes far too long for me to say in Chinese. I get blank stares in return. In any event, for these brothers, encounters with foreigners are not really debates or exchanges of information. They're release valves for their frustrations with an outside world that can be so hostile and critical of China. It's their way of saying: *We're finally catching up with the modern world, and you the historic polluters are lecturing us about climate pollution? We are making low-cost products for consumers, earning pennies, and getting beat up about it?*

The original brother jumps in, this time to rescue me. "America. We like the people, but not the government. They just want to be everyone's policeman. For China, it's best to be number two, or maybe number three in the world. Otherwise, we'll attract too much attention."

He offers a toast to my mother and me and—voilà—he has expertly saved face for me, and for him, and for China. I ladle some food onto my plate and wait for someone to please change the subject.

When my grandparents Carleton Sun and Mildred Zhao married, he was studying at Shanghai's elite Fudan University. During my 2013 trip, I have plopped myself down on a curved bench on the campus of Fudan University. I have been running for a month, racing across Japan and China for small bits of history that may or may not fit together. My father is waiting for me at a nearby hotel. I still need to catch up with Ayi, our old nanny, and interview my cousin and my uncle. Cathy and kids want to know when I'm coming home.

And then I stop myself, and wonder what it must have been like for Carleton Sun eighty years prior. By the time he got to Fudan in his late twenties, he'd lost his father and brother, joined a movement to kick foreigners out of Hankou, survived the world's worst flood on record, and seen his village property taken by bandit warlords. He'd have needed this bench more than I.

Like many universities in China, Fudan was designed by a foreigner—specifically, Henry Murphy, the same American architect who'd designed Ginling Women's College in Nanjing. Fudan University was set up in 1905, by dissident professors and students from the Jesuit Aurora University across town. The word *fudan* means roughly "return of the dawn," chosen by its founder to symbolize China's new, outward-looking future.

There are a lot of similar examples. The medical center at the elite Jiao Tong University in Shanghai has its roots in an 1844 facility founded by a British missionary. Fudan's medical college was founded by a Chinese public health doctor who graduated from Yale. The list goes on: the Rockefeller Foundation helped fund Nankai University in Tianjin, the US Congress supported the original Tsinghua University in Beijing. American financier Edward Harkness donated to Xiangya Medical College in Hunan. The century of humiliation sure left behind a lot of lasting institutions.

Approaching the entrance of the university archive, I once again rehearse my pitch to the staff: Chinese American, looking up family history, my grandfather went here, requesting records. The only person in the small entry room is a middle-aged woman at a wooden desk. "*Yao shen ma?*" What do you want?

Before I get very far into my spiel, she interrupts. "*Zhen jian.*" Document. I hand over my passport, along with Carleton Sun's from 1949. "Wow," she says, reaching out with two hands as if she's taking communion at church. She flips to the main passport page, to the section written in both French and English.

The Ministry of Foreign Affairs of the Republic of China requests all civil and military authorities of Friendly States to let pass freely

[handwritten] SUN I, CARLETON
a national of the Republic of China, going to
[handwritten] USA, CHILE, ARGENTINA, BRAZIL, VIA ALL NECESSARY
COUNTRIES
and afford assistance and protection in case of necessity.

"How did you get this?" she asks.

"My mother kept it all these years."

"And how did she preserve it so well?

This is my opportunity to say *bu tai qing chu*. It's not so clear. I present a few more supporting documents as a male student walks in and stands right behind me. The woman gatekeeper's lengthy pause troubles me.

"Can you prove this man Sun Honglie is your relative?"

Ouch. This is the question I'd prayed not to come up. This same thing happened in Tokyo. I have no documentary evidence that Carleton Sun fathered my mother. In fact, I haven't even brought my own birth certificate.

"*Bu hao yi si,*" I say. Sorry, this is all I have.

"Hold on." She disappears through a door behind her. The student behind me sighs. And then, relief—she returns in two minutes with a slim 8-by-10-inch envelope. "You can't take these with you." Neither am I allowed to photocopy them. "But you can take pictures with your phone. Go over there to do it. *Kuai dian.*" Hurry.

The "hurry" sets me off, but my back turns before I roll my eyes. Then I open the envelope and pull out the contents: Yellowed papers. Folded handwritten letters. Report cards the size of 5-by-7 index cards. A course sign-up sheet: Chinese name. English name. Major (banking). Student number (5711).

The report cards tally his grades from both Wuchang Zhonghua University and Fudan. Carleton Sun, it turns out, was not a great student.

World Trade Theory: B−
Economic History: C+
Banking History: D
Modern Political Systems: B−

Banking Systems: A−
American Political Systems: C+
Question of Chinese Accounting: C−
History of American Literature: D+
Commercial Banking: D+
Japanese—Basic: B−
History of Chinese political theory: D
History of Economic Thought: C+
Rail Transportation: B−
Japanese Language: D−

Wow, okay. For some reason I treat the report card as a secret document, looking over my shoulder and assuming the protective crouch I employ at the ATM. And I start snapping pictures.

The year 1934 was a defining one for both Mildred Zhao and the Chinese Communist Party. It was the year of the Long March, when the Red Army, decimated by the Guomindang in Jiangxi, retreated to a four-thousand-mile trip across punishing and frigid terrain. The men who survived ended up in Shanxi and began plotting their military and political comeback.

In Shanghai Mildred Zhao and her husband built a private grade school and started enrolling students. "I had planned for three years to open a girls' middle school before I asked my two friends to join me," she wrote Anna Graves. "I always think that this will be the better way for we girls to do some solid work for our country. . . . We had ninety-two students the last term. In spite of the danger, I am very happy and interested in my work."

She named the school *hai guang xiaoxue*. Light of the Sea Primary School. When my mother and her sister talk about their old days in Shanghai, it's *hai guang* this, *hai guang* that. Mildred wrote:

The name of the school is Hai Kwong Primary School. "Hai Kwong" means the light of the sea. I do wish this little light could guide our small people in the dark.

The school went up on Avenue Tenant de la Tour, Lane 431. The road was named after a French lieutenant and World War I flying ace surnamed Tenant de la Tour. Or Lado Road, in Chinese. Based on an address directory from that time, if Mildred walked south down the avenue toward the Catholic cathedral, she'd have passed the China South Weaving store and Yung Ching Rice Shop. Her neighbors were surnamed Virsky, Grant, Dietrich, Savitsky, Kardosvskaya, Robin, Munson, Jaubert, and Green. Going northbound, she'd encounter the Southern California Oil Company, an outfit called Le Champ de Cours Français, and Shanghai's main Jewish synagogue.

It was an international neighborhood, but Mildred and Carleton only partially embraced it. In certain respects, Mildred lived a culturally Chinese and inward-looking life. She avoided dealing with Jewish merchants and described them in unkind ways. Clinging to old traditions and beliefs, she served pig's foot to her daughter Lily on the eve of Lily's trip to the Holy Land, on the assumption that eating feet strengthens your own for walking. She cooked pig's brain for the same reason. Often she dreamt about burning incense and paper money to dead ancestors.

At the same time, she loved classical music performances—except for the parts when she nodded off. "I was listening!" she would later claim. When designing the school, she splurged on notable Western technology upgrade: flush toilets. And for hours every week, she wrote her English-language letters to her contacts in the States. Mildred still had aspirations of studying there.

This was the source of conflict with Carleton, who hardly spoke any English. If they were alive today, he'd disparage her as a "banana"—yellow on the outside, white inside, insufficiently Chinese. And yet, Carleton was a culturally hybrid man himself. He wore both Chinese coats and Western suits. He danced the tango and fox-trot when he went out. They lived in a "patchwork town," in the words of historian Marie-Claire Bergère, and thus lived patchwork lives.

It all seemed very promising at the outset. Their first child, Lily, arrived in 1935. Then Constantine in 1938. School business increased, and by the late 1930s enrollment exceeded four hundred students. During the occupation of China by Japan in World War II, the Light of the Sea Primary School was remarkably safe and secure. "Comparatively we suffer very little during the hostilities," Mildred wrote in 1939. "My address will not be changed at least for 20 years."

That same year, Mildred brought in a business partner to administer the school as dean, a woman named Zhang Qiong. She later became the godmother to Mildred's son, my Uncle Eddie. But there was one thing about Zhang Qiong that was unknown to anyone at the school at the time: she was an underground member of the Communist Party. In the meantime, Mildred's husband was being recruited for a high-profile political job back home in Wuhan.

The unraveling would soon begin.

PART TWO | The Great Interruption

Chapter Seven | THE DAY THE JAPANESE WAR DEVILS CAME

He grabbed a piece of paper and drew a Japanese flag on it. And put it on a bamboo pole to welcome them.
—Villager Tong Guangde

During World War II in China, my great-grandfather saved the Tong village from slaughter. At least that's what villagers tell me— all the villagers. This is the challenge of oral history. On one hand, several people here corroborate the basic story and details, so it seems hard to make something up in such a coordinated way. This passes the two-source rule of journalistic confirmation. On the other hand, I wonder about historical groupthink, how so many memories can converge on the version recalled by the best story-teller. Or the loudest or most frequent storyteller. In this case, the people I'm talking to were either quite young at the time, or they'd heard the story from elders.

By this time in World War II, the Japanese had taken advanced positions across China, occupying key rail and river strongholds. Many of these were the same locations controlled by European powers a century prior: Tianjin, Qingdao, Shanghai, and the Yangtze cities at the bottom of the Grand Canal. When the Japanese marched on the river cities of Changzhou, Zhenjiang, and Yangzhou, and then took Nanjing in horrific fashion, they were just 120 miles south of the Tong village. News came quickly, even to this Jiangsu backwater.

"Pregnant women, they raped them," Tong Daren's niece tells me during my village visit with her. "Stabbed with bayonets."

My great-grandfather was still living in Nanjing when the Japanese came, and somehow he escaped the bloody winter of 1937/38. His son, my grandfather, had retreated to Sichuan in the remote southwest with the forces of Chiang Kai-shek's Guomindang. There in Sichuan, his wife bore a son—my father—before she succumbed to tuberculosis four or five years later.

Much has been written about the Rape of Nanking, but there is one account most searing to me: the recollection of Japanese soldier Deguchi Gonjiro, recorded in activist and filmmaker Tamaki Matsuoka's book *Torn Memories of Nanking*. His words are imprinted on the wall of the Nanjing Massacre Memorial Hall—in a section describing a Japanese soldier's confession:

> On the day when Nanjing was seized, the corpses outside the city wall piled into hills when we entered the city. I felt something soft under my soles, so I lit a match and found the ground was covered with dead bodies as if it was covered with mats. There were women, children, old men and old women. . . . I once saw they took women on their shoulders and raped them, even old women were captured and they were killed immediately after they were raped. It was extremely cruel.
> Now we must apologize to the Chinese people.

After the Japanese took Nanjing, and then Wuhan further west, fighting in the China theater came to a relative standstill. Tong Zhenyong left Nanjing and went up the Grand Canal to the Tong village. Around 1940, according to oral interviews, Japanese troops approached the village. And my great-grandfather went up to talk to them.

"Tong Zhenyong told us, 'Don't be afraid,'" Tong Daren's niece says. She was less than ten at the time. The story from her and several villagers goes something like this: Tong Zhenyong hosted the Japanese troops in a village granary for about three hours, talking to them, feeding them, and pleading for them to spare the village. "He saved us," she says.

I ask, "I heard he cooked something for the Japanese soldiers to eat—some kind of egg?"

"*Dan cha.*" Poached egg with sugar.

"And did he wave some kind of white surrender flag?" One villager had mentioned this to me.

"Don't know anything about a flag."

Among the people I try to confirm all this with is the despised Tong Guangde, the tall man with the hat from Tong East. I meet him at an outdoor table in the village just outside his house. This time he's wearing a baseball cap.

"*Xun gen?*" he asks. Searching for your roots again? As we exchange pleasantries, another elderly man joins us. This always happens here. A stranger comes, the people pounce. Representing himself as in his eighties, this man would have been a teenager in 1940. His hair is jet white, as is his thick moustache. He is wearing blue sweatpants and a red warm-up jacket with a logo of Michael Jordan soaring for a dunk. "I remember your great-grandfather," Moustache Tong says. "I grew up here and then moved away. I'm just back from Anhui province."

Hat Man Tong interrupts with the requisite host greeting: "Did you eat?" Moustache Tong waves his hand to reject the offer. I do the same and say yes, I have eaten, which is a lie. There is no time for lunch. It's already midday, and I have two precious hours to gather information, grab my suitcase, and hustle onto the bus for Shanghai. Chinese hospitality is many things, but it is not efficient.

I move on quickly to the "Tong Zhenyong Saves Village" story. "I hear a hundred Japanese soldiers came that day?"

"No," Hat Man says. "Not more than twenty." Already he is sketching out an alternate narrative. "When they came, he grabbed a piece of paper and drew a Japanese flag on it. And then he put it on a bamboo pole to welcome them."

The flag details also differ. I'd heard about a white flag, not a Japanese flag. There is something extremely challenging about these oral histories. It's a bit like that party memory game where you place ten items on the table with a sheet over it, and then lift the sheet briefly for everyone to see. You re-cover everything and see how many items each person can list. But in this case, the actual event has been covered for more than seven decades. Each person's recollection is colored by his own thoughts and narratives. Who knows, perhaps Tong Guangde remembers a pro-Japan flag because my great-grandfather had a Tokyo past. The problem isn't that people remember differently. The problem is that they speak with absolute *ken ding* certainty.

He leans in. "You know the Japanese soldier who first arrived in the village? He was a relative of your great-grandfather." He leans back.

I put down my notebook. "What did you say?"

"Yes, he was a relative of Tong Zhenyong's wife. She was Japanese, you know."

"Yes, that I know."

"That soldier was his wife's brother's child."

I try to process this. If this is true, it could explain a surprising act of mercy in a war without any.

But then Moustache Tong turns his face directly to Hat Man Tong and delivers an incredulous look. "Aah?" He is calling BS. "Aah? That is not true."

Hat Man is emboldened. "I know this story! The next day he explained all this to us." He goes on to say the Japanese soldiers who'd approached had been stationed temporarily at Ping Qiao town, about six miles away. "They walked through, saw nice houses with shingles, and wanted to come loot the place."

At this point, Moustache Tong assumes I need a primer. "Your great-grandfather went to Japan. And he had a Japanese wife. When the Japanese devils came, he saved the village." I nod.

Hat Man Tong: "He was a hero, very respected."

This last part I know to be only partially true, at best. Several villagers have told me that during the great famine, the Tong East leaders dug up my great-grandfather's grave and sold the wood from his casket. Then there was the issue of the historical discrimination that Hat Man's Tong East waged against Tong Daren.

At this point a woman joins us—someone I've met before. Her mother took care of my great-grandfather before he died; she was his nanny (or, rumor has it, something more). The nanny's daughter once visited me in Shanghai, subtly suggesting I take her seventeen-year-old grandson with me to America. I have learned to speak carefully around her.

"Did you eat?" she asks. Before I have time to mention *we just went over this*, she presents several watermelon slices. Our conversation turns to my great-grandfather's personality, much of which I've heard before. Intellectual, good skin, tall, liked to spit.

I have to go soon, so I try to run a few more questions by them, as quickly as Chinese Time allows. Did Tong Zhenyong come from a family of wealthy landlords?

A rapid-fire exchange ensues.

Hat Man Tong: "Yes, he came from a landlord family."

Moustache Tong: "You're wrong."

Hat Man Tong: "I was here!"

Moustache Tong: "Go ahead and say it. You're wrong."

Another question: Did my third cousin Tong Daren indeed receive a letter from my grandfather in Taiwan? Does anyone know what happened to the letter? This is often cited as the reason Tong Daren had had such a hard life—his relationship with an anti-Communist relative in Taiwan.

Nanny's Daughter: "I know about this."

Hat Man Tong: "No. If he did, I would have heard about this."

I sigh and put down my pen. There are too many competing agendas and narratives, but more fundamentally, I have come too late with some of these questions. Too much time has gone by, and too many Tongs have departed.

"Stay for lunch," Nanny's Daughter says. "Just two dishes and a bowl of soup. That's all. It will be quick." Again I decline and make my exit, not knowing when I'll return or how many of these old people will still be around then.

———

On December 8, 1941, hours after the attack on Pearl Harbor, Japanese gunboats turned their sights on Shanghai. They fired on the last British vessel anchored on the city's Huangpu River. Japanese foot soldiers stationed in the Hongkou northern section of the city marched into the heart of the International Settlement and took it without resistance. Japan's wartime truce with the treaty ports of Europe and America was over.

They crossed the Garden Bridge, where the Suzhou Creek dumps into the Huangpu. This is a famous bridge, a signature image on Shanghai postcards, and may be my favorite one in town. The metal lattice structure reminds me less of China and more of a railroad bridge over the Susquehanna River in Maryland. The bridge was built by an English construction firm in 1907, replacing an old British toll bridge that Shanghai locals despised; it served as an entryway to a park reserved only for foreigners in the International Concession. As a vestige of beat-up-on-China colonialism, it is as good a symbol as any.

Once the Japanese took the International Settlement, the city of lights went largely dark. In accordance with martial law imposed, curfew began at 9 p.m. The residents in Asia's most open, anything-goes city in the 1920s and '30s found themselves under a strict registration and surveillance system. Guards at barbed-wire barriers demanded to see residence papers. Americans walked around bearing red armbands, for citizens of an anti-Japanese enemy country.

The occupation brought food rationing. The Japanese controlled the river and the railways, cutting Shanghai off from inland farms. These shortages brought starvation, and corpses appeared in the streets—often those of children. On the black market, rice prices skyrocketed, and the inflation robbed people of purchasing power.

But where Mildred and her family lived, further south and west in the French Concession, they enjoyed a semblance of normality. The Japanese afforded the French Concession some protection and freedom, as France's Vichy government was controlled by a Japanese Axis ally: Germany. So Shanghai residents seeking a wartime haven poured into the concession. The massive influx helped enrollment soar at Mildred and Carleton's Light of the Sea School, to six hundred students. The war provided opportunity for them.

Mildred's health improved, and she overcame a bout of rheumatism. "Chinese medicine and vitamin pills plus injections gave me a [sic] strong health now," she wrote Anna Graves. "I am quite fat now. If you meet me on the road perhaps you could not recognize me."

In late 1942, Mildred delivered her third child. Like the earlier two children, this infant girl was delivered at the Shanghai Red House Maternity and Infant Hospital, established in 1884 by American missionary Margaret Williamson. The baby had the one quality universally desired in Chinese society: light colored skin. "Small and cute," Sanjie described the baby seven decades later.

"The youngest daughter is a darling to us," Mildred wrote. "She is very cute and very clever. We all love her. Therefore we gave her your name."

The name of Anna. But there was a small problem: they had already named their older daughter Anna. So they simply swiped the name from the big sister, as if it were the last cookie from the jar, and gave it to the baby sister. The baby was Anna Sun, my mother.

"I recognize this," my mother says as we turn down Lane 431 in Shanghai, the site of the old Light of the Sea School. It is July 2013. The road Tenant de la Tour has been renamed since 1949 and is now Xiangyang South Road. Lane 431 goes down two blocks, just past a public men's room with no door. The facility is being used.

We've walked south from the metro stop on Line 1, following the signature leafy plane trees of the French Concession. During the old treaty port days, Parisian expats planted them to provide a rare bit of shade. The trees boast thick, knobby trunks that rise from the ground and grow into strong Y-shaped arms. They're perfect for climbing, except that our kids learned quickly that climbing is not allowed.

Down the lane, the building in front of us does not resemble the two-story-schoolhouse pictures from the past. This one is new, with four floors, plus office workers and an electric fence. "Doesn't look right," Mom says. We knock repeatedly at the gate, but there is no answer.

We walk around the block to a parallel lane to get a look from another direction. As we approach, an old man looks down on us from the second floor of a very old apartment building and comes out to talk. He is wearing a tank-top undershirt as old as I am. One minute into our chat, his wife emerges from the kitchen.

"I've lived here my whole life," she says.

"Do you remember the Light of the Sea School?" Mom asks. "I lived here as a girl."

"Of course! I went there," the wife says. They don't, however, recognize each other's names.

"My mother was the principal," my mother says, at which point everyone gives a reverent pause. The woman points down the alley, apologetically. "That is not the original building. It's been torn down." She explains that the original structure continued to be used as a school for two decades after my mother left. Then, in the 1970s, it became an education site for special-needs kids, before falling into the hands of a Hong Kong developer. The woman lowers her voice to speak quietly, and we have to lean in.

"The developer built this new building. He was connected to the military. What happened was, soldiers rented space here to people, to line their own pockets. They're all corrupt! If you knock, they will never let you in."

To make matters worse, the new, taller building has robbed her and her husband of natural sunlight they once enjoyed. She gives an unforgiving stare. Damn the profiteer landlords from the People's Liberation Army.

It was time for a new topic. "Did you know Han Huilu, the teacher?" the woman asks. The name vaguely rings a bell to my mother. "We think she was actually an underground Communist spy."

By the time the Light of the Sea School went up in the 1930s, members of the Communist Party in the city had descended far underground. Just a few years prior, the Guomindang strongman Chiang Kai-shek betrayed his Communist allies and began a brutal Communist extermination campaign. Chiang's ally, the Shanghai mafia godfather Du Yuesheng, carried it out. His Green Gang men forced their way into residences of union leaders and Communist safe houses, pulled out leftist leaders, and executed them on the spot. By one estimate, Du's men murdered ten thousand Communist leaders.

Purged from key cities, the Communists went into survival mode in the countryside, leaving party operatives in Shanghai to fend for themselves. They set up study groups, quietly recruited, infiltrated key organizations, and bided their time.

Among them: the woman who worked as dean at the Light of the Sea, named Zhang Qiong. Zhang was a native of Hunan, the home of Mao Zedong, and protégé of Mao's deputy Liu Shaoqi. According to her official party biography, Zhang joined the Communist Party in its second year of existence, 1922, and became a factory union organizer. She moved to Shanghai, and before long moved into a senior position at the Light of the Sea School. It would only be a matter of time before party members came out from the shadows.

| Chapter Eight | LOST AND FOUND
Grandmother's Voice
on Cassette |

The only way was to find this ship. If I didn't go, maybe I'll still be in Shanghai. Maybe I died.
—Mildred Zhao

I first heard my grandmother's voice in a Boston University library. It came from a scratchy audio cassette tape recorded more than forty years ago. This was an accidental find in the summer of 2013. At the base of a box filled with archived letters and photos of Welthy Honsinger Fisher, there was a stack of dusty tapes, the same kind my friends and I used in middle school to make mix tapes of Hall & Oates, and Foreigner and the Police.

There is something about hearing a person's voice for the first time—any person, really: Franklin Roosevelt, Margaret Thatcher, Charles Lindbergh, Kim Jong Un. Even more than archival video, I want to hear a person's phrasing and cadence, the volume, any stuttering and ums. It is, to me, a window into that person's self-confidence. It's one thing to turn up hundreds of pages of precious letters from a person to establish the basics of a grandmother's life. It's an altogether different experience to hear her speaking out loud, as if she's talking, for one moment, just to me.

It happened at the Howard Gotlieb Archival Research Center at BU, which houses the archive collection of documents, photos, and other artifacts from the life of Fisher—my grandmother's old teacher. There are very special rules here. First, visiting requires an appointment. Even though you don't know what specific items are in the archive boxes, you must schedule a trip to Boston and hope to get lucky. Upon arriving, you surrender your bag, books, personal items, and cellphone to a storage locker. Laptops are okay, as are pencils. Only then can you view a summary of each collection, or "finding aid." The materials are organized by box, so you check off the boxes you'd like, and wait.

By the time I've sifted through more than twenty boxes of letters and pictures, it is midafternoon and the library will be closing soon. That's when I spot the tapes buried at the bottom and riffle through, one hand holding back the papers on top, the other scooping and digging through the bottom. And there it is: *Interview Mildred Djao—1972*.

Upon my request, the librarian brings out a boom-box tape player of the same vintage as the cassettes. I insert the tape and waste five minutes listening to side B before realizing I really want side A. When I finally fast-forward—or perhaps rewind—to the right place and push *play*, half an hour remains.

Welthy Honsinger Fisher's longtime assistant Sally Swenson is interviewing Mildred Zhao for a biography about Fisher. The fidelity of her voice is remarkably crisp. But there is no time to ponder. I hit play and transcribe the interview as fast as I can type. Sally asks what year Mildred went to the Baldwin School. The answer is 1911.

"Third grade. Primary school," Mildred says. "There is a famous Methodist mission school over there. So the principal wrote a letter for me, and introduced me to see Mrs. Fisher."

"How did you know you wanted to go there?" Sally asks.

"Because my father took me there. My father came back from Japan, and he had worked in Nanchang. I was the only daughter in the family. It seems to me my father and mother took me there."

Her words flow very smoothly, with a comfort many Chinese immigrants take decades (if ever) to attain. Her voice is high pitched and has a staccato cadence, quick and piercing. The voice has an ever-so-slight accent: not exactly Hong Kong, and not typical mainland Chinese either. It's the spoken English of someone who learned it at an early age. This, once again, punctured my image of a two-dimensional cutout Chinese grandmother who was supposed to be bossy, accented, and unreflective.

The voice keeps talking and I keep typing. "Everything is changed now. Even my own school is changed to Communist. You see, just one week before the fall of Shanghai, I left Shanghai. The fighting was still going on. The only way was to find this ship. If I didn't go, maybe I'll still be in Shanghai. Maybe I died. I just took sixty US dollars to live."

I type up seven pages of notes, and by 3:50 I'm done. So is the librarian, who nudges me out.

Walking down Commonwealth Avenue to my rental car, I begin to process what has just occurred. It dawns on me that I have just had, in a way, my first and last conversation with the grandmother who never got to America. She would have loved to attend Boston University, walking into classic red-brick classrooms and worshiping in the Gothic chapel with the river just behind. Indeed, her daughter eventually made it here, as did her ashes. What I hadn't known is that her voice had also been captured in the United States for decades.

After World War II ended, Mildred hatched a plan to attend Colorado State University. By then she was in her forties, and still sending in applications and money. But wartime inflation made the Chinese CNC currency barely worth the paper it was printed on. As part of one application, Mildred deposited a thousand dollars in an American bank to demonstrate her ability to pay tuition. She went to the Chinese black market to exchange money.

"I have paid C.N.C. $8,000,000,000.00 for the exchange of one thousand dollars," Mildred wrote Fisher. "Is that terrible? The exchange rate is even higher these days. It is very difficult to buy dollars at official rate."

I count nine zeroes. Eight billion Chinese yuan. Chinese money was worth so little that people spent it on Monday before it lost value on Tuesday. Shoppers engaged in panic buying, and hoarded goods. Banks declined to make loans for more than a month, as they were unsure debtors could repay. The Light of the Sea School banned students from paying tuition in cash, which was losing value by the hour. It only accepted a commodity that held value over time. So, like the emperors in imperial China, they took payments in large sacks of rice.

By December 1948 the political situation turned very uncertain. A Communist victory over the GMD was becoming increasingly clear. The uncertainty at home convinced Mildred to stay in China rather than leave for Colorado. "It is impossible for me in leaving my work and family during such a trying time. Of course it makes me very disappointed, but one cannot help it. When the fighting is getting near to us I begin to feel that is God's will."

Then she flip-flopped again, and left. Mildred found her way onto a military boat bound for Taiwan, getting her off the mainland. Her final destination: Greeley, Colorado.

The Communists took Shanghai without resistance. By then, almost the entire Guomindang leadership had retreated. On the evening of May 25, 1949, GMD remnants staged one final "victory parade" along the Bund before fleeing after dark. At dawn, the first members of the People's Liberation Army streamed in: peasants in ragged green uniforms and sandals. The liberation was oddly smooth; church bells welcomed the new regime, as did local police and a big city banner. Shops opened at the normal time. *Hamlet*, starring Laurence Olivier, played in some theaters, *I Wonder Who's Kissing Her Now* in others.

Carleton and the children remained in Shanghai when it fell. Aunt Lily recalls that in the days after, "there were lots of *huodong*," movements and parades choreographed by the new occupiers. "Many parades. We kids stood on the sidewalk and played little drums as the soldiers marched by. And we danced. There was this harvest dance—everyone did the steps in formation on the school courtyard."

Carleton was angry. He'd long objected to Mildred leaving China, where he had to support his mother and his brother's widow and children. They never agreed on the best place for the family. "They blamed each other," Aunt Lily says. "He said, 'You should not have left.'"

As it turns out, Mildred never continued on for the United States. The turmoil and uncertainty of the new Communist era convinced her to stay close and head for Hong Kong. A lot of families found themselves in the same situation: one person hedged against the future by exploring Taiwan or Hong Kong, and another would stay behind to see what the new regime would bring.

"I have only heard from you once since you went to Taiwan," Carleton wrote in a letter to Mildred. "And I have not heard from you since. This is my third letter to you in Hong Kong. Everyone in the family misses you. Folks now are puzzled about your going there. Things are not running smoothly in the school.

"I think the best scenario is for you to come back to Shanghai at once. Preferably before summer break. Then you can clear up a lot of rumors. If you come back, you can assign people to their proper positions. And then go abroad. Finish this, and then you can go."

But Mildred never returned home. The situation in Shanghai grew worse. The new regime took over newspapers, associations, factories, and universities. Residents started calling each other "cadre." And instead of wearing colorful Western suits and leather shoes, men donned the high-collar cotton tunics Sun Yat-sen suits. By March 1950, Carleton had seen enough. He sent the kids to join their mother in Hong Kong, staying behind himself to run the school.

"I dropped them at 4:25 p.m. on the train," he wrote Mildred, "then I went home alone. It feels so empty I can't describe it. The last few years I was so busy at work, worrying about our jobs and income. But when I got home, spending time with the kids made the worries dissolve.

"*Da mei* [Lily, the oldest] is so very mature. She helps comfort me. . . . Now that she's gone, so many things seem pointless. In Shanghai, business is not good. We have some money to live, but I've spent most of it down. I hope to finish up some things here so I can rest awhile, and eventually save up to invest in a new business. My heart is so unsettled."

At the bottom of the letter, he wrote a few words for the children, in simple sentences:

Anna, after you boarded, what did you eat? I bet it was hard to sleep. How did you go from Canton to Kowloon? I can't go with you

in person. I cannot put into words my pain. Every second, every
quarter hour, I pray for you to arrive safely. . . .
My heart always follows you. I hope you can go to school. You
left your playing cards behind. I hope you can find something else
to play.

The key detail my mother remember from the trip to Hong
Kong was the heat. The travelers got warmer and warmer the further south they went: Shanghai, Hangzhou, Nanchang, Changsha,
Guangzhou. "We kept taking off layers," she told me. "We were like
refugees." They *were* refugees.

At the border they crossed the narrow Luohu Bridge over the
Shenzhen River into Hong Kong, where Mildred was waiting.

With hindsight, the decision of Mildred and then her children
to escape to Hong Kong was a no-brainer. They avoided two and
half decades of Mao's terror. "What would it have been like if we'd
stayed?" my mother's brother, Uncle Eddie, often says. At the time,
though, this decision was questionable at best. Mildred Zhao went
with just $60 in her pocket to feed herself and three children. None
of them spoke Cantonese, the local dialect, and the kids found
themselves teased by local children. "They pointed at us and said,
'Communist! Communist!'" my mother recalls.

They settled in a sordid shantytown known as Ngau Chi Wan,
alongside thousands of other mainlanders. Only my mother went
to school; there wasn't enough money for the others, so Lily and
Constantine stayed home and rolled sweet *tang yuan* dumplings to
sell. Mildred was by all accounts a lousy seamstress, but she made
Anna's uniform nonetheless.

On April 26, 1950, Anna received this letter from her father:

Little one,
Thank you for your letter dated April 14. I am so happy to read it.
How is your Cantonese coming?
Did you like the honey I sent? Do your shoes fit? I will be in Hong
Kong hopefully in 3 weeks.

Then a week later:

Little one,

In two weeks, Daddy can visit you in Kowloon.

Your classmate Chen Huang came up the stairs today looking for you. I told her Sun Ailian [Anna Sun] went to Hong Kong. So she left.

Carleton visited the family in Hong Kong at least three times, and always returned to Shanghai, exhorting Mildred and the children to go back with him.

"Mildred, this year you spent down 90 percent of your savings," he wrote. "You don't even have transportation money. You and I can starve. But we cannot let our kids suffer. . . . Don't be so suspicious and paranoid. Just bring the children back to Shanghai for now. We can save and get by. We can live together and die together."

Somewhere between the spring of 1951 and the summer of 1952, he was arrested.

Chapter Nine | THE WARTIME COLLABORATOR IN OUR FAMILY

It's no problem to talk about this now. This is history.
—Wu Mingtang, Wuhan archivist

The gunmen first came for him one midnight in 1947. Thugs burst into the family living quarters on the second-floor residential quarters atop the Light of the Sea School in Shanghai. Mildred and the children jumped awake. "It was the first time I ever saw a gun," Lily says. She was fifteen at the time.

The men directed Mildred to a small table at the foot of the bed and interrogated her for hours. "For his sake, I was faced with pistol by a man (or detective) rushed to my bedroom one night urging me to hand over my husband to him," Mildred wrote Anna Graves. "If not by the help of telephone, a number of board of trustees came to the rescue, I was killed that night."

Carleton, meanwhile, was on the run. He'd anticipated this, and had relocated to a "safer place," Mildred wrote. A second close call came months later. "Carleton came back to Shanghai, where he was walking on the street one day. He was caught. Just before putting in prison while he was still in the detained house, many friends rescued him."

He would not be so lucky a third time. As Aunt Lily tells the story, the thugs pursuing him were hired by the ruling Guomindang. After the war, GMD leaders emerged from their mountain hideout in southwest China and began settling scores. They hunted down suspected traitors—particularly those suspected of collaborating with the Japanese occupiers. That was Carleton's war crime, the reason they were after him.

This is the part of the story where it'd be easiest to turn away. Anyone who has ended up on the "wrong" side of history surely has wished for some kind of do-over, now that they know how things turn out in the end. I wish that in the fog of war he had not joined the occupation government controlling Wuhan—that is, the puppet state of the Japanese. To many relatives, and most of the billion Chinese on the planet, this is an unforgivable source of shame, particularly in light of what we know about the 1937/38 Rape of Nanking.

Like most English readers, I learned about this event from Iris Chang, author of *The Rape of Nanking*, one of the first English-language accounts of the atrocities. I met her once in the late 1990s. Chang came to the studios of the *PBS NewsHour*, where I was working, to be interviewed about the book. When she spoke on the screen, what I remember most about her is her eyes—searing with hate as she spoke of Japanese Imperial Army soldiers tossing Chinese babies up in the air and spearing them, half-burying Chinese soldiers and having German Shepherds finish the job. Chang was around my age, which made the account that much more accessible to me (she committed suicide not long after). Chang's critics say she was more activist than historian, at times favoring emotion over evidence. But to me that day, history became sermon.

This was the hardest part about looking up this chapter of my grandfather's history: I already knew how the movie ended. I could only interpret what I was learning through the lens of hindsight. In real time, Carleton Sun made his decisions in a Shanghai of the 1930s swirling in uncertainty and intrigue. The city served as a hub for agents and spies from Russia, Japan, Germany, France, the United States, and England. Alongside them were dueling Chinese political camps, rival drug gangs, and fence-sitters playing all sides, waiting out what would turn out.

A key question at the time was what to do about Japan, which had already occupied Manchuria in northern China and a section of Shanghai. I'd always learned about this period as one of unbridled Japanese aggression. But in fact, the two sides engaged in a number of overtures before all-out war. Guomindang strongman Chiang Kai-Shek penned an article in 1934 asking whether Japan was a friend or foe. A year later, Japan's foreign minister explored a possible détente with China. The secret back-channel peace talks involved a group of GMD leaders who called themselves the "low-key club." Central to the consultations was a man my grandfather will forever be linked with: Wang Jingwei.

He is, bar none, China's most notorious collaborator—its Pétain, or Quisling, or Judas Iscariot in the public imagination. At the very least, Wang was a man of complexity and contradictions. I have seen him variously characterized as: misunderstood, baby-faced, idealistic, traitorous, womanizing, pragmatic, vain, hoodwinked, outmaneuvered, reckless, naive. But most often: puppet.

Someday Wang Jingwei may get a fair shake from history, but I don't imagine I'll be around for it. As soon as you throw out a term like "collaborator," people's minds are made up. Imagine I told you a story about someone who decided to join the Islamic State, or the Klan, or the political party you cannot stand. The rational side of our brains would turn off and we'd default into right-versus-wrong mode. Wang joined the early wave of Chinese intellectuals studying abroad in Japan (the same wave as my great-grandfather), and signed up as an early member of the Tongmenghui, Sun Yat-sen's secret Revolutionary Alliance with designs on overthrowing imperial China. Wang saw himself as a true believer, an ideological heir of Sun's "pan-Asian" vision of Eastern geographic unity. Surely that was better than aligning with Western hegemons. Wang criticized the Chinese Communist Party for allying with the Soviet Union, and later blasted the Guomindang for its ties with the British and Americans. At the same time, he fancied himself a realist in the face of the Japanese occupation.

To many observers, the war by 1939 was unwinnable for China in the face of Japanese aggression. After Nanking fell, Hankou burned to the ground. Chongqing suffered its worst bombings to date, and a rotten harvest made food prices skyrocket. At this point, there was no hint of Pearl Harbor, no suggestion the Americans would join the Pacific Theater and support the GMD in retreat. This set the stage for Wang Jingwei's dreadful miscalculation.

Seeking to end the conflict and the killings, he sought a deal with the Japanese, to trade land for peace, space for time, and to cut Chinese losses. In return for Chinese territory, Wang wanted Japan to end the bombings, give up key mines, and promise to pull back in two years. This would end the conflict and preserve the nation. In the end, his plan was built on two mistaken assumptions: that he understood the patriotic pulse of China, and that his GMD colleagues would back him up. They abandoned him, leaving Wang isolated and with little negotiating leverage. In the end, he accepted a very bad deal, in which Japan gave no commitment to eventually evacuate or cede territory. He had been outplayed.

In 1940 Wang signed on to run a government in central China under the control of Tokyo. At the ceremony to recognize the founding of Wang's "Republic of China" collaborationist government, tears ran down his face as he declared, "I hate it, I hate it."

When the time came to recruit officials in Wang's government, Carleton Sun was offered a position and he took it, leaving back in Shanghai his wife and three children. He was in a way returning home. I imagine the move had several upsides for him: He could move back to his home province, speak the local dialect, eat the local food, and support his widow mother and widow sister-in-law's family nearby. His work would oversee food distribution to local Chinese. And he could work an important government job, something he'd pursued for years. Could all this have been part of his thinking?

"There are several possibilities," says Yuan Jicheng, a retired economic historian in Wuchang. He speaks with a clinical detachment to such an emotionally charged issue. Like many Chinese analysts and academics, he makes his points in numeric order. "One, a small portion were actually traitors who sided ideologically with the Japanese. Two, some had business arrangements with the Japanese. Three, some did it against their will, but were forced or blackmailed into it. Four, some needed jobs so their families could eat, so they were desperate. Five, some were tricked into it." That's his list.

I note this is not the black-and-white view of most.

"Chinese historians, we all *luan chao*," copy each other like crazy, he says. "It's time to rewrite history."

I don't imagine this will happen soon. American historian Timothy Brook writes in his book *Collaboration*: "Every culture tags collaboration as a moral failure." Once you say "collaborator" out loud, Brook writes, it "superimposes a moral map over the political landscape." To him, this allows for a common narrative of World War II occupation: that most people resisted the Japanese and German aggressors, whereas a tiny smattering of cowards joined them. The problem, Brook argues, is that this oversimplifies the reality we now know. In German-occupied France, many people in fact aided the occupiers, for one reason or another. They hedged their bets, sat on the fence, and took the jobs available to them. By the 1970s, enough time had passed for the French to consider a more nuanced view.

Not in China. The difference is, the French have seen scores of regimes come and go, whereas in Beijing, the party in charge still subscribes to its founding myth: we the Communists beat the Japanese and founded the republic. We the revolutionaries, we the underdogs, we the redeemed. Thus, Brook writes, the Chinese "are at a much earlier stage in coming to terms with their occupation."

At ten the next morning, I'm walking into the Wuhan Municipal Chronicles. A "chronicles" office is basically a local records building. Ten in the morning is the earliest most morning meetings take place in China, as only the odd foreigner would talk shop over breakfast or coffee (typically the lunch "hour" is noon to two, so much of the midday is off-limits too). Male archivist Wu Mingtang buzzes me into the gated complex, as Chinese history here is indeed a gated enterprise.

"I believe he was sentenced as a *hanjian*," I begin, wiping the sweat off my face in his large office stacked with books and binders. I put the embarrassing information out there immediately, figuring it might get us straight to the point. It does.

"He *was* a *hanjian*," he says. Wu pulls over a stack of fifty or so pages he's prepared. Most are copies of government meeting minutes, attendance lists, and speeches. He asks: "Can you read Chinese words quickly?" I hesitate, just long enough for him to continue. "Never mind, we can talk it through." What strikes me is his confidence and continuous eye contact.

The document he places in front of me says "Reorganized National Government," the name of the Japan-controlled puppet regime Wang Jingwei ran. It claimed to represent all of China, though a map of reality would include only a portion of central and eastern China. In 1940, three Chinese leaders claimed to represent the true people, each portraying himself as a political descendant of Sun Yat-sen: Wang Jingwei in the eastern center, Chiang Kai-shek in the southwest, and Mao Zedong in the northwest.

The name on the documents says Sun Ditang, the name Carleton used while he was here. It was not unusual at the time for people to have several names in their lifetimes (which makes deciphering genealogies particularly challenging). In Shanghai, he went by Sun Honglie, and a decade later, his passport name read Sun Yi. Sun Ditang represented a kind of new identity for my grandfather's new job working for the Japanese. Surely he understood the risk: depending on who won the war and how its history would be written, he stood to go down as a realist, saving Chinese lives, or as a sellout.

According to the papers, he held the lofty title of president of the Social Mobilization Committee for the Hankou Special Municipal Zone. "This suggests he was wealthy," Wu Mingtang says. "Or that he had good *guanxi* connections."

"His hometown was Mianyang, not far away," I say.

"That would definitely have helped."

Archivist Wu explains that the job of the Social Mobilization Committee was to promote Japan-China unity. Carleton Sun Ditang's unit spread this message to Boy Scout troops, business organizations, medical and education groups, drama clubs, book clubs. This job, of public messaging, later fell under the category of "cultural traitor," as opposed to "political traitor" denoting people who made actual governing decisions. Many political traitors were executed after the war.

I ask Wu if it was plausible Carleton took this job because he had an anti-Communist streak, mentioning old letters indicating that Communist-allied bandits confiscated his family property in the 1920s.

He confirms this. "*Hen jiandan.*" It's very simple. "During land reform here, the Communist Party took people's money and property. That meant he couldn't afford college."

Carleton Sun Ditang served in Wuhan for at least three years, and in 1943 he played a small role in a political change affecting his family back in Shanghai. In Europe, the Vichy government of France (under the occupation of Germany) gave up its historic concession in Shanghai. The territory went to Germany's Axis ally—Japan. So after a century, the famed leafy French Concession was finished. For my grandfather, suddenly the Japanese regime he served under controlled the very section of Shanghai where his family lived.

In reality, the French Concession had been good to him and Mildred. It gave them the peace and space to open the Light of the Sea School and raise a family. But his day job required him to blast the devil French colonialists. He spoke in August 1943 to a business group, according to a speech Wu, the archivist, has tracked down.

Shanghai is the country's economic capital. One hundred years ago, Westerners occupied it. They controlled everything. They were invaders, and we became a colony. We lost our rights and territory. This is a cancer, and if we don't cut it out, our country cannot be independent.

Before leaving, I put to Wu Mingtang the question I have really come to ask: "All this is embarrassing to my mother, her family, my family. What do people today think about this issue of collaboration? Is it okay to talk about this?"

He knows what I'm asking: whether today's China still judges Carleton Sun, aka Sun Ditang, a traitor.

"It's no problem to talk about this now. This is history."

I give out a sigh of relief. He has, in a way, granted permission to start turning the page on my grandfather's shameful past. And it seems he knows it. "Call any time," the archivist says as I walk toward the exit gate. "We're friends now."

The next day's research can only be described as comical. A local history professor has volunteered a male undergraduate student to assist me for the day.

"Teacher Tong, can I carry your bag?" Li Honggong, the student, greets me in the morning at the entrance to Wuhan University. Teacher Tong. The first hello requires some kind of honorific title.

"You don't have to call me Teacher Tong," I say. But I pause because there's a problem. I can't think of something different or better, yet still appropriate. Calling me by my Chinese given name, Tong Zhigang, is not something a person two decades younger does. Addressing me by my English name sounds odd. And "Mister Tong" is too formal. We're stuck.

He says: "I'll call you Teacher Tong. It's appropriate."

Our plan is to scour local Wuhan-area local history volumes suggested by the professor, and scan for any references to my grandmother Mildred Zhao's father. He's an important player in the whole story—the man who presumably decided to unbind her feet and pay for her education. Some of Mildred's letters suggest her father studied in Japan, but we don't even know his name. We start at the library of Wuhan University, but again, there's a catch.

"Teacher Tong," Li, the student, begins, "it's like this."

It's like this. *Shi zheyang.* As day precedes night, *shi zheyang* always precedes bad news. *Shi zheyang—we don't have your hotel room ready yet. Shi zheyang—I cannot process your refund. Shi zheyang—I quit.*

Shi zheyang, Li says—he's not a student here, and we can't get into the library without university IDs. So he has to call a friend who studies here and borrow some. We have to impersonate other people. This is something I haven't done in two decades, and now I'll pretend to be someone just a couple of years older than my son. What could possibly go wrong?

As we wait, we discuss Chinese economic history, which Li is currently studying. He explains Chinese universities are changing the way they teach. The old dogmatic view—of a century or more of humiliation and suppression by Western imperialists, followed by Maoist liberation—is evolving. "We used to think 1911 was a failure," he says, referring to the toppling of the Qing dynasty and imperial China. Traditionally, this had been taught in the People's

Republic as a bourgeois revolution rather than a real one. "But now we see differently, as a step along the way."

Then the student says something surprising. He cites Chinese scholars from, of all places, the United States. First, Li mentions John King Fairbank, the father of China studies in America going back to the 1940s. Fairbank emphasized the influence of the West in China's modernization—Western ideas, Western thought pushing its way in from the outside. The good white men. The newer framework, Li says, emphasizes change from within. "But today, we look at both."

This is a refreshing conversation. Typically in China, I hear history described as *This is how things happened.* There is correct history and there is incorrect history. But I throw Li a far more basic question: "Why are you studying China through the lens of American historians? Why not Chinese historians?" Imagine a reverse situation, of American intellectuals adopting a Chinese take on the US Civil War: Confederacy General Luobaite Yi Li losing to his Union counterpart, Youlixi Si Gelante.

He thinks for a second. "Maybe it's because China produced no history books for several years. There was too much chaos."

The student IDs show up. Neither one looks like either of us. My mission is to pretend to be a young adult with shaggy hair and thick-frame spectacles. I have neither of those. "Should be no problem," Li Honggong says. "Let's try it."

We wave the cards over the digital readers, and the turnstiles open. Still, I walk through and brace for an alarm and the possibility of uniformed men coming from four directions. Nothing happens. We make our way to a reference section of finding aids: books that serve as indices to other books. Li Honggong starts flipping through records of Mildred Zhao's county, Hanchuan, writing down in my notebook the names of various people surnamed Zhao.

Zhao Zhoujia: information located in Hanchuan County volume, scroll 2, article 9, female name. And so on: *Zhao Guozao, Zhao Dezhi, Zhao Cheng, Chao Zhen, Zhao Shiyou, Zhao Mengzhu, Zhao Ping, Zhao Benxi.* My plan is to run these names by my mother and her contacts in the village, to see if any ring a bell. It's a ridiculous quest, really, as Zhao is the seventh-most popular surname in China, shared by twenty-seven million people. It is the Davis of China, though there are twenty-five times more Zhaos than Davises. I mention to Li Honggong that this seems an inefficient way to do research. He shrugs, as if to say, "This is the best we have." Then he spots a librarian walking briskly in our direction. "Let's go. Now."

Li Honggong seems to know what's about to happen. He flings the volume back into the stack and directs me to dart toward the stairwell. Not exactly done, we speed-walk out of the library and pursue plan B. I have flown eight thousand miles for this.

Next stop: Wuhan city archives. A second student, a woman, joins us there around 11 a.m. In my experience, most records offices in China are not self-serve operations: you submit your identification and what you're looking for, and a person behind the desk does the searching for you. But first, that person interrogates you.

"Why do you want documents on Sun Ditang?" the elderly male archive staffer asks. I explain he's my grandfather, knowing what the next question will be.

"What are you going to do with them?" This is the equivalent of a public relations officer back home asking me the angle of the story I'm chasing. Will this be a hit piece, or a positive story? Gatekeepers are gatekeepers. If any information put out there can be used to make an organization look bad, it's better to restrict or deny access. I figure it's best not to mention that this may show up in a book published overseas.

"To research family history," I say.

He follows up: "So, this is just for family use?" I stay quiet as he directs us to a waiting area that looks like a set of church pews. Indeed, I can use a bit of divine intervention. Once again, I am waiting for China to serve its history to me, on its schedule and its terms. Forty-five minutes later, the archivist calls us over and says he's located some documents: handwritten speeches, minutes of government meetings. Which ones do I want?

"All of them," I say.

He cocks his head in a show of irritation. "All of them?" A Chinese negotiation requires this type of performance, but I have come a very long way and refuse to back down.

"Are there a lot of documents?"

"Quite a few."

"All of them, thank you."

He appears to relent, but as the clock approaches noon calls us back up.

"It's like this," he says. *Shi zheyang.* "We have to make copies of the documents. But now it's lunchtime. We'll start after."

Li Honggong moves in. "We're in a hurry, as Teacher Tong is visiting from America. When do you open again after lunch?"

"Two o'clock."

"Can a staffer do it now, and go to lunch later?" No. Can we make our own copies? No. So off to lunch we go as well, but by 2 p.m. they are just starting to photocopy. This project is taking a full day.

The documents here cluster around one important date. July 7, 1942 was the fifth anniversary of Japan's invasion of China. In one internal memo, Carleton Sun Ditang of the Social Mobilization Committee writes that the puppet government should "not over-emphasize" this anniversary. There is also a copy of a speech my grandfather gave on that anniversary, focusing on Sun Yat-sen's vision of a "Greater Asia Co-prosperity Sphere." "Listeners will be very touched" by Sun Ditang's speech, the minutes indicate. "They will denounce the Western imperial powers."

So after all this, it's becoming clear my grandfather was a political messenger for the pro-Japan regime. This comforts me—perhaps because back home in Washington I'm surrounded by people in the same business: political framing. They craft and sell narratives. *It's important for American companies to still manufacture things. The best food is grown locally. Solar energy should be subsidized. Solar energy should not be unsubsidized. The best way to exercise is in a warehouse.*

It's late afternoon by the time we leave the archives, so the workday is pretty much over. I bid goodbye and thanks to my student accomplices, and on the subway back to the hotel I come to a realization: anything I find here will reflect my grandfather's public life, the 9-to-5 version of him in a highly political environment. It's not as if I'll uncover his private, unguarded thoughts as to why he made what turned out to be a colossal mistake.

In the Wuhan city of Hankou, Carleton lived in a modern, Western-style apartment during the war. Sanjie, his niece, says he lived on the second floor of an apartment. "Two bedrooms, one for him and one for his mother." Sofa, coffee table, record player, calligraphy on the wall, and a piano. He owned a rickshaw pulled by a laborer to get him around town.

My mother and I visit this apartment building during our trip. It still stands today, having survived wartime bombardment by the Japanese in 1938 and the US B-29s in 1944. This is rather impressive for Hankou; the city twice burned to the ground (in 1844 and in 1911) and has flooded over countless times.

First, we notice the arch entrance, leading to an alley. This is the signature design of hundreds of structures in Shanghai and Hankou, "stone-gate houses," or *shikumen*. "Yan Qing Li," she says, reading the sign that hangs over the arch. A local historian has told me Yan is the surname of the builder who erected this structure soon after the historic flood of 1931. Atop the concrete face of the arch it reads: "A 1933 D"—AD 1933 , I assume. Inside the alley there are entry doorways to individual apartment units on either side. Suddenly a man emerges from one door, slapping his back with a towel as if he's just emerged from a shower. He is wearing boxer shorts and nothing else. Perhaps sixty or so, this man is entirely comfortable with his bald head and protruding potbelly. We approach.

"Do you live here?" I ask. He nods but makes no eye contact. He whips his towel across his back again. My mother asks if anyone still lives here who was around in the 1940s. He shakes his head.

"This place once belonged to a capitalist," he says. "Before liberation." The owner rented out units until the Communist government took ownership, and the tenants have all changed over.

"My father lived here," my mother says, and the man turns toward her. Now he's interested. He looks at her, in a purple blouse and silk summer pants, and says to me: "*She* looks like a capitalist."

"My grandfather's name was Sun Ditang," I tell him. "Have you heard it?"

"No. He must have been rich."

"I'm not sure," my mother says.

"You said he had a rickshaw. Of course he was rich. That's pretty simple." Towel slap, towel slap. He lifts his chin to bid us goodbye and walks into his house.

————————————

It seems to me there is a lot more space in today's China to discuss the once-touchy issue of collaboration. Not at the official history-book level, but in less formal contexts. China historian Rana Mitter of the University of Oxford referred me to oral histories on the topic, noting specifically a set of video interviews produced by a noted Chinese state television anchor named Cui Yongyuan. Cui interviewed hundreds of people about the war, in an online series called *My War of Resistance*.

In one section, several men now in their eighties explain their own collaboration with the Japanese side. Here are three reasons from three different men interviewed:

"I decided to try working for the Wang Jingwei navy. I figured, 'If it's good, I'll stay. If not, I'll go to Chongqing [to join the KMT].' Today we would call it bourgeois thinking. Back then, I wanted to get promoted and make money."

"Wang Jingwei came and saw that I could speak well. And I dared to speak. So I joined him."

"We had no food to eat. I needed to take care of my family. Joining the [Communist] Eighth Route Army would have meant too much suffering and poverty. So I opted against that."

These were self-interested men, looking for the best deals for themselves and their families. Self-interest over ideology. And then there is collaboration in film. In 2007 when I was in Shanghai, the award-winning director Ang Lee released the erotic spy thriller *Lust, Caution*. Based on a 1942 wartime novel by Eileen Chang, it received lots of attention on the mainland, mostly for its adult NC-17 rating. The mainland version redacted the raciest scenes, though curious, tech-savvy Chinese netizens found easy workarounds. The *Marketplace* Shanghai bureau intern at the time, Edward Sheng, said the main reason young people used these web proxies to jump over "the great firewall" was to view the forbidden scenes from *Lust, Caution*.

In the film, the female lead is sent to assassinate a dashing male Shanghai collaborator working for the Japanese occupation. It all goes south when she falls for him and they become lovers. Not to give it all away, but the whole setup of Good Girl taking out Bad Guy turns murky in a hurry.

Wang Jingwei died in 1944, an utter failure. Outmaneuvered by the Japanese in 1940, he did not envision the United States entering the war. When this happened, Wang told his son that if the Washington-Guomindang alliance won, his family's honor would be lost. This, of course, happened.

But here is a footnote to the story that I find fascinating. Wang's widow was put on trial, in a case that challenges the narrative of good resisters versus bad collaborators. Her name was Chen Bijun. In June 1946, GMD lawyers tried Chen Bijun as an enemy traitor in a Suzhou courtroom, though in reality it was just a show. Publicity materials described this as a "traitor trial." She was charged with colluding, on behalf of herself and her late husband Wang Jingwei, with the Japanese prime minister, at a time "when all Chinese were united against Japanese aggression."

Chen Bijun flipped the script entirely during her defense, delivering a rage-filled indictment of the GMD. She argued that the GMD army were the cowards, retreating into the mountains and then selling out to US and British foreign interests. Meantime, Chen argued, Wang Jingwei's regime kept the Chinese people fed and alive, even under Japanese occupation. She blasted the Chiang regime for postwar hyperinflation and mass unemployment; life after the war was worse than during it. And Chen cited a saying that went around at the time, that GMD leaders were corrupt and cared only about gold bars, cars, houses, women, and face. It's snappier in Mandarin: *jinzi, chezi, fangzi, nuzi, mainzi.*

Chen Bijun received an ovation from the public observers in the courtroom. She was mobbed for autographs. After receiving a sentence of life in prison—a foregone conclusion—she slammed the GMD's attempt to "deceive three-year-old children" about who the real war heroes were. Chen died in jail in 1959.

After the war ended, Carleton Sun laid low from politics and shifted to the business of honeybee production and needle trading for several years. His letters to Mildred make reference to needle import taxes, tax rebates, and Guangzhou honey prices. Here is one from November 1950:

> Guangzhou honey prices are low. Shanghai prices also fell 10 percent. But that's okay. As for needles, we can't sell #22, but we can ship over #32. If the price is good, let's pursue that.

He was arrested, as best we know, at some point in the next year. Mildred wrote in 1951:

> There is still no information from my husband yet. About a couple weeks ago I tried to get in touch with him indirectly. But in vain. . . . No letter came since April. War brings us bankruptcy and separation.

By then, two purges were under way on the mainland. Mao unleashed the Campaign to Suppress Counterrevolutionaries in October 1950, exhorting citizens to turn in spies, agents, journalists, students taught abroad, foreign company workers, Catholics, and remnants of the old GMD and Wang Jingwei regimes. Many were executed, as Chairman Mao set execution quotas of 0.1 percent of the population in some areas.

This campaign overlapped with another, called the Three-Antis Campaign, whose triple targets were corruption, waste, and profiteering government officials. Bureaucrats deemed crooked were fined and tortured, and sometimes executed. Bankers famously committed suicide by jumping out of high-rises, prompting Shanghai's mayor to ask, "How many paratroopers are there today?"

The exact date of Carleton Sun's arrest remains unclear to me. The records in various Shanghai offices conflict—or at the very least, they don't go together. Property records in the neighborhood police station near the Light of the Sea School show he was sent to prison on March 26, 1952. An officer at the city's central police station in Shanghai told me my grandfather was arrested in July 1951, and then convicted in July 1953 as a counterrevolutionary. He was sentenced to fifteen years, Aunt Lily recalls, based on conversations with mainland relatives in the '70s.

It was also very confusing to Mildred and the children in Hong Kong. In June 1952 she wrote: "I got the definite information three weeks ago about Carleton's custody in Shanghai. More than a year ago he lost his freedom. That's why I could not get his letter.

"For the sake of the children this is really a great shock to me. The last time when he was here, I persuaded him to stay. He refused and urged us to go back with him. If I did go back, I am sure I will be put in prison too. It is very easy for anyone to lose one's freedom or to commit suicide."

The question is, who turned in Carleton Sun? During our trip in 2013, my mother and I found the chief suspect in a document found at the police local station. The household registration book lists the various tenants of Alley 431 South Xiangyang Road over time:

~~Property head: Zhao Zhizhen, Hai Guang (Light of the Sea) Primary School.~~

My grandmother's name, Zhao Zhizhen, is crossed out, replaced by: "Principal Zhang Qiong." The former dean and underground party member.

"Zhang Qiong!" My mother whispers. "I bet she turned in my father." Later, Aunt Lily surmises this is "probably true."

In the next column, also crossed out:

~~Sun Yi (Carleton), male, born 1905, Mianyang, Hubei, post-secondary.~~

And below, these handwritten words in blue ink:

Moved out 52.3.26.
Counterrevolutionary
Tilanqiao prison

Two other Shanghai relatives implicated Zhang Qiong, who would have had a motive: nudging Carleton Sun out of the way would have given her control of the property and its revenues. She later went on to become a celebrated cadre in the Shanghai city education department, gaining membership into an elite party consultative conference. She died in 1981. A memorial plaque for her is on display at a Shanghai primary school. The woman is immortalized, even as her former partners at the Light of the Sea School have literally been crossed out of the public record.

At the outset, I would spit out Zhang Qiong's name when I mentioned her. It took me awhile, though, to step back and think: like my grandfather, she too gambled on the outcome of wartime China at a time when the outcome was highly uncertain. It turns out Zhang herself was interrogated by Guomindang authorities in the 1930s.

"She was forced to sit on a *laohu deng,*" or tiger bench, my mother's cousin Cai Su told me. Under this particular torture, you sit along a bench lengthwise, with your hands tied behind you. Your knees are tied down in front of you, and then they put a brick under your feet, and then another as your feet are forced higher and higher up. The point is to induce unbearable pain and dislocate the prisoner's knee joints before she passes out.

Chapter Ten

FROM PRISON TO MAO'S GULAG

I have written all these things because I have a responsibility to history. But the political situation has changed.
—Carleton Sun

It was known as the Alcatraz of the Orient. Two years before Carleton Sun's birth in 1905, the British built the Ward Road Gaol in the International Settlement. It stood on the street named for Frederick Townsend Ward, a Massachusetts sailor who led an imperial Chinese army—the Ever Victorious Army—against the Taiping Rebellion. Being named for its street address seemed a bland description for the world's largest prison at the time. Its state-of-the-art execution chamber hanged prisoners with a trapdoor directly over the morgue. The design was imported, inspired by penitentiaries in Singapore and Canada.

Later it became known as Tilanqiao Prison, located in the northeastern Hongkou section of town. During my assignment in Shanghai, I hardly knew anything about Tilanqiao and its role in city history.

The first time I visit, in 2010, I notice the black metal gate surrounded by high concrete walls, perhaps three stories high. A plaque next to the gate denotes the building's "heritage architecture":

Designed by Shanghai Municipal Council. Brick-and-concrete composite structure and reinforced concrete structure. Built in 1901–1935.

When Carleton Sun was a prisoner there, he was in his mid-forties, the age I am now. One visitor came regularly: his elderly mother. She was illiterate and had bound feet, making it hard to walk. Yet she was a feisty woman who made the trip requiring two city bus transfers. Often she went bearing hard-boiled eggs. The rest of Carleton's family stayed away, having "drawn clear boundary lines" to insulate themselves from his crimes.

Reconstructing this part of his life turns out to be challenging, which shouldn't have surprised me. The prison system is one of the most opaque features of Chinese society. What's more, Carleton Sun was imprisoned early on in a new regime just starting its recordkeeping system. I manage to track down one surviving prisoner from roughly the same period in the early 1950s. He tells me inmates then were required to stay silent all the time, or risk electric shock punishment. Prison cells were packed at the time, as the new regime arrested so many people it had nowhere to put them.

Carleton Sun was transferred to the burgeoning *laogai* "reform through labor" prison labor camp system. First he was sent to a gulag at Dafeng city in northern Jiangsu province, then transferred to a labor camp in the remote northwest, to the Siberia of China: Qinghai province on the Tibetan Plateau of the far northwest. At that point his trail goes missing, at least to us.

The French historian Alain Besançon argues that the twentieth century was the "century of concentration camps." During that time, the British put Boer women and children in South African internment camps. Japan imprisoned captives in Southeast Asia. The United States forced Japanese Americans into internment camps on the West Coast. And then there is Hitler, Stalin, Pol Pot. But at the turn of the twenty-first century, only one world power entered it with a thriving concentration camp system: China. This is according to Philip Williams and Yenna Wu, authors of *The Great Wall of Confinement*.

Estimates vary, but somewhere between 1.3 and 8 million Chinese prisoners were sent to the gulag. The Chinese system—which the government of the People's Republic says it abolished in 2014—forced inmates to work. This was a long-inherited practice: the building of the Great Wall required forced conscripts; an estimated one million died doing the work. The dredging of the Grand Canal exacted similar casualties. Chiang Kai-shek's Guomindang National Revolutionary Army in the 1930s and '40s forced peasants to fight its wars and construct rail lines and roads.

The idea of a labor camp system was one imported by Mao from Stalin's Soviet Union. But the Chinese system added a twist. Williams and Wu write that what whereas the Soviet system focused on work and production, the Chinese gulag sought to reform prisoners' thinking—to convert convicts into socialist disciples. Thus the term *laogai*: "reform through labor." Inmates attended "struggle sessions," where they confessed to their own moral errors and accused others of sinning. They were rewarded for informing on one another, undermining inmate solidarity.

"If you inform on other people, you get advancement. Something good comes to you," says former Qinghai inmate Wei Xiezhong. He is one of three men from Qinghai's original labor camp in the 1950s (my grandfather's era) who agree to tell me their stories. Wei now lives in Nanjing but has met my father and me in Shanghai.

"It makes you not trust people. The camps turn you into an animal, like a dog. Today I don't even trust those around me, even my spouse. When it comes to making people inhumane, there's Hitler, Lenin, Stalin. None compare with Mao."

Wei hosts us in his daughter's apartment in Shanghai. He is tall and strong for an eighty-year-old, wearing a white Nike Air Jordan golf shirt that somewhat covers a bulging belly. We're joined by another labor camp survivor, named Zhang Shouchang, a smaller, frailer man. Time is running out for China's generation of labor camp survivors to tell their story, and Wei understands this. "We are all sufferers," he says on meeting us. "Let's ditch the formalities."

First we watch a video—Wei's amateur recording from a recent trip back to Qinghai's Delingha city, where his labor camp once stood. The camp has since shut down, and now the place is a paved city with a vast plaza. Wei slaps Zhang on the back. "*That* wasn't there back then, was it?" I'm curious why he would return to this place of bad memories, but it may not be too different from war veterans returning to the scene of battle.

Wei and Zhang were arrested and sent to Qinghai in 1957, perhaps three or four years after my grandfather arrived there. The two men were college students, rounded up with thousands of others as "Rightists." They'd joined a series of campus campaigns a year prior, known as the Hundred Flowers Campaign. At the time, Chairman Mao encouraged students and intellectuals to freely express their opinions about the new socialist regime. But quickly, the student denunciations of the Soviet-style education system and failures of the economy got out of hand for Beijing. The regime changed course. The flowers and the freedom shriveled up, and a crackdown known as the Anti-Rightist Campaign ensued.

Wei knocks his head softly with his fist, to dislodge old memories. During the crackdown, Wei went south to Shenzhen to get to Hong Kong, but was arrested by border police. "I received a five-year sentence, including three years of no political rights." An estimated half a million intellectuals were jailed or killed. Wei was sent off to the first of two labor camps, in all spending twenty-three years in the gulag. Wei points his finger at me. "You can't comprehend this."

Prisoners were sent out west on freight trains. Zhang recalls the trip lasted four days or so. "We sat on the floor of a cattle car. Maybe a thousand prisoners in all."

"Did you know where you were headed?" I ask. "Did they tell you?"

"No. The guards didn't tell us. And we didn't dare ask."

Zhang's group got off the train in Gansu and boarded the backs of large, open trucks. There were no rail tracks to Qinghai at the time, and hardly any roads—the literal end of the line. So prisoners built the roads. Along the way, the men built their own houses and dug irrigation trenches. In the days before houses, prisoners slept in earthen caves dug into hillsides.

"Your grandfather probably did that," Wei says, adding that he and Carleton Sun likely were sent to the same gulag—the Delingha

Reform through Labor farm. This was the first of many camps built in the 1950s. Traditional jails were bursting at the seams, and prisoners needed to be sent somewhere. The mass incarcerations in the early Mao years went hand in hand with the building of a new socialist state: secure the border; consolidate authority; define enemies and punish them. The simpler the narrative, the better.

Wei and Zhang start talking rapid-fire, their recollections gaining momentum like a boulder rolling downhill. Qinghai was so dry that the ground never got soaked when it rained. Temperatures in the winter fell to 20 below. Prisoners who broke the rules risked extended sentences, solitary confinement, or execution.

During struggle sessions at night, prisoners had to criticize themselves or someone else in the room. Often a session would focus on a single culprit and turn into a full-blown violent attack on that person. The inmate would bow his head contritely and confess guilt, Zhang says.

"That was more powerful than torture. You couldn't be silent, or else others would attack you."

At the Delingha camp, the food rations were reasonable in 1957 and 1958, until the famine of the Great Leap Forward. At that point, each prisoner received just two steamed rolls and a bowl of rice gruel, twice a day. Starvation became the most common cause of death. Wei takes a long pause. I look up from my notebook and realize tears have formed in his eyes.

"Whenever I have a nightmare, it's about this time period."

I don't have time to take the exact same slow-moving rail trip to Delingha that Carleton Sun presumably did. Instead, with my father I fly west, first to Dujiangyan in Sichuan, where another labor camp veteran lives. He has written lengthy blog entries about the labor camps under an Internet pseudonym. I'll call him Sichuan Man.

"This is my responsibility to history," he says, taking a seat in our hotel room. Sichuan Man was also deemed a Rightist: during the Hundred Flowers Campaign, he criticized a party member who fell in love with a high school classmate and then abruptly dumped her.

"She went crazy in college," Sichuan Man says. "I thought, 'You can't have sex with someone and throw her away and drive her crazy.' Our generation had to hold people responsible."

Along with ten other classmates, Sichuan Man wrote a "large character poster" denouncing this party member. For this misdeed he was deemed a Rightist and transferred to remote Qinghai to finish college. He was assigned a job as an agricultural worker at the Delingha camp, and gained access to labor camp information files.

Sichuan Man proceeds to draw a map of all the main camps, each one represented by a triangle surrounding massive Qinghai Lake. Jotting every point he makes as if this is his school chalkboard, he explains Delingha was the first camp, built in 1954. Prisoners from Carleton Sun's era were sent there, initially to dig irrigation and build roads, he says. "Build a mile, walk a mile." Just about every prisoner was a counterrevolutionary, a broad category that included rich landowners, GMD soldiers and military police officers, spies, thieves, robbers, Rightists.

Early on, the prison terms handed down were arbitrary, he says. "Back then, they could just decide you got fucking five years."

"Could you appeal?" I ask.

"Little Tong, you don't understand. There was no system or procedure. Back then, they could just execute people."

I ask if prisoners were treated better or worse based on their presumed crimes. He shakes his head. Any rewards went to the men who produced more. While some camps produced clothing or work tools, Delingha was a farm that grew barley, rapeseed, and potatoes. It was too cold and dry to grow rice or corn or cotton. The camps needed as many workers as possible, so there was hardly a possibility of early release.

"Almost all the camps shut down in the 1980s," he says. "They lost money." Young, healthy prisoners from the 1950s had aged or died out. The revenue from inmate production no longer covered costs.

I start to wonder if I'll get to see anything useful in Delingha. Sichuan Man tells me the camp was one of the first to shut down and convert into a state-owned farm. The way he describes it, the gravesites are likely plowed over, and who knows where any documents are. "You can't find it," he says. "No way."

Then he issues a warning: there are hucksters at the camps, purporting to have prisoners' remains and ashes to sell to family members. "They will cheat you. They will give you just a pile of dirt. Or horse or cow ashes."

At this point my father and I commit a tactical error. We suggest that Sichuan Man publish all this information, perhaps abroad in the United States if it's too sensitive for Chinese censors. Suspicion crosses his face. "If you want me to publish this, then it's a problem. I have children and grandchildren who have to be protected."

After all this time, is this prison camp information still so sensitive? Sichuan Man is convinced: "It doesn't matter what happens to me, I'm already old. But the political situation has changed." He is referring to the regime of Xi Jinping and its increasing intolerance of any internal criticism.

We suggest a lunch break, and Sichuan Man initially agrees. But then, after a bathroom break, he returns and abruptly changes course. "I have to go. My tongue is not well and I should go home to eat. This is all I have to say." He walks out. We have spooked him. It starts to dawn on me how taboo China's prison labor camp history may still be. Either that, or the experience has instilled in these men a paranoia that never goes away.

My dad and I split up for a few days. He takes the train to nearby Chongqing, the old treaty port where he was born. I fly to Qinghai's capital, Xining. On the plane, the overhead video monitors play a series of slapstick comedy videos—the usual fare. During our *Marketplace* assignment in Shanghai, our children's favorite segments were those of the British buffoon character Mr. Bean, the tweed-suited child of a man with a knack for getting a turkey stuck on his head.

Upon landing in a city at high altitude, I realize I've forgotten two things: lubricating eye drops and sunglasses. It is dusty, bone dry at 7,500 feet. The sun simply beats that much brighter. At a street peddler selling shades, I choose a conservative metal-rimmed pair over the seller's recommendation of a flashier model. "They make you look more *yang xing*." More Western character. Here

I was, researching a grandfather who "dressed too Western" for his own relatives in Shanghai, now encouraged to be more Western character.

This frontier of China has no shortage of diversity. I hear all manner of accents, see pedestrians in Tibetan garb and women in head coverings. A significant population of Chinese Muslims lives here, which may explain two things: a wealth of mutton restaurant options (mutton chops, stewed mutton, mutton kebabs, mutton noodle soup, and my favorite—mutton soup with bean threads and unleavened bread chunks) and a striking scarcity of cold beer.

The manager of the travel agency/hotel where I'm staying is ethnic Tibetan. The prison labor camps "remain a sensitive topic," he says. Many camps are three hundred or four hundred miles west by train. "But I don't think foreigners are allowed into some of those areas."

"Why not? Because of the labor camps?"

"No. Weapons testing."

I later learn Delingha is smack in the middle of the Los Alamos of China.

That evening, I take a long walk to get dinner (mutton soup, bread chunks) but move slowly as I adapt to the altitude. For a break, I step into a convenience store to buy some room-temperature beer and a bottle of "iced" tea. Reaching into my khaki shorts pocket, I groan: I've left my small bills in another pair of pants, so I pull out a hundred-yuan bill (about $15). China can be a tolerant society, but not when it comes to big bills.

"Fine. I'll break it." The elderly shopkeeper woman flings my change onto the counter, adding a glare for good measure. I linger a second and to my right see a younger woman with the same exact round face. Surely she's the shopkeeper's daughter. She clutches an infant wearing the one thing every Chinese baby does in the summer: a one-piece jumper with a massive slit on the bottom. This allows for real-time potty training anywhere—just squat and go.

"Can you tell which part of him looks like a boy?" the elderly woman asks, no longer surly. We both laugh, and the ice breaks. She asks me what has brought me to the end of the earth, and I give my abridged tale: Chinese American, Tong village, Grand Canal, Subei province.

She cuts me off. "I know *all* those places. I used to work on the Grand Canal," on a freight barge that began in Shandong province in the north and motored all the way down to Zhejiang province, near Shanghai. The trek took three weeks each way.

"Wow. It must have been hard work."

"No, not really." I hardly hear Chinese people admitting this. "We'd work till we stopped at a port for loading and off-loading. Then we didn't push off until the next morning."

I must have gotten stuck on her accent, because she stops talking. "Do you understand what I'm saying?" I nod. Eighty percent is getting through, which for these purposes is enough. I learn her grandson is coming up on his hundredth day, and she asks about my children. I pull out my mobile to show her a few.

"IPhone," she says, and then turns her focus to the images. "Will your kids go to Harvard? Harvard is the best, right?" This is an important question to her. "What's second best? Third?" She wants her grandson to attend Harvard, then changes her mind. Too far away.

New topic. "When will you retire?" she asks.

I shrug. "Too early to think about."

"As long as I can get my kids through college and married, and my grandson raised, my work will be done." This strikes me with two thoughts: how quickly China is changing now, allowing regular people to prosper; and how long it took to finally get here—after false starts, war, floods, famine, and internal witch hunts. Finally, with this generation, the seeds of change my ancestors helped plant are taking root.

My beers are getting warmer, so I grab my shopping bag and snacks and vow to stop by again. In truth, we both know I won't. "We have a connection," the shopkeeper says. "When you walk out, I'll be sad."

I have arrived in Xining with two promising contacts. The first is a mysterious distant uncle of a friend. He works for a government office that keeps records from the camps. The uncle walks into my hotel in a suit, which is unusual—perhaps he's high up.

He can only meet briefly. I ask him where records go when a prisoner dies. Do they still exist?

"When someone died, they contacted the family" to come and retrieve remains and possessions, he says. "But back then, there was no phone, no e-mail, no cellphones. So after a while, if we didn't hear back, the body was just buried."

I ask if he can help me gain access to department files. The uncle says he'll try, which means no.

"What's your name?" I ask as he heads to the door. He gives the pause of a man savvy enough to survive in this system.

"Just call me 'old man.'"

Contact Number Two gives his name immediately, perhaps because he's retired. Mr. Jin worked as a manager at the prison department, and he in fact is the son of a Delingha prisoner. His father was convicted as a "historic counterrevolutionary" for aiding the GMD before the 1949 liberation. But unlike Carleton, his father survived his sentence.

Many ex-cons stayed in Qinghai to work in the prison economy. There are opportunities here, and their pasts make them unemployable back home. "Your record, your history, it never leaves you," my uncle Tong Qi in Changzhou once told me.

Mr. Jin takes me by cab to his old department to hunt for records. "Maybe they still have his sentencing document." Mr. Jin is short and half bald, and makes extended eye contact in a way that tells me to never cross him.

"What about his personnel dossier?" I ask. I'd received conflicting information as to whether a person's file was destroyed upon his death. Historian Frank Dikötter of the University of Hong Kong once told me he stumbled upon old personnel files for sale at a Chinese outdoor market—a fitting marriage of authoritarianism and capitalism.

"They're supposed to be kept forever."

The department is housed in a large tan building with a sign on either side: QINGHAI PROVINCIAL PRISON MANAGEMENT DEPARTMENT on the right and QINGHAI PRISON ENTERPRISE GROUP LIMITED COMPANY on the left. Privatization has come to this place. In the front hallway, Mr. Jin flashes an ID card to the guard and signs a registration book. "He's with me," he says to the guard, shooting me a look of *keep walking and don't pull out your passport.*

The file room is filled with ceiling-height file cabinets, almost like a corporate human resources department. Two women work at desks facing each other—they are the gatekeepers. Mr. Jin explains we're looking for files for a man surnamed Sun. Perhaps it's listed under Sun Honglie. Or Sun Ditang. Or Sun Yi. I give all three names.

"Sit." One of the women motions us to a set of nice soft leather chairs. Perhaps this is the private-sector Qinghai Prison Enterprise Group Limited Company. The woman walks to one cabinet and pulls a handle revealing a set of card catalogs, like an old library's Dewey decimal system back home.

Indeed, the woman looks stereotypically librarian-ish: wire-rimmed glasses, no-nonsense straight hair, humor challenged. Her two fingers walk through a set of cards, then another. "Nothing," she says, returning to her desk. We approach. Are you sure? Yes. Did you check all three names? Yes. Are all the files from labor camps here? (I'd received conflicting answers to this question.)

"We *have* all the files," she says, not a bit perturbed. "Except for *laojiao.*" There were two types of prisoners in the system. *Laojiao,* or "reeducation through labor," was in concept a shorter-term punishment for lesser convicts. Carleton Sun fell under the more severe category of *laogai,* or "reform through labor."

We walk out, stuck and lacking options for the moment. I need a bit of air to think about the next step, though Mr. Jin needs something else. "Lunchtime," he says. "I'm taking you to eat mutton."

Mr. Jin has his own fascinating story. After working for the prison department that put his own father in the gulag, he retired and took a job at a direct marketing consumer goods company. This company just six years prior had been declared a lawless "evil cult" by the central government. Now the firm is a thriving, legitimate enterprise pulling in $3 billion a year. Mr. Jin is a salesman for Amway.

He warns me about going to Delingha. "You can't take a train there. They won't sell you a ticket." Indeed, it is a nuclear weapons testing zone. The safe bet is to take a long-distance bus ride, which means eight or nine bumpy hours at high altitude. "You'll be able to buy a bus ticket no problem."

We return to the prison department/company two days later. "Did you find another name for him?" the same woman asks. I've called three people in the States, but only come back with an additional nickname of his that's highly unlikely to be the right one here. She confirms this—nothing. I pepper her with more questions: "Any chance the system got one character wrong in his name?" *No, I've tried alternatives.* "Can I flip through the card catalog myself?" *Only staff members.* "Are there any records stored elsewhere?" *No.* "Can I look at one of the cards?"

On this she relents, passing me a yellowed prisoner-registration card. It reads:

Prisoner number.
Personnel dossier (*dang an*) number.
Name.
Additional names.
Sex.
Age.
Date of birth.
Component social status.
Hometown.
Address.
Ethnicity.
Job prior to arrest.
Sentence.
Crime.
Starting/ending date.
Date jailed.

The woman reaches to take the card back, then lowers her voice to say something that contradicts her previous statement. "Basically, we *don't* have all the files from Delingha camp." Perhaps it was true that when the camp shut down in the 1980s, its files had nowhere to go. They got destroyed, or misplaced. "Even if we had a card for your grandfather, it wouldn't have much information.

Many don't even list the date of death." In some cases, I'd read, authorities lied outright about a cause of death, to cover up mass starvation during the famine. Some simply listed the cause as *bing*, disease.

"I suggest you just go there and see it," she says. "You came so far from America. A lot of prisoner relatives have come here looking for the same thing. The best thing you can do is take some soil from the labor camp and bring it home to bury it. It's very meaningful. You should do that."

This presents a face-saving solution for both of us. She exits the situation without admitting failure, and I have a symbolic gesture to pursue. I bid goodbye to her, and then Mr. Jin, and walk in the direction of the long-distance bus station.

Part of me anticipates the long bus ride ahead. In my experience, slow, long-distance travel is the best chance to see a fight.

Once, in 2007, in the dead of night in middle-of-nowhere Zhe-jiang province, a migrant teenage woman bus worker whose job was to take tickets on the bus simply lost it. She was teased by a tall young man who refused to present his ticket and demanded the driver take a different route. She tried to shush him, he badgered on, and the ugly words escalated. A bathroom break temporarily defused the situation. "Ten minutes," the girl declared as the bus pulled over on a dark stretch of two-lane road. All the women got off and went left toward the shops. The men, including me, peeled off to the right to urinate directly into a concrete ditch on the shoulder (in these moments, the Chinese man is an unparalleled multitasker, able to conduct his business, operate his cellphone, and light a smoke all at once).

Bus Monitor Girl and Passenger Boy started up again on the edge of the ditch. Suddenly a crowd materialized around them. Passen-ger Boy must have delivered a piercing insult, because Bus Monitor Girl rushed him, swinging wildly and screaming something fierce. Unfortunately for her, he had four inches and perhaps forty pounds on her. He grabbed her and flung her into the ditch.

She pulled herself up and screamed something primal again. The bus driver stepped between them and shouted for everyone to get back on. Show over.

A more vivid boy-versus-girl fight came at close range a couple years later. My assistant Cecilia Chen and I were taking a slow train in Hunan. Our timing was terrible. The trip came on the most traveled week before Chinese New Year, the largest movement of humanity on the planet.

Any seats were long gone by the time we boarded. We carved out a bit of space by the door, squeezed in with two dozen other people. Amazingly, a pair of girls—perhaps teenagers—boxed out enough fellow travelers to make room to sit on tiny four-inch stools, around a rice pot. They were migrants from the countryside with no makeup, no discernible hair product, no deodorant.

From time to time, they'd pop the top of the rice pot and dig into their meal, which consisted entirely of bright-red Hunan peppers atop white rice. One girl, upon closer examination, looked mentally challenged—her eyes didn't focus quite right, and it appeared she hadn't combed her short hair in days. The other, perhaps an older sister, wore a round face and midlength ponytail, constantly directing the other what to do. An hour later, she unveiled a pack of dried watermelon seeds and the two worked on them, cracking them with their front teeth, swallowing the meat and spitting the shells into the rice pot.

At the first stop, one or two passengers boarded and dove into the crowd, incident-free. Stop two, though, was a major city. The door opened and a pack of five or six teenage boys, each with cheaply dyed orange hair, rushed off, bumping the Hunan Pepper Girls. The ponytailed one cursed. A minute later, another man with regular black hair came running to exit before the door closed. In his haste, he knocked over the Pepper Girls' rice pot and bowled over the confused-looking sister. He almost took me down as well.

He cussed. The ponytailed Pepper Girl screamed back. This all took place in a local Hunan dialect, but, really, when you've been worn down by heat and human density, the language doesn't much matter. Everyone speaks venom.

His dignity at stake, the young man countered with some rude comment. He stepped off and they continued yapping at each other. But the physical distance—him outside, her inside—seemed to sap the energy of the exchange, and we stood there awaiting the door to close.

It didn't. So the Pepper Girl spat a wad of watermelon seeds—

and associated saliva—at the man, accurately enough to nail him in the face. He paused for a moment, and then dropped his duffel and charged her.

I don't exactly remember what happened next, as I found myself in the middle of the swinging arms and fists. I ducked my head into my arms but still got struck by glancing blows. This was one of those silent fights, with only the sound of combatants exhaling. And in a moment, it was over. Neither party seemed to win the bout. The combatants flung one last set of insults, and the man stepped off.

The door finally closed, at which point the Pepper Girl gave one last grumble. And then, remarkably, life on the train resumed as if nothing had happened. In America a dispute like this would prompt travelers to ask if she was okay. There'd be outrage at a boy fighting a girl. The event would be mined for some broader meaning about society.

Not here. The Pepper Girls reached into a bag and began working on a third snack.

The bus ride to Qinghai turns out remarkably uneventful. Silently we cross the frontier of traditionally defined China. Historically, the territory of ancient China was described as the land between Four Seas (*sihai*): Lake Baikal in modern Russia to the north, the South China Sea below Hong Kong to the south, the East China Sea off the eastern coast, and Qinghai Lake to the west. Delingha exists well beyond the lake.

However Delingha might have looked back then, today it welcomes visitors the way other Chinese cities do: with bright lights. Well past midnight, I awake to see a well-lit, official-looking building that spans two or three football fields. Alongside it runs a manmade marine-blue river, lit from the bottom like a swimming pool. The Chinese infrastructure boom has stretched clear from the eastern lip of Shanghai to this little-known missile-testing city on the Western edge.

"Welcome." The simply dressed middle-aged man I'd arranged to meet waits at a quiet street corner that doubles as a bus stop. I'll be staying with him, as I'm told Delingha hotels are off-limits to foreigners. "Tomorrow we see the *nongchang*," he says, the farm.

My host's father had been a Delingha prisoner as well, around the same era as my grandfather.

When I meet the old man the next morning, he shares a few of his own memories and then looks straight at me through cataract-clouded eyes and points a crooked finger: "If you write about this, don't use my real name."

No wonder this Chinese story is still so largely unknown to its people. Far more has been written and spoken about the Mao Zedong's twin tragedies: the mass famine caused by the Great Leap Forward and the political witch hunts of the Cultural Revolution. Those events involved far more people. There were far fewer forced labor convicts (1.5 to 8 million) than those who starved in the famine (thirty million to forty million plus) or persecuted during the Cultural Revolution (hundreds of millions). The gulag era also began earlier, so there aren't many survivors left. Another factor could be that there is no widespread, acclaimed Chinese version of Aleksandr Solzhenitsyn's book on the Soviet prison camps, *The Gulag Archipelago*. But I also get a sense after meeting with several prisoners of that era that they're also scared to talk. Six decades after the blame and indoctrination sessions, fear of the state apparatus remains.

I'm not sure how I'll react to being in Delingha. There's been so much buildup to this moment—talking to relatives, chasing documents, reading and rereading family letters, interviewing old prisoners, promising to keep identities private, listening to my mother and her sister talk about their father Carleton Sun for hours at a time. What does this moment mean? So much is made in Chinese society about *xun gen*—searching for your roots. But when you physically come as close as you can to the actual roots, what happens then?

The first reaction is entirely physical and unemotional: breathlessness, from the altitude and my asthma. Asthmatics often describe their struggle as breathing through a straw, but here it's more like a coffee stirrer. On the first day, I can only walk a couple hundred yards before resting.

The other reaction is that of being tardy. One phrase keeps replaying in my mind: "You came too late for this." Sun Peipei, my mother's second cousin and Carleton Sun's great-niece in Shanghai, has said this more than once. It's too late to find anyone still alive who remembers Carleton's politics, or his arrest, or his imprisonment or death. It also seems too late for documents. So what am I really here to see?

"Here it is." The driver turns left off the main road a half hour outside Delingha city, to the grounds of the old prison labor camp. It doesn't look like we've turned into, well, anything. It all looks the same here: yellow-brown dirt and gravel and dust—the monochrome look of a moonscape. The only interruptions to the scene are a few trees, a smattering of barley and oil vegetable plants, and several goats. I finger a plastic bag in my pocket.

"There are no people here," I say. The place reminds me of the entirely abandoned town in West Texas I'd visited for a story: Happy, Texas. More than a decade after farmers overdrilled and drained the aquifer dry, the place ran out of water and everybody moved away. My host and driver look at me as if to say: *What did you expect?*

We pull over at an old-fashioned irrigation ditch, so rudimentary it might go back to the 1950s. "Do you think the early prisoners dug these irrigation trenches?" I ask. Shrug. Maybe. Driving on, we spot a few signs of life: two very old houses with clay walls and holes in the roofs, a primitive water well, and a wheelbarrow from a long time ago. And more goats.

Then we come upon an old graveyard. It is a wide-open space with no headstones or identifying names, just a vast stretch of oval mounds, one per body. "These are probably from the '70s," my host says. That's too recent. I ask to see an older makeshift cemetery, which looks pretty much the same—except with darker-colored sand. It looks eerily similar to the shallow graves I saw at a Somali refugee camp in 2011, though in East Africa the mounds were topped with sharp tree branches to deter foraging coyotes. In much of the world, this is the way you leave it—simply and namelessly.

A wood plank sticking up from the ground just about trips me. It's maybe twice the size of a small cutting board. The planks, my host explains, once had the names of the deceased—etched on it or written in ink. By now, the board was perfectly blank, smoothed over by heat and snow, sand and wind. Literally airbrushed from history. I can only make out one other plank. Perhaps the others are covered under sand, buried with their owner, or never even existed at all in this vast tomb of the unknown prisoner.

I bend down to grab a fistful of graveyard soil, with an image in my mind of Willy Loman in *Death of a Salesman*, frantically planting seeds at the end of an unfulfilled life. Surely my grandfather had similar thoughts in this place, I tell myself. I fish out the plastic bag from my pocket and toss in the soil—just as the bureaucrat woman suggested—to bring with me back home.

Given the vague and thinly documented information I have on Carleton Sun, I am left with a few dozen pieces of a five-hundred-piece puzzle. There are academic books and others' memoirs from the gulag; a documentary-style film, *Jiabiangou*, on the topic; and the personal recollections of a handful of prisoners. If he'd have kept diaries or letters, those would have been confiscated. There are no remains or prison belongings still around; mainland relatives vaguely recall that a few of my grandfather's personal items were returned after he died, but they were very young children in the 1950s and their parents are gone. Indeed, I waited too long to start chasing all this.

I also have my imagination. So I've decided to put the following three letters in Carleton's words, as he might have described life in the Delingha prison labor camp. To be clear, what follows is a passage of fiction. These are not his direct words, though several passages come directly from anonymous sources I've met. This type of allegorical writing is common among Chinese writers today, to convey a certain reality and still detour around government censors. To me, it gives voice not just to Carleton Sun, but to the millions who perished alongside him.

1955
Zhen,

Two years have gone by since they put me in a freight railcar and banished me far to the west. They took everything—my watch, my books, my clothes. Even my hair. We were all shaved after arriving, and got matching black clothing and cotton quilted jackets. In the winter it is colder than I can imagine. The dryness of the mountain air is just as bad, bringing cracks to my lips and fingers and heels.

Are you still living in Diamond Hill in Hong Kong? Life is so hard for you there. Did you manage to make enough money to send the children to school? Did the Dai family help you get visas for Argentina or Chile? Every day I wonder where you are. Is my mother still alive?

One of the hardest things is not being allowed to talk during work. If we break the rule, we pay for it at the struggle session. Repeat offenders get beaten, not by the guards but other prisoners. One man, a skinny guy with glasses, tried to run away and escape, but he was caught and executed by firing squad. Intimidation fuels this place. The thing is, even if anyone got out, he couldn't survive Qinghai. It is so barren. There is nothing here.

In struggle sessions, they brainwash us. I think it's working. First we criticize ourselves, like confession in a church but in front of everyone. We all tell bad thoughts. Bad deeds. They pick a person each night to criticize, and we have to join in or we're the next target.

Honglie

"During that period, we were like Roman gladiators. If you kill someone else, you live." This is how Wei Xiezhong, the former Delingha prisoner, describes the *Lord of the Flies* environment there. Wei tells me about the time he betrayed another man.

"There was this prisoner, named Liu, from northern Jiangsu. He'd been sentenced to twelve years for being a counterrevolutionary. Privately, he told me all his thoughts and experiences. Then, when food got scarce in 1960, we only got 18.5 *jing* of food per month." That comes out to about three hundred grams per day—half of what the World Food Program deems a survival ration.

"We were all in bed, preparing to die. But the farm still needed workers. Liu was strong and wanted to work. He said it helped him to go outside, forage for food and steal. He kept bugging and annoying me to let him do it."

Wei adjusts his glasses briefly and looks down. "So I informed on him. I told leaders Liu still had counterrevolutionary thoughts. I assumed being an informant would shorten my sentence. It didn't. But Liu got a longer sentence. I met him years after we both got out and was so ashamed. He knew what I did, and I know what I did. These betrayals give us the most shame. And now all these years later, we are dealing with guilt at the end of our lives."

He asks if I know what it's like to give confession in a Catholic church. I shake my head—not exactly in that way. I need a bathroom break and hurry over, experiencing my own surge of sorrow for the first time during this project. The gulag system, far from turning out politically reformed men, did something else: it stripped them of their humanity. Wei Xiezhong became a shadow of himself in Delingha, and surely my grandfather did as well.

Looking into the bathroom mirror, I can hear my mother's words coming back to me. *Perhaps it's better not to know everything.* I take a breath, splash some water on my face, and wipe away the tears before rejoining the group.

1957
Zhen,

I wish you could tell me about the children. How is Constantine? The girls work hard, but I hope he can focus on schoolwork. I hope you have found a way for them to keep going to school.

Yesterday they asked us to fill out forms to put in our dossier, to write down the names of all our relatives and where they live, where they work. Who is your wife? Who is your uncle? Who is your grandfather? What is their work unit? We cannot skip any details. I'm afraid for you and other family members to be connected with me, but if I don't write the truth and the Party finds discrepancies in our family, this will bring trouble for everyone.

All our dignity has been taken away. You and the children are suffering in Hong Kong. And I am here, criticized for the choices I made. Some things I say are true, some are lies. We all manufacture lies to attack others and protect ourselves.

Always we carry shovels to dig. When I first came, we dug roads and rail paths through the mountains. Now we dig trenches for irrigation so we can plant enough food to feed ourselves. We eat potatoes and mantou dumplings with no filling. They are hard to chew and digest, because the flour is less refined. Right now the food is enough.

Leaders can't kill us all, so they put us to work. Officially, they say reform is the number one goal and production is number two. Not true. Production is the most important thing. It is hard for us intellectuals to do labor, we're not as strong. But we must keep up. It doesn't matter what your crime is, so long as you produce.

Remind the children about me. Tell them they can still get ten peanuts for each spoonful of cod liver oil. Tell them if they eat the root at the tip of the peanut, be careful: a peanut plant will grow out of their heads.

Honglie

By 1959, China's great famine had arrived and starvation was the main cause of death. "At that point, only the thieves survived," Wei says. "Me too. Stealing is the only reason I survived. During the harvest, everyone did, otherwise the food we grew would have shipped to somewhere else."

Wei does not offer specifics as to how he stole food. When I ask him if he feels guilty for surviving at someone else's expense, he shakes his head. "There's a twisted logic in China today. It's okay to steal from the government, but you cannot steal people's private things. Private property is sacred. It's as if we go to dinner and fight over the check. If I say, 'I can write it off on my expense report,' we all stop fighting. People are immoral today because of this past. This is why we have so much corruption. Because of the Mao era."

1959
Zhen,

I don't think I will survive this 15-year sentence. Food is so scarce now. Our grain rations are half of what they were a few years ago. Many men do not go out to work anymore. They are too weak. For now, I can keep going, but barely.

It is hard to focus on anything, because we are always thinking of hunger and food.

We know someone has died when a horse comes by. It pulls a cart with a body inside, wrapped in a large sheet and tied up. Each corpse gets what they call a soft burial. Of course there are no caskets, just shallow graves arranged haphazardly because men are dying so fast. Every day gets quieter.

Not too long ago, I still had hopes of seeing you and the children. I assume everyone is still alive. By now, Lily and Constantine are adults over 20. Even Anna must be 16 or 17 by now. I cannot believe what I have missed. Likely my mother is gone by now.

We have run out of hope here, for new ideas, for a new and strong China. Wang Jingwei said he did not believe the Communists would bring a better China. I fear he may have been right.

Honglie

The record is uncertain, but Carleton Sun died either during the famine, or just before it hit.

Chapter Eleven

THE BROTHER
LEFT BEHIND
IN THE WAR

It's best you don't write about these things.
—Uncle Tong Bao

The older brother held the hands of an adult on either side as they
boarded the boat. The grownups were his father and his father's
mistress, but the boy's younger brother was not there. The trio had
only two tickets, but somehow, as the crowds pushed onboard like
cattle, they all made it on. The three took a set of stairs down to a
dark, bottom-level cabin with barracks-style bunk beds.

Already the room was filling up with people, but this was the
safest place for the three to be discreet, just in case ticket checkers
came. The boat, named *Zhongxing*, which means "resurgent," was a
converted cargo vessel, designed to carry perhaps five hundred passengers. More than twice that many had boarded.

The location: port of Shanghai. It is February 1949.

These three had been running from the Communists for weeks.
The father had to get out: he'd taught law at a university whose
president, Chiang Kai-shek, headed the Nationalist Guomindang
government, and now the GMD was in full retreat. One month
prior, the rival People's Liberation Army forces took Beijing in the
north and headed south toward the capital city, Nanjing.

The three had left Nanjing two months before it fell. They'd boarded a bus in a hurry, and as it pulled away, the older brother spotted a dog trying to chase down the vehicle. "It was a small dog, maybe white," the boy recalls six decades later. "I think it was my dog." The older brother is my father.

The bus took them to a Shanghai-bound train packed to the rivets. Some passengers were so desperate they clung to the outside rails; others balanced atop train cars, until the tunnels.

"When the train went through the tunnel, those people got wiped out," my father has said many times. This is his enduring war memory, although he didn't see it himself. "The people on the train told us this."

They waited in Shanghai for more than a week before boarding the boat to Taiwan, and thank God they waited. By the time the *Zhongxing* steamed across the Taiwan Strait—passengers huddled, seasick, vomiting for days—they arrived to learn that another ship ferrying war refugees to and from Taiwan had sunk. One night before Chinese New Year's Eve, the holiday in Asian culture, the *Taiping*, meaning "tranquility," sailed with its lights off, due to wartime Shanghai's night curfew. The ship struck a small cargo boat and sank in frigid January waters in half an hour. The *Taiping* had been licensed to carry 580 people, though in reality more than a thousand—perhaps as many as 1,500—got on. Only thirty-six survived. The estimated casualties are on the order of those from the sinking of the *Titanic* in 1915.

Like so many refugee stories, my father's escape story is stacked with close calls that can bring you to your knees. Why did his father choose to take him, and not his younger brother? How did they get space inside the train bound for Shanghai? Why didn't they get tickets on the *Taiping* before it sank?

My father landed in Taiwan at the age of ten and quickly climbed the education and economic ladders. You've heard this zero-to-60 immigration story before: He became a starting point guard on the high school basketball team and studied engineering at National Taiwan University. He met an American GI stationed on Taiwan and got baptized in a Lutheran church. In the early 1960s he joined a small wave of students to study in the United States, during a peak in US–Taiwan relations. He attended graduate school at the

University of Minnesota, where he met the woman he would marry at a Chinese Student Association dance. Then he got a high-salary job at the only company he ever wanted to work for: IBM. He drove a 1967 Ford Mustang—four-door, yellow.

Having heard this story a number of times, it now makes me wonder about the flip side, about the brother who did not get out. In a normal distribution, for all the winners of history there would be a proportional set of losers. Perhaps these losers were born in the wrong place at the wrong time and serendipity worked against them. Wouldn't it be nice to have a parallel case, of a brother in the same family who traveled one road while my father traveled the other?

That person is my uncle, the younger brother left behind.

Technically, Tong Bao is my half uncle. Tong Bao and my father share a father—and thus the surname Tong—but were born to different mothers. But in my Chinese conversations, I can't ever remember hearing the word "half" in this context. Family trumps accuracy.

To be honest, my uncle can be a challenging interview. If I were reporting this story as traditional journalism, I would not choose him as a source. Sometimes you shake a tree all day and a single mango drops. Or to swap metaphors, Uncle Tong Bao can float on the surface of a conversation for hours, as if he's wearing an emotional life jacket that doesn't let him dive deep.

Yet over time, I discovered his story of survival, abandonment and exile, public humiliation and reinvention, and redemption. The Tong Bao movie would have a dramatic soundtrack. But there is one problem: he doesn't want the story told.

"It's best you don't write about these things," Uncle Tong Bao says at the coffee table in his modest apartment in northeast Shanghai. It is the summer of 2014. This was the last of dozens of conversations we'd have before I start drafting this book.

I put down my pen. "Why not?"

"*Bu bi.*" It's not necessary.

"But this book will be published in America, not here."

"I have friends in America. They might read about my private affairs."

"Friends in America. Do you have a lot?"

"Six."

I sit on a low couch, looking at the last of some sixty pages of notes I've just scribbled about his extraordinary life. Six friends.

"You should write the book this way," Tong Bao offers. "You should focus only on my mother's life, before 1945."

"Drink tea." Aunt Qi Menglan enters and pours hot water in my teacup. She sits to my right on the couch, as Uncle Tong Bao leans back on a chair to my left. "Why don't you write a novel?" she suggests. "You can change the names."

Goodness. "Which parts are *bu bi*?" I ask. "What part of your life should I keep out?" The signature scene from the 1980s film *Amadeus* flashes, the one where the emperor tells Mozart that the composer's masterpiece contains "too many notes." My insincere reply is the same as Mozart's: *Which few did you have in mind, Majesty?*

I don't let a source decide what goes in or out of a story. It's as absolute a rule as there is in journalism. Yet this situation feels different, as we're talking about my uncle. The Professional Me is colliding with Filial Me. I repeat my offer: What sections should I take out?

"*Bu guangrong de.*" The parts that are not glorious.

I sip my tea. By now, the leaves have steeped so long it's very bitter. I've avoided this confrontation, this conversation, for too long. Yet this moment was coming, one way or another.

"This is *my* book," I say, surprising even myself as the words came out. After so many years in China, I am tired of exercising self-restraint: *Take the business card and smile. Drink the alcohol that goes down like Drano.* This story has to be told in a real way—setbacks, infidelity, arrests, labor camps—to humanize what so many people have overcome. It has to be real.

My uncle says nothing. So I kept talking, filibustering. It's hard to litigate this kind of argument in your second language. "This is not a product of advertising or public relations. A book about just the glorious parts would be your book. Not mine."

Uncle Tong Bao looks away and folds his arms. "Then go ahead and write it." It is an answer of resignation rather than permission. This is the first time I can remember angering him. Aunt Qi

Menglan breaks the silence. "Then just write a good book. Write it beautifully." She speaks in a more direct, unfiltered way about herself and her past. "I like books that are transparent. Honest."

This uncomfortable exchange has played and replayed in my mind ever since. How can I tell his story, and still honor him? So I have decided to change his name, at least somewhat. This is not a wholesale alias. Early on in his life, my uncle had his surname changed from his father's to his mother's. But here, I will use his true-but-long-discarded name of Tong Bao. Here is how I think about it: for the first three decades of his life, Tong Bao had many things taken away from him, robbed from his life experience: Warmth. Desire. Opportunity. And most of all, trust. Naming him would turn me into the next thief. So here goes.

When Tong Bao was born in 1947, his father (my grandfather) was a widower attempting to put his prewar life back together. My grandfather had spent seven years hiding from Japanese air raids in the western mountains of Sichuan province, alongside members of the Nationalist Guomindang government of Chiang Kai-shek. In Sichuan, my grandfather's wife gave birth to their second child: my father. This wife, my father's birth mother, died shortly after from tuberculosis. My father remembers nothing of his birth mother.

Upon the Japanese surrender in 1945, my grandfather returned down the Yangtze to Nanjing. He fell in love with the woman who would become his second wife and Tong Bao's mother. This marriage to Wife 2 lasted two years before my grandfather left her and left China. Wife 2 would suffer for decades, on account of her marrying a GMD professor for two years.

Before leaving wartime China, my grandfather found time to meet a third woman, a Ms. Wang of Shanghai. "He represented her in a legal case," Tong Bao says. "She was the daughter of a capitalist." He pulls out the term "capitalist" in a room furnished with a nice piano, a flat-screen TV, and a $5,000 racing bicycle.

To make things worse, Tong Bao's mother—the spurned Wife 2—was pregnant with their second child when my grandfather left her. "She never talked about this," my uncle says.

Aunt Qi Menglan jumps in: "Mistresses were very common then. They say a good man has nine wives."

Tong Bao's mother at the time did not even know her husband had left, or who he went with. She later received a letter from a friend in Taiwan who'd run into my grandfather and his mistress.

"This was when mail still went back and forth from Taiwan," Tong Bao says. By the summer of 1950, though, Beijing and Washington entered the Korean War, the US Navy's Seventh Fleet sailed into the Taiwan Strait, and all communications between Taiwan and the mainland ended. Tong Bao was two years old then, and has no childhood memories of his father.

China's political system, though, does not forget. Tong Bao bore the stain of being a GMD son. There was one incriminating phrase that kept haunting him, a phrase stamped atop his dossier: the political status of *haiwai guanxi*. Overseas relations.

I first met Uncle Tong Bao in 2005, when *Marketplace* sent several journalists to the mainland for a special series of live programs from China. This was a common thing. In the first decade of the twenty-first century, virtually every major news organization in the world went over to "discover" China. This was our turn.

He lives in a walk-up apartment on the fifth floor of a solid but modest neighborhood. I hardly remember anything about our interaction. Aunt Qi Menglan did much of the talking while he slaved in the kitchen, frying up one dish after another. This, I learned, is what Shanghai men do: cook and clean while the women appear to be in charge. Once during an early trip to Beijing, I told a cab driver I lived in Shanghai, prompting a strongly worded reply. He warned me: "Don't come up here and say you're a Shanghai man. They're wimps. They talk and talk but they never fight. *Bu nan bu nu.*" Neither man nor woman.

Uncle Tong Bao is not so much androgynous as overlooked. If you passed him on a Shanghai street, you might look straight past. Medium height, slight build, round face. His eyebrows slant down toward the edge of his face, almost as if he's sad all the time.

On the first trip, he spoke mostly of logistics: where to get a cab, how Shanghai lays out on a map, what to eat and not eat. Only later would I realize that these everyday details are Uncle Tong Bao's way of showing affection. Just before I left that night, he presented me with several thick cotton sweatshirts to bring home for the kids.

"We have sweatshirts," I said. I pack light, and there was no way I'd squeeze these in the suitcase.

"*Yisi yisi*," he said. Just a little something for meaning. He shoved the oversize shopping bag in my hand, walked me down five floors, and delivered me into a cab.

Building a relationship with Uncle Tong Bao is like putting pennies in a jar. Each visit is a small deposit. Most of the times I met him, I asked him to help me explain something for a story I was chasing: *How do the currency controls work again? What do you make of the slave labor scandal? How do you deal with Internet censorship? What was it like before there were direct flights to Taiwan? Will you attend the Olympics? The Shanghai World's Fair Expo?*

The ice begins to break in 2011, the year after we've moved back to the States. I fly back specifically to start researching family history. It's summer vacation, so I've brought along my older son, Evan, who is eleven. Uncle Tong Bao and Aunt Qi Menglan insist we eat at their place for dinner. And sure enough, once we arrive, he is cooking up a feast: bamboo shoots, tofu, shrimp stir-fried with ginger, braised pork, snap peas with potatoes, soy sauce–boiled eggs.

Quickly we learn there is a problem. We've arrived an hour before the appointed dinnertime, and Evan is starving.

"It's still early for dinner," Aunt Qi Menglan says. Still, she has to offer something, so she walks out and reappears with a bakery box filled with individual cakes. "Eat cake." As we settle into the small living room couch, I nod my consent to Evan and he digs in. Better to spoil an appetite than a relationship.

At dinner my aunt doesn't so much sit as roam. She explains she can't eat much on account of bad teeth. Mostly she hovers around Evan, with a pot in one hand and a spoon in the other. It seems to me she's making a mental tally of every bite he takes, the way an umpire tracks balls and strikes.

"He eats so little," she complains. "Why isn't he eating more? What does he like to eat? We'll make it." No need, I say. Perhaps it's just jet lag.

"He doesn't want to eat," Uncle Tong Bao says to her. "You're pressuring him."

Evan sits back from all this attention and says he's not feeling so well. "I might have a fever," he says in English.

"What's the problem?" Aunt Qi Menglan requests a translation as I ask for a thermometer.

Request denied. "No fever!" she declares, with the kind of Chinese certainty that shall not be challenged. "If he had a fever, he'd feel cool, not hot."

The logic confuses me—perhaps she's referring to the chills from the patient's perspective—but now is not the time to seek clarification. Instead, I direct Evan to lie on the couch for a few minutes and ask if they have beer. And then Uncle Tong Bao begins talking.

"I was always put in the back of the line," he says of his childhood. "So long as there was a front and a back, I was in back."

I ask: "What kind of lines?"

"All of them." Uncle Tong Bao was deemed ineligible to attend the best middle schools, even though he received top grades. He grew up in the city of Changzhou, in between Nanjing and Shanghai—his mother's city. She and Tong Bao crammed into a small apartment with his younger brother (named Tong Qi), her own brother and his two children, and her mother. "There were so many political movements in the 1950s, celebrating loyal revolutionaries and criticizing the rest of us."

The status of *haiwai guanxi* followed him like a shadow. When the time came during the Cultural Revolution to exile teens and young adults with bad political status to the countryside, Tong Bao received a long sentence of ten years (though one of my mother's nieces actually was exiled to Guangxi province for thirteen years).

But he focuses on the treatment of his mother's persecution during the Cultural Revolution, at the hands of Red Guard youths enforcing ideological purity. "They came to dig up your roots." Party members went back into everyone's dossiers to hunt for family connections to real and imagined enemies of the regime. Red Guards targeted teachers and school administrators in particular; Uncle Tong Bao's mother was a vice principal. "She was a leader," he says. "So long as you were a leader, you were targeted."

"They called it 'cleaning up the classes,'" Aunt Qi Menglan says. "Some teachers were forced to sit in public and have their heads shaved—but only on one side of their head. They called it the 'yin-yang' haircut." I'd read about cases of students beating teachers to death with baseball bats and belts, but this was an altogether different experience, hearing it directly from participants and victims in my own family.

As for Tong Bao's mother, "they criticized her on *dazibao*," he says, describing the handwritten "big-character posters" that went up on walls across the city. *Dazibao* turned up everywhere: in outdoor spaces, work units, and notably schools. Some signs parroted propaganda slogans or poems; others directly targeted key leaders to whip up revolutionary frenzy. Some *dazibao* denounced key leaders as bourgeois intellectuals, historical revisionists, or counter-revolutionaries. Periodically, a sign would simply describe a hated person as "Guomindang's bitch."

He looks at me for a moment. "She never talked about any of this."

| Chapter Twelve | CURSED BY OVERSEAS RELATIONS |

I was so lucky to find a frog on the way home. My grandmother would cook it for us to eat.
—Uncle Tong Bao

Soon after escaping mainland China, my father tasted Coca-Cola. This was in the early 1950s, when Taiwan enjoyed the protection of the US Cold War umbrella. It began with the conflict in Korea that mainlanders knew as the War to Resist US Aggression and Aid Korea. Six hundred thousand Chinese soldiers and thirty-six thousand American troops died. By the time of the cautious truce in 1953, Washington and Beijing were outright enemies. The United States folded Taiwan into its Pacific alliance, joining Japan, South Korea, Australia, Thailand, and the Philippines.

Into Taiwan came American money and influence. As the US Navy's Seventh Fleet patrolled the waters of the Taiwan Strait, American GIs, diplomats, and missionaries landed in Taipei. My father remembers attending a Boy Scout camp with wealthy American boys. At the time, the typical person in Taiwan made just $900 US a year—around the same per capita income as Ghana or Kenya, but one-tenth that of America. "Everyone was poor," he recalls, "but we were equally poor."

On the radio, my father remembers Taiwanese deejays playing

rock-and-roll hits by a foreign star known as *mao wang*, the Cat King. "I don't know why we called him that." The Cat King slicked his hair, and his music was bolder than what the 1950s Taiwan audience was used to—Pat Boone, the Brothers Four, Connie Francis. The Cat King was, of course, Elvis Presley. My father and his friend knew other stars through film. Theaters in Taipei played *Casablanca, Gone with the Wind, A Streetcar Named Desire*, all with Chinese subtitles, giving students the illusion they understood English. In truth, he found the Southern accents of Blanche DuBois and Scarlett O'Hara particularly hard to follow. Even now, after six decades in the States, "I still don't understand" the accent.

Taiwan's economy in the '50s and '60s began to rev, for a number of reasons: intellectual elites from the mainland, the GMD's iron-fist authoritarian rule, American money, and legacy Japanese colonial investments in roads, electricity, and education. Turbocharged by capital from the US Agency for International Development, Taiwan became a low-end manufacturing titan, churning out textiles and transistors for the world.

At the age of sixteen, my father met an American sergeant from Allentown, Pennsylvania. Bill Bloss had transferred to Taipei after serving in the Korean War, and his new tour came with a house, cook, driver, and Jeep four-by-four. Before long, Bloss ventured across the street where he lived—Dragon Spring Street—and chatted up a group of local teenage boys, including my father. Bloss offered to teach them English, and joined them at ping-pong and snooker, the British billiards game. He drove them around in his Jeep. "He had a record player with an automatic changer," my father recalls. "It was totally fantastic to us."

Bloss took them to a Lutheran church, where my father and a couple friends got baptized. He even helped them choose English names: James. Jerry. Carl. David. My dad chose Alvin. Eventually the American GI offered a room in his house for Alvin Tong to sleep in. The two men spoke English every day, and Bloss bought my father luxury items from the PX, including cotton underwear as an alternative to the cheap, sandpaper-like boxers local boys tended to wear. My father can talk about Bill Bloss's influence for a long time, most of all the positive image this friendship gave of the

United States: "It was always the goal to go to America. It was the obvious choice for all of us."

By the time my father graduated with an electrical engineering degree from National Taiwan University, Taiwan was sending two thousand of its best and brightest to the United States for graduate school. Alvin Tong would join them, inspired by Bill Bloss from Allentown. It was, in a way, a passing of the industrial baton. One century after America's post–Civil War industrial boom had brought fortune to the ironworks centers of Pennsylvania, post–World War II Taiwan was having its own manufacturing boom. It was 1962.

That same year, my father's younger brother Tong Bao on the mainland was eating tree bark and grass to survive. In the mainland city of Changzhou, he was a teenager in the worst famine in recorded history.

Tong Bao would not have told me any of this had I not asked about it. Like many of his generation, he does not sermonize about the bad old days. I have to squeeze out the information as if it's the last toothpaste left in the tube.

I'm sitting at his dinner table in Shanghai, asking about the *sannian ziran zaihai*. I've heard of this period of the Great Leap Forward described as the Three Years of Natural Disasters. But he looks at me as if I have two heads.

"It was not a natural disaster," he says. "It was a totally manmade disaster. There was no flood. There was no period of no rain. We had to eat tree bark and grass."

"How did you eat the bark?" I ask. "Did you just pluck it off the trees and eat it?"

A pained looked comes upon his face. Of course not. "We stir-fried it, with a little soy sauce, scallions, and water."

"That was just to make it a little salty," Aunt Qi Menglan chimes in. "To go down with the rice." I'd later learn from other relatives and interviews that people scraped bark off trees, soaked it in water from limestone quarries to soften it, and then fried it up.

This was when things were the worst, Uncle Tong Bao says. "I was so happy to find a frog on the way home. My grandmother would cook it up for us to eat."

The food started to become scarce when he was twelve. China followed a strict Soviet model of central planning, built on five-year plans. In 1957, the last year of the first Five-Year Plan, grain production grew only 1 percent—not enough to keep up with the growing population. In Changzhou, the government issued ration coupons to buy eggs, fish, pork, rice, noodles, cloth, and beans. Tong Bao's family received fewer food rations than others, he says, suggesting it was punishment for *haiwai guanxi*, overseas relations. "You got more coupons, or fewer, depending on your status."

The government launched the Great Leap Forward a year later, directing farmers what to plant: yes to the "eight essential crops," no to the "five eliminates." Many in the countryside were recruited to communal industrial projects, siphoning them away from tilling, sowing, and reaping. Food production plummeted.

China's motivation was a familiar one in the country's history: to throw off generations of backwardness and reclaim its place among the elite nations. To catch up and surpass. This motivated the Qing reformers in the late nineteenth century, the May Fourth demonstrators in 1919, and Deng's free-market reforms of the 1970s and '80s, and motivates the leaders in Beijing today. University of Hong Kong historian Frank Dikötter writes in his book *Mao's Great Famine* that Beijing during the Great Leap Forward sought specifically to overtake Britain in fifteen years, as measured by steel output.

Under the Great Leap, bureaucrats had to meet unreasonably high quotas for steel and grain production. So they lied about achieving them. Behind the fake numbers were mass shortages. Based on various estimates, somewhere in the neighborhood of thirty-six million to forty-five million Chinese starved to death during this period.

In prison labor camps—like the one I assume my grandfather was sent to—prisoners were known to trade briefcases and wristwatches for food. They ate the scabs that formed on the edges of their lips, as well as lice from other inmates' heads. In one harrowing scene from the semifictional documentary *Jiabiangou* (The ditch), one man falls over and throws up. Another immediately mines the vomit with his fingers and stuffs chunks of the returned food into his own mouth. "There was not a single county where cannibalism was not discovered," wrote a county party committee deputy secretary in Anhui cited in *Tombstone*, an account of the famine by Chinese journalist Yang Jisheng. Yang wrote that people sliced human flesh off the buttocks and legs of corpses and ate it—sometimes cooked, sometimes raw. One Shanghai intellectual and author, over a smoothie at a Western-style coffee shop, told me the story of his friend in Henan province during the famine: the man somehow came into possession of a pig, and buried it to hide it from his own friends and family. At night, he secretly dug it up to eat, and survived the famine.

"1960 was the worst," Uncle Tong Bao says. "We even needed ration coupons for pots and pans." Then he looks at me and asks: "Why talk about this? It doesn't change anything." He always gives off a certain hopelessness about the past. There is nothing empowering about it, no cliché about learning history to avoid repeating it, no need for a museum of bad memories.

In my experience, a lot of people from his generation agree, which means many stories from their generation will die with them. "Older people don't talk about their suffering," Aunt Qi Menglan says. "They show it by sacrificing for their children. It's their way of saying, 'Never again.'"

For the first few months after my family and I moved to China, I barely saw my uncle, mostly because we were so busy getting settled. Five Tongs had to cope with a clothes washer one-third smaller than our Kenmore back home. There was no dryer. All our daily tasks seemed to take longer: cleaning the grit and dust from our clothes and shoes, grocery shopping, delivering the kids to school and back, getting to church in the French Concession.

It took three months to have the contents of our shipping container delivered, even though the container sat in the port of Shanghai. Here is the ridiculous bureaucratic story: releasing the container required that we present residence papers. Those papers required Cathy and me to undergo dodgy physical examinations (a few pokes, chest x-rays, $120 each). And they required a copy of our housing lease, a copy of my work permit, and proof that our children were actually our children.

This was the most absurd part. The kids' birth certificates sat in a file inside a cabinet *inside the shipping container*. In the end, after emergency document requests by relatives stateside and a threat by Shanghai authorities to deport our one-year-old, we resolved the situation. "Your head was going to explode," Cathy often reminds me.

Meantime, I worked and traveled endlessly. I reported on the new auto age; state-owned PetroChina's mammoth $11 billion initial public offering; industrial pollution in lakes ringed by illegal paper mills; millionaires tasting Château Margaux for the first time; parents hiring brokers to marry off their lonely twenty-something only children. In 2007, China's economy grew by a whopping 14.2 percent, by World Bank estimates.

And yet there were signs of slowdown. Many factories in coastal cities were losing competitiveness. As in previous low-cost manufacturing locales in history, Chinese labor costs were rising, as were the costs of electricity and raw materials like iron ore. Was the miracle over?

For this I consult Uncle Tong Bao. One day we meet at a Shanghai factory where he works as a consultant. We begin at the cafeteria. "First, we eat," he says. "This cafeteria food is not good." Then we walk the floor of a small workshop making dental machines that screen for plaque and cancer. He notes that the struggling factories are the ones with low-technology easy to replace in another country. But these dental machines are hard to make elsewhere.

"And, we can charge more," he points out, "to customers in Japan and Europe."

Tong Bao is good at explaining economics. China's transition has coincided with his own. He thrived during the earlier, simpler era of China Manufacturing 1.0, when factory owners made money off the backs of the world's cheapest workers and the practical advice of engineers like him. But China 2.0 requires a new recipe. The vast pool of what economists call "surplus rural labor" is drying up. Fewer young people are around to make more than they consume.

"I have five *danwei*," or places of employment, he tells me. He teaches engineering at Shanghai's elite Tongji University, but like many academics, he makes most of his income from business consulting gigs on the side.

————————

In the United States, my parents got married in 1965. My father finished his engineering doctorate at the University of Minnesota, where my mother worked the grill at a restaurant called the Big Ten. My older brother, Tony, was born. Soon after, they moved to the IBM town of Poughkeepsie, where Dad joined the IBM Country Club volleyball team and became known simply as "Al."

Alvin Tong had completed his transition from China refugee to white-collar American. His is a story of risk taking: living with an American GI in Taipei, postwar Taiwan's bet on trade and globalization, studying in the United States.

But for his brother on the mainland, the key in the late '60s was to avoid risk. This was the time of the political cleansing known as the Great Proletarian Cultural Revolution. Tong Bao and his brother and mother tried to keep their political heads down, but it was no use.

Buried in his mother's personnel file was an accusation that she'd received financial help from a person living in enemy Taiwan. In the 1950s, she was seen walking out of what was known as a Friendship Store. These enterprises catered to foreign visitors with a hankering for peanut butter, or Hershey bars, or uncensored versions of the *New York Times*. Some Chinese shopped there as well. All purchases required what are known as "foreign exchange coupons."

Tong Bao's mother bought comforters and blankets at the Friendship Store with coupons from a mainland friend who was member of the Communist Party. But upon her exiting, one of her teacher colleagues saw her and reported this to authorities. The assumption: she got the foreign exchange coupons from someone in Taiwan.

"This was the key issue" for her punishment, Tong Bao's younger brother, Tong Qi, once told me. "But she got the coupons from a friend, not anyone with the Guomindang." The informant, he said, was actually a family friend. This event was dredged up as evidence of disloyalty during the Cultural Revolution.

Uncle Tong Bao describes the beginning of this purification campaign one evening in our Shanghai apartment. My in-laws are visiting us from Toledo, Ohio. After dinner, our kids are down and the subject of everyone's childhood comes up. In 1966, when my in-laws Chuck and Sue Thayer were graduating from Wooster College in Ohio, Mao was proclaiming the Cultural Revolution.

"We heard the announcement on school loudspeakers and speakers from cars," Uncle Tong Bao says. In Changzhou, youth members of the Red Guard intent on purifying the party barged into people's homes, looking to destroy evidence of China's bourgeois, landlord past. Tong Bao's mother took preventive measures, smashing anything porcelain, including a Qing-era bowl that had been passed down several generations. She burned a set of classic books with wooden covers. "We threw our rice bowls into the trash can," Tong Bao says. "Destroyed photos. And the china. We had no choice. Some neighbors had seen our china and told the authorities."

Chairman Mao orchestrated the Cultural Revolution as part of his political comeback. Marginalized following the disaster of the Great Leap Forward, he returned to the public eye thanks to a well-publicized swim. Even though Mao was already in his seventies, he demonstrated his physical vitality by appearing in a white robe in Wuhan in July 1966. This was a repeat performance of a political trick he'd performed ten years prior, when he "swam" across the Yangtze River in Wuhan three times. This time, he disrobed to his trunks and crossed the river "relaxed and easy," reported the official news service. "He stayed in the water a full sixty-five minutes, covering a total distance of almost fifteen kilometers." This would have represented a world-record pace.

A month after this feat, the Great Helmsman stood on a platform atop Tiananmen gate in Beijing to observe hordes of fanatics chanting and waving copies of *Quotations from Chairman Mao*, also known in the West as Mao's Little Red Book. He wore a military uniform—fitting for the estimated one million self-styled "red guards" standing below. Before long, the Red Guards demolished old buildings and temples, attacked teachers and school leaders, even their parents.

"Students kicked teachers, punched them," Aunt Qi Menglan says. "Screamed at them like a mob. It was a mess! Hit them in the mouth. People were crazy. The crazier the better. There's no way you could comprehend it. We even attacked our parents for not being revolutionary enough." One coworker informed on her father. "Because he was a capitalist," she says. "If you don't participate, you're not a revolutionary."

She pauses briefly. "We don't like to talk about the past, because we're ashamed of what we did."

Fanatical students targeted Tong Bao's mother. She went to school and found herself locked inside during the day, pressured into confession. Members of the Red Guard dredged up the Friendship Store event, claiming she'd been aided and abetted by friends in Taiwan. They called her a "historic counterrevolutionary," a designation for persons—and associated relatives—who had defied the Communist Party before the 1949 liberation. They resurrected language from an old campaign, calling her a "Three-Antis element" for a person presumed guilty of corruption, waste, or profiteering.

"She couldn't sleep," Tong Qi once told me. "The interrogations affected her emotionally, being forced to admit something she didn't do." Some of the punishment took place outdoors as well. One time, in the winter, she was made to stand for hours in the cold, with her head bowed forward so icicles above could drip inside her collar and down her neck.

Tong Qi says this wore her down so much she started having trouble thinking clearly. She started to wonder if she had indeed joined the GMD. She became suicidal. But she never confessed. "She never talked about this," Tong Bao says. "We heard about it through other friends. There are things that happened in that classroom that we will never know."

Tong Bao graduated from high school at the worst possible time. Just when he was preparing to take the nation's university entrance exam, it was canceled by party authorities, ostensibly to let young people work as full-time revolutionaries. He was exiled to the countryside along with millions of other students with declared bad backgrounds, to "learn from the peasants." From his classroom of forty-five students, most would be sent down to the countryside in Liyang, Jiangsu, about sixty miles away. "Only four or five had a choice of where to go," because they had connections, he says. "Others like me had no choice." Within days, he packed a suitcase and clambered aboard a bus. He was nineteen.

In the countryside, Tong Bao first slept in a cow shed with six other young men before they moved into a rudimentary house. The walls were made of brick with mud in the cracks ("no mortar") under a roof of rice husks. They grew rice and attended mandated political meetings and self-criticism sessions.

This was his lost decade. The good part of this story is that he stayed long enough to meet the woman who would become his wife. A broken radio helped bring them together. He'd learned to fix them on the side during the Cultural Revolution. Qi Menglan, the woman who would become his wife, was teaching grade school in Liyang. "I liked him then," she says during one conversation, before he shushes her. No further romantic details are forthcoming.

Uncle Tong Bao's comeback story after the Cultural Revolution began when he was around thirty, when he took the reinstated college entrance examination. This came just after Mao died in 1976. Out of the messy leadership-succession process emerged the market reformer Deng Xiaoping. As part of his reforms, Deng pushed literacy and education. He believed sending bright students to the middle of nowhere for physical labor made for a waste of time.

Five million students took the reinstated test in 1977, including my uncle. What's curious is why so many decided to take it. "It doesn't make sense," economic historian Thomas Rawski told me. "For so many years, there was no reward to education." Going to school did not help you move up the ladder. Rawski believes the best explanation is historical continuity: the roots of education run so deep in society that the Communist Party could not dig them out.

As a thirty-year-old taking the two-day examination, Tong Bao sat alongside kids as young as eighteen. Of the five million test takers, only 272,000 earned university slots—a 5 percent pass rate. My uncle passed. This is his favorite story, and he deserves to tell it. Tong Bao enrolled in the Nanjing Institute of Technology. But sadly, his mother did not live to see him graduate and build a life she could not provide. She died in Changzhou of cancer in 1980.

Uncle Tong Bao married Qi Menglan—the woman who had him fix her radio a decade prior—shortly after graduating. A year later, their only son was born: Tong Chengkan. He is my cousin.

PART THREE | The Great Resumption

| Chapter Thirteen | MY COUSIN AND HIS SHANGHAI BUICK |

You know the problem with Chinese people? We're too good at obeying.
—Cousin Tong Chengkan

During our last year in Shanghai, 2010, a soap opera took China by storm. It was called *Snail House*. In a way that captivated millions, the show captured the tensions so many young urban adults face: betrayal, corruption, tenuous relationships, and—most of all—the housing arms race. As an American, it was hard for me to grasp the importance of home (or apartment) ownership in China. For a man in Shanghai, it has just about become a prerequisite for matrimony; a woman will not marry you without the financial security of a home. You pretty much cannot take a cab ride without discussing *ping fang mi*, the local price per square meter.

Housing prices are out of reach for so many, as the soap opera title suggests. When I first arrived in China, my uncle Tong Qi did some ballpark math: In Arlington, Virginia, we figured a typical house sold for roughly ten times an annual salary. In Shanghai, it was on the order of thirty years. By one wonky ratio—housing prices divided by income—China is home to some of the world's priciest markets.

Snail House starred two young professional sisters. The older one was taller, with a no-nonsense short haircut, the younger sister sporting longer hair with bangs; she was a bit more glamorous, a bit more whiny. Big Sister rented a tiny apartment with her husband, while Little Sister shared a room with another couple.

The plot gets busy quickly when Big Sister receives an anonymous envelope with the equivalent of $5,000—enough to start house hunting. It's from her Little Sister. And the money is dirty.

It turns out Little Sister has been cheating on her boyfriend, sleeping around with a rich, crooked Communist Party member she met at a work function. The official is married, but the political sugar daddy is hunky—a viewer favorite. Even as he takes bribes from property developers, the dirty politician has a soft personality and good hair. In the show, he dials up mistress Little Sister to background piano accompaniment.

Yang Junlei, a professor of comparative cultures at Shanghai's Fudan University, told me the show "hit on a very relevant problem in China today: infidelity, mistresses, housing. *Snail House* really nails it. It's hot.'"

But the viewer knows it can't last. Little Sister's boyfriend eventually discovers her infidelity. There is lying, guilt, covering up, a pregnancy (naturally), and a showdown between the wife and the mistress. In the end, karma even catches up with the two-timing cadre: he dies when his car crashes into an oncoming truck— perhaps an ominous metaphor for the Shanghai housing market.

"*Snail House*—so accurate," my cousin Tong Chengkan says over dinner in the summer of 2011. "Society is so materialistic." This is something he talks about a lot, where traditional values have gone. There is a paradox here: we are sitting smack in the middle of Overpriced Showy Shanghai, at a Western-style brewery in the French Concession.

Tong Chengkan is the son of Uncle Tong Bao. Like his father, Tong Chengkan no longer goes by the surname Tong. He uses the maiden name of his father's mother. But I'm referring to him as Tong Chengkan to provide him a measure of anonymity.

He himself still lives with his parents, which is a particularly sore spot. Most young professionals can only afford to buy their own places if they get help from their parents. But Tong Chengkan's don't have that kind of money, and in any event would prefer to spend it on their own lives. Fair enough.

"It has to be hard to buy without your parents' help," I say.

My cousin puts down his fork. "It is just about impossible." Tong Chengkan works a respectable job—what you and I would call middle-class employment—as a factory maintenance manager at the General Motors plant in Shanghai. It churns out Buicks and Cadillacs for the world's biggest new-car market.

He makes a reasonable salary, but since he lives at home, he is handicapped in the marriage market race—which disappoints his parents, even as he seeks to avoid them. And on this night it's actually worse than that. I ask about his girlfriend, someone he works with at the plant. "We're no longer together," he says, and then delivers the stunning reveal. "She is now dating someone else—my best friend at the factory."

"What? Are you serious?" I ask.

"He owns his own apartment."

Ouch. "Is that the real reason she's now with him?" At this point I have pushed too far.

"What do you think?"

He is running, and yet at the same time not keeping up. It's a bit like the "Red Queen's race" from Lewis Carroll's *Through the Looking-Glass*. In the story, Alice (from Wonderland) runs and runs, yet doesn't get anywhere. The Red Queen explains: "Now, here, you see, it takes all the running you can do, to keep in the same place. If you want to get somewhere else, you must run at least twice as fast as that!" Alice exits the race. Cousin Chengkan does not.

In another marriage market, Chengkan would merit a higher value for his earnestness. He always picks me up at the airport when I come. He makes a point to visit my folks when they fly in from Oregon. But earnestness doesn't pay the mortgage. Here is his problem: six decades after supposedly overthrowing the bourgeois landowners, too many mainlanders want to be bourgeois land-owners, pushing up the price.

"What if you quit, try to get a new job?" I ask.

He laughs. "Too risky. My parents would never allow that." In the past he's told me the problem with Chinese people is they are too *tinghua*, too good at obeying.

Yet there is some good news here. Already Tong Chengkan has another prospect: a fetching viola player he met in the community orchestra. He plays clarinet. "I've given her a ride home a few times."

"That's great. Tell me more."

"Well, there's a problem." The musician woman hails from a relatively poor province in the north, Henan. In Shanghai, any reference to people from Henan is typically unkind. It would represent marrying down.

"Why does this matter?" I ask.

"It's not just me getting married—it would be our whole families getting married. Think about it: her relatives would want to move to Shanghai to get jobs, and use our connections to do it. What if they are farmers? That's a problem. Do they celebrate Chinese New Year different than we do?"

It's clear he has thought this out. He continues: "Then if we have a child, her mother will come to care for it and live with my family. There will be conflicts. We all have different standards."

I blink in a way that he knows means I don't understand. So Tong Chengkan gives an example of his own parents. His father grew up in Changzhou, whereas his mother is from Shanghai. "And this is always an issue." Indeed, his father—my uncle Tong Bao—has told me, "To Shanghainese people, any other place is a small town." The upshot is, marrying down brings problems, yet it's also unlikely he'll marry up. He's stuck.

This captures something fundamental about today's young Chinese. From far away, they are the rising, scary Chinese middle class, pilfering American jobs. The competition. But in reality, it's like watching a duck swim: smooth and graceful on the surface, yet paddling madly underwater to stay afloat.

My cousin insists on paying the bill, as he always does ("you're the guest here"), and we walk down a curved street in the leafy French Concession. This is our favorite part of town. Tong Chengkan gestures at a large single-family house with a yard. A gate and a guard stand between my cousin and a house he'll never afford. "I bet you," he says, "that a government official lives there."

_____

When I first meet my cousin in 2007, I fail to notice any pressures or anxieties. He has come to the airport with his father to pick up seven Tongs from America—Cathy, me, the kids, and my parents. Tong Chengkan is tall and lean, and even though he's cursed with the bushy Tong eyebrows, his arc in a way that make him look curious and friendly. It's like a question mark is always hovering over him.

During our frenzied first week, he comes over and whips out a digital Canon SLR camera bigger than mine. The camera has a sensor technology known as EOS, which explains his e-mail address at the time: eosfans@hotmail.com. Later, he pulls out an IBM Think-Pad laptop that is sleeker and slimmer than mine. It all seems rather overdone at first glance.

There are a couple things I don't realize at the time. First, I'm looking straight into the face (and the eyebrows) of what economists call convergence. Or catch-up. He embodies in a single lifetime the turbocharged boost China has pulled off. The story has happened on his watch. Just to compare, this path from starvation to show-off took the industrial West two full centuries, according to Nobel economist Michael Spence in *The Next Convergence: The Future of Economic Growth in a Multispeed World*.

Spence offers a number of explanations for this, but they all exist in Tong Chengkan's experience: his parents saved like crazy to invest in him; he and his father work in sectors where China can sell what it makes to the world; and their country has imported the outside world's lessons about globalization dos and don'ts, so it doesn't have to relearn everything.

Here's the other thing I miss: that brand-name goods carry more social currency and value here. They help you stand out from an enormous Chinese pack. Back home, Cathy and I proudly proclaim our brand and logo fatigue, that we are *so above this*. It doesn't so much work this way in Shanghai, where material goods can bring more material benefits. "When people see my girlfriend's Louis Vuitton bag," my former intern Sheng Liyu once told me, "they treat her differently. She might get a job interview that she wouldn't without the bag." He paused to smile. "Assuming it's not fake."

Indeed, my cousin has reason to invest in himself. In this race for scarce opportunities, he is an only child bearing the burden of unmet expectations. It can be soul crushing. Often when I think about China's new Generation Me, I compare or contrast cousin Tong Chengkan with my longtime *Marketplace* bureau assistant, Cecilia Chen. Both are culturally hybrids, adaptable to both very Chinese and very Western environments. They're around the same age, and have worked for multinational companies.

And yet they've turned out remarkably different. Cecilia rebelled against these expectations and became, to my mind, very culturally un-Chinese. Tong Chengkan, though, turned out proudly national- istic. It is a striking contrast of two thirty-somethings, both born at a key moment in time: the start of the one-child policy.

Tong Chengkan was born in 1981, two years after the rollout of the strict family-planning regime. The policy was a reversal from an earlier position. In the 1950s Chairman Mao proclaimed that a large population was "a very good thing." In fact, during the Cold War he went toe-to-toe with US Secretary of State Dean Acheson, who suggested China could not feed its growing population. An angry Mao fired back. "He said, 'Of all things in the world, people are the most precious,'" anthropologist Susan Greenhalgh, author of the book *Just One Child: Science and Policy in Deng's China*, told me in an interview. But China could not feed its people during the great famine of the late 1950s and early '60s.

Despite his rhetoric, Mao began to explore population controls. The first rules were voluntary, nudging couples to delay pregnan- cies and space out their babies. And these rules showed promise. The fertility rate plunged from around six births per woman to fewer than three.

But then the controls became mandatory. Greenhalgh told me of the two competing camps: one advocating a softer policy, the other hardline; the hardliners prevailed. This served the interests of Deng Xiaoping, who staked his legitimacy on making people wealthier. One way to do this was reducing the amount of people. The strict policy took effect in 1979.

Two years later, Tong Chengkan's mother was in the third term of her pregnancy. She called into work sick to fake an illness. That way, she could still receive her full-time salary, even as she was in labor. At the time, she was living in Liyang city, but she went to Shanghai—sixty miles away, and where her mother lived—to deliver. This was against the law: having a baby outside your place of residence violates the household registration, or *hukou*, rules. Uncle Tong Bao describes this violation as "black *hukou*. But don't write too much about this."

After Tong Chengkan was born, population officials gave his mother a special certificate for abiding by the policy. It entitled her to a payment of five renminbi per month. "You could buy a lot of meat for five renminbi," my uncle says.

"But what if officials found out you got pregnant with a second child?" I ask. "Would they take away the payments?"

"Immediate abortion. Everything is done through the work unit. And if they find you have a second kid, you're fired."

For the first month, Aunt Qi Menglan's mother did not let her bathe or wash her hair, or brush her teeth, for an entire month. This, as the belief goes, prevents new moms from getting sick. Qi Menglan's mother fed her the same food every day: eggs, raw sugar, dates. "It was terrible," she says.

Baby Cecilia Chen arrived two years prior to that, in the northeastern city of Dalian. She almost came home from the hospital as one of two babies, and this is not a twins story. Cecilia was born a few months before the strict one-child policy took effect, but the voluntary system provided powerful financial incentives. During pregnancy, Cecilia's mother wrote up a pledge at work. "It said, 'I promise to only have one child,'" Cecilia says. "She got one hundred days of vacation instead of only fifty-six." Her father, then in the army, would have missed out on promotion if he'd had a second child.

But the maternity ward provided them a two-for-one offer. Newborn Cecilia's mother and father struck up a conversation with another set of new parents with an infant boy. The boy's parents did not want to keep him, as he was born out of wedlock. So they offered to sell him.

"The price was forty kilograms' worth of grain ration coupons," she says. To me this is one of the most remarkable parts of this bizarre story: the ration coupons were more valuable than cash. Cecilia's parents went home that night and pondered, and returned the next morning with their ration coupons in hand. They were ready to buy. "But by then he was already sold."

During Cecilia's and Tong Chengkan's teenage years in the 1990s, China was making a bumpy transition to a market economy. McDonald's outlets started to open up, and my cousin remembers the day he first tasted Coke. At the same time, grains, meat, and milk still were scarce and rationed. To supply him with enough milk, his parents obtained extra milk powder by *zou hou men*, "taking the back door." This situation stayed in place right up through high school, at which point I presume they'd left poor old China behind. After all, by the late '90s, I was grooving on a Windows computer, the state-of-the-art Excite search engine, and an AOL e-mail account. Wasn't everyone?

I was wrong. At dinner one night (we went to many, many restaurants), I ask if he still keeps in touch with old high school friends from the '90s.

He looks at me. "It was hard to keep in touch with them, even back then," he says.

"Why? You had their phone numbers."

"Phones? We didn't have phones then."

China's great housing chase began in the '90s, and Tong Chengkan's family bought in. Privatization reforms allowed them to purchase the university apartment they'd been living in (technically, land belongs to the state, though individuals can buy and sell "use rights"). "We were the first group," his father, Tong Bao, says. They paid twenty thousand renminbi for the flat, or around $2,300 US. It would easily go for half a million today. "We should have bought more then," Tong Bao adds ruefully.

China's internal reforms went hand-in-hand with foreign trade and investment, which in my cousin's family was translated as Black & Decker—or *bu-lai-ke and dai-ke*. The company, which dates back to the Qing era on the Chinese calendar, put out the world's first portable electric drill. It made fuses and ordnance shells for the Allies in World War II. It brought us the magical Dustbuster.

But the company's growth slowed after the war. Germany and Japan rebuilt their economies and delivered high-quality, affordable alternatives to the market. In this newly competitive global market, Black & Decker closed plants in England, Ireland, and the United States, moving production to lower-cost locations like China. In the Shanghai industrial zone of Songjiang, Black & Decker contracted with a no-name manufacturing plant to take advantage of the so-called China price: a typical Chinese worker at the plant made one-sixtieth of the average American. This plant brought in the engineering professor Tong Bao to consult.

"This was ODM manufacturing, not OEM," he says proudly during the plant tour he gives. An original equipment manufacturer (OEM) is basically a direction follower—for instance, the iPhone assembly firm Foxconn does exactly what Apple tells it. It takes a blueprint from a client and follows instructions. Chinese workers contribute relatively little brainpower and thus receive meager profits.

Original design manufacturers (ODM), by contrast, take a rough idea and figure out themselves how to design and make it. They're given responsibility, freedom, and a bigger share of the money pie. This kind of incremental innovation is what China Inc. tends to be very good at.

In my uncle's case, Black & Decker came in with a concept, and he consulted on plant design, materials, assembly, and quality control. This kind of gig was what globalization was delivering, and the trend would soon speed up. One year later, China joined the club that enshrined this collapse of distance around the world: the World Trade Organization.

One reason Chinese parents apply so much pressure to their children is that they, the parents, have sacrificed so much to get where they are. My first bureau assistant, Linda Lin, compares it with the American kids' book *The Giving Tree*. One year I gave this book to her son (along with *Goodnight Moon*, which he preferred less), and Linda told me that the story of a tree giving up everything for a child (its leaves, branches, trunk) is exactly the kind of sacrifice Chinese parents make. The issue is, by the time the parents have been reduced to mere stumps, their child better make something of his or her life.

Cecilia faced this kind of pressure at a very early age. She grew up in the old treaty port of Dalian in northeast China. (It's one of those places that has changed hands several times. Russian lease-holders in the late 1800s called it Port Arthur [and also Dalniy] until losing the 1905 Russo-Japanese conflict to Japan, which renamed it Dairen.) By the age of three, she could recite Chinese poems, and she started English lessons at five. That left little time to see her favorite monkey stage-show at a nearby park, where she'd watch with a caramel from a street peddler in her small hand. It cost 0.02 renminbi—one-fifth of one penny.

When Cecilia was nine, her mother forced her to learn electronic keyboard. "We had no electric fan in those days," Cecilia wrote in a *Marketplace* blog post, "so when I practiced on hot days, my mom would sit beside me and fan me." Later, her mother switched her to accordion, all the while monitoring Cecilia's grades as any good helicopter parent would. "On Chinese New Year of fifth grade, I ranked 10th out of 53 students, 7 places lower than my previous ranking," Cecilia wrote. "My mom scolded me the entire day, and I didn't eat the most important meal of the year: New Year's Eve dinner."

She grew to be tall and lean, with a defined set of cheekbones. On the eve of the entrance examination for high school, her mommy dearest delivered the following threat: if she scored too low and didn't get into high school, she'd "grow up to be a kindergarten teacher." In the blog entry, Cecilia wrote that she longed for a sibling not so much to play with as to share the harsh parental spotlight.

Cecilia's grades slipped in high school. "She didn't focus on her homework enough," her father told me over lunch at a seafood res-taurant in his home city of Changzhou. "Listened too much to her

Sony Walkman. We weren't strict enough." He'd become a busi-nessman by then, and described his daughter in market terms. "I invested so much, but there has been no return." Negative parent-ing ROI.

Still, Cecilia did well enough to enroll in Dalian Marine College and receive an associate's degree in industrial electricity. The prob-lem was, she graduated into a glut of college students. The central government in the late 1990s promoted university enrollment to upgrade its skilled workforce, and campuses starved for revenue were happy to oblige. As a result, too many degreed students were chasing a limited number of jobs. "You needed a degree even to get a job cleaning hotel rooms," Cecilia said.

Then, unexpectedly, her family moved to Canada. Unbeknownst to Cecilia and her mother, her father had applied for a special Cana-dian visa for immigrant investors and entrepreneurs. When it came, they all moved to Vancouver—well, sort of. Cecilia settled in, but her folks became what Chinese Vancouverites call "astronauts," floating in and out of Canadian airspace, landing just frequently enough to maintain visa status. Mostly, they stayed in Dalian to work while Cecilia lived alone in Vancouver.

Cecilia became a barista and hung out with Chinese twenty-somethings from the mainland, Hong Kong, and Taiwan. And she went back to school, enrolling in the University of British Colum-bia to study psychology. The problem was, learning psych termi-nology "was a pain in the ass, especially for people not born" in Canada, she said. So she switched into communication arts—but again, this disappointed her father. "She could have stayed with psychology and become a psychiatrist," he said, shaking his head. "Could have made a lot of money."

In 2007 Cecilia was forced to return to China, and it didn't go well. Her father had failed to adhere to the Canadian visa rules and got them kicked out. So Cecilia became what mainlanders call a "sea turtle." It's a pun. *Hai gui* out loud means both "sea turtle" and "oversees returnee." Sea turtles, given their overseas education and experience, are often targeted by multinational and Chinese firms looking for workers with English language and critical think-ing skills.

Cecilia took a public relations job at Carrefour, the French big box chain. But inside the company, the structure was still "very Chinese," and she did not last long. The issue was, Cecilia's world-view had changed. At Carrefour, prime assignments were given out based more on connections than merit. Yes-men and yes-women became vice presidents, and from what she could tell, appearances and connections meant everything. The brownnosing environment discouraged the honesty and blunt talk she'd become used to. "It's easier to deal with non-Chinese people," she often says.

She got annoyed with Chinese society in general. It bothered her when a journalist friend regularly showed up forty-five minutes late at a restaurant, without apologizing (this is very common on the mainland). "So I stopped calling him." While she liked to read books, her friends went on about stocks and bonds and property prices. So for a fresh start, Cecilia quit her job at Carrefour and eventually landed at *Marketplace*. And she began dating a white guy from Albany.

The live woman's voice comes from inside the car speaker, speaking Mandarin: Hello—OnStar service, may I help you? Yes, please hold. Here are your directions, thank you.

I'm on a road trip with cousin Tong Chengkan, in his Buick LaCrosse sedan. We are driving to Changzhou, about two hours away, to visit a mutual uncle—the brother of his father and mine. I want to ask about one particular family sore spot: our grand-father Tong's first and only return to China in 2000. It came more than five decades after my grandfather fled. Aligned with the anti-Communist Guomindang, he and his mistress and my father boarded an overloaded vessel bound for Taiwan when it became clear the US-backed GMD had lost the mainland to the Commu-nists. Left behind were Uncle Tong Bao and his brother still in their mother's womb, Tong Qi. Tong Qi is the brother now living in Changzhou.

I don't know if I buy the concept of closure, but for sure this trip would have been the right time for my grandfather to return to China and apologize to the sons he had abandoned. After arriv-ing in Taiwan, he built a white-collar life as a lawyer in Taipei and eventually retired to Northern California. Surely he thought of Tong Bao and Tong Qi all these years—or did he?

The Buick purrs smoothly in on the left lane, overtaking vehicles creeping dangerously slow. The further out one ventures from a Chinese city, the less predictable the adventure gets. Just past one exit off-ramp, a VW sedan is driving backward up the shoulder. Obviously the driver had missed the exit. "The car's from Anhui province," Chengkan grumbles, shaking his head. There is a certain Shanghai view of the world, kind of like the distorted *New Yorker* magazine cartoon cover we've all seen: the less-important people and vehicles in the distance barely register on the sketch. Half an hour on, a box truck has jackknifed on the right. "Drivers stay on the road too long and they get tired and fall asleep," he says. "They all want overtime."

This trip is a long time coming, with a cousin I'd never met until I was well into my thirties. We'd talked about it for years, but the scheduling stars never aligned. I was constantly on the road for *Marketplace*, and his General Motors factory job demanded inconvenient shifts. On more than one occasion, I'd wondered about my "what if" life. What if my dad had been the sibling left behind? What if I were the mainland cousin, driving—of all vehicles—a Buick?

My cousin has no time for theoretical musing. "No point in thinking about that." Each day has enough trouble of its own. From the driver's seat, he starts uploading random thoughts about the present. "European films are very philosophical, whereas American movies are all shooting and blowing things up," he says. Chinese films are *luan qi ba zao*. A big mess. His favorite composers are Chopin, Shostakovich, and Bach. My cousin doesn't understand why Americans like Brad Pitt are so obsessed with a certain frontier province in the Himalayas, as if the treatment of monks there matters to regular Chinese people. "Don't write about that part."

Tong Chengkan reveals he has a new girlfriend, but again there is a "however." He is sinking under her expectations of gifts and declarations of love (editor's note: they have since broken up).

The OnStar lady notifies us we've missed a turn near Changzhou, prompting him to sigh and scramble. "Changzhou drivers are crazy and break the rules." This is indeed a lower-profile city without the trophy high-rises of Beijing or Shanghai. "Here, you can buy an apartment for ten thousand renminbi per square meter," he says, instantly rattling off a property statistic like so many in China. "In Shanghai that would buy a place *way* outside the city."

We meet Uncle Tong Qi and his wife and son (an architect) at their apartment. Like his brother, Tong Qi was also exiled to the countryside for a decade. And after the national college entrance exam returned, he took it and also aced it. By the time we settle into a Changzhou restaurant, I ask about The Grandfather Reunion.

It turns out my grandfather waffled on meeting his own sons—he almost didn't show. In 2000, Grandpa Tong was taking a group tour of China. Before the tour began, he'd made plans to see them but didn't commit to a time or a place. By the time the tour hit Shanghai, my father and his siblings spent hours on the phone convincing my grandfather to meet Tong Bao and Tong Qi. He almost backed out.

"He eventually decided to meet with us, but by then there wasn't much time left in his schedule," Uncle Tong Qi says. The tour was about to move on. The only option was to meet very late at night in Shanghai's Hua Ting Hotel, where the tour group was staying. "I had a big exam the next day," Tong Chengkan says, but there was no choice but to go.

From Changzhou, Uncle Tong Qi's family rushed onto the soonest train. "It was so late. We booked a return trip on a 3 a.m. train." The uncles and their families arrived at nine, and Grandpa Tong came two hours later. Finally, they came face to face: these brothers and the father they never knew.

The meeting was, by all accounts at the table, a bust. They exchanged greetings and small talk. My grandfather commented on "how tall we were," Chengkan says. "And how the Tong family has no short kids!" After an hour, my grandfather excused himself to go to bed, and that was it. There was no talk of the 1949 abandonment, no questions about political suffering or icicle torture or the famine—all because of his politics. I suppose, to be fair, my grandfather could not have anticipated Mao's crackdown against these Tongs and so many millions. But to not even ask about this after so many years? This was unconscionable.

The sons offered to meet again the next day. But their father did not call again.

"Just one hour," Tong Chengkan says calmly as he eats.

I am the incredulous one. "That's it?"

"It was not particularly successful," Tong Qi says, as if he were commenting on a game of cards.

The dinner comes to an awkward end. A creature, perhaps from the roach family, surfaces from bottom of the sea cucumber soup. As the guest from America, I choose not to be the one to discover this and try to eat as normal. Soon after, Uncle Tong Qi's wife, Luo Jiana, shrieks. She hollers for the female manager, who takes a little too long to commit to action. In front of all of us—and now the entire restaurant—the manager ladles out the critter and starts walking away with it. "I took it out," she declares.

Aunt Luo Jiana explodes. "That's all you're going to do? We can't eat this now!"

The manager glares at my aunt and takes away the entire sea cucumber platter. Minutes later she comes back with the same dish in a suspiciously similar-looking bowl. I suspect she has simply gone into the kitchen and executed a slow U-turn. And then a fly turns up in the noodle soup. Aunt Luo Jiana does not know what to say by this point. And since we're just about done, we get up to leave. She demands that the dinner be free, on the house. I don't think she gets what she asks for, and I look away as she settles the bill at the front of the restaurant. Cousin Chengkan and I drive back to Shanghai.

I start speaking about my grandfather in a way Chinese grandsons are not supposed to—how he left behind a pregnant wife and toddler for another woman; how he stayed away for five decades, how he didn't even ask his sons left behind about the horrors of the Cultural Revolution. I'll never forget Uncle Tong Bao's words about his mother's torture at the hands of her students: *There are things that happened in that classroom that we will never know.*

To be honest, it's hard to fume in your second language, but my cousin understands the point. He just nods amen to the sermon, and then speaking with his inside voice. "Why would he just give us an hour?" he asks rhetorically. "Didn't he care what happened to us?"

Then he pivots and says something that makes me turn toward him. "I've always wondered whether this runs in the family."

"What do you mean?"

"Selfishness. Do you think we'll turn out the same way?"

My grandfather died in 2011, at the age of 101, in Northern California. I served as pallbearer alongside my brother Tony, our cousin Calvin, and Uncle John and Uncle Simon and Uncle Jimmy. My dad happened to be traveling overseas in Taiwan at the time, and called his brother Uncle Tong Bao in China to share the news.

"Dad died," my father recalls saying. Tong Bao gave a respectful "Oh." And that was the end of the conversation—the end of a relationship that never was.

A year later, cousin Chengkan and I meet for dinner at a small Cantonese-style restaurant on Shanghai's west side. I break some bad news to him. My grandfather's widow (his third wife) years ago had taken control of his estate. Seven-eighths of the money went to Wife 3's three daughters, born in Taiwan. The son from Wife 1—my father—got one-eighth. That meant the mainland sons born to Wife 2—Tong Bao and Tong Qi in China—received nothing. One final slap.

"I want to tell you my feelings," Chengkan says after a few minutes. This time he is a little less diplomatic. "When Grandfather died, it meant nothing to me."

I nod and say nothing.

"This may not sound very nice. But I feel no relationship to the Tong side of the family. No connection."

Chapter Fourteen	LONELY AND SMOTHERED
	The Only Child

Why does everybody want everything Western?
—Cousin Tong Chengkan

On the one day he needed to perform spectacularly on a test, Tong Chengkan did not. I've never heard him mention the nationwide university entrance exam, but his mother does. It's a difficult conversation in their apartment, as if the entire family underperformed. The result has dictated much of his adult life.

"He did not attend a top university," she says. Tong Chengkan is out of the apartment at the moment, as he often is, perhaps cycling his high-end Giant road bike or rehearsing with the community orchestra. I imagine the point is, at some level, to avoid conversations like these.

I'm a bit confused. "I thought he attended Tongji University, like his father?" Tongji is an elite university in engineering and architecture. She shakes her head.

"No, no. There's Tongji *professional* school, and Tongji *trade* school. They're entirely different." Tong Chengkan graduated with a trade degree in electricity and mechanical automation before taking his job as an equipment manager at the GM plant. The plant assembles Cadillacs and other vehicles for the Great China Market. For most American parents, this would be a perfectly acceptable career path, but something else is eating at his mother: before he took this GM job, he somehow passed up an opportunity at a better one, an office job with a state-owned company. She speaks as if this were unforgivable. We all turn quiet, as if we're all conducting the same thought experiment: What if my cousin had done better? Where would he be now? Married and living in his own place?

It's hard to overstate the importance of the entrance exam. It makes all the difference in where you attend college, and that academic pedigree matters far more than it does in the United States. It's as if your whole life boils down to your SAT score (thank goodness for me it did not).

Tong Chengkan's blue-collar job seems quite good to me. He inspects and repairs assembly-line machinery, making a middle-income salary at what in China is a superstar company. There are no bad Buick jokes here. In fact, our grandfather would have been proud to know he works for GM and drives a Buick. In the 1980s in Taiwan, Grandpa Tong would sit on his couch and wax about his favorite auto brands, all American: Cadillac. Oldsmobile. Buick. The bigger the sedan, the better. Today on the mainland, American branches have a certain cachet: Krispy Kreme, Apple, Nike, New Balance, Disney, JanSport, Walmart, even Howard Johnson. This is despite geopolitical tensions. Young Chinese "don't wear their nationalism," a market research consultant once told me.

The Buick brand's success in China helps explain why the brand still exists at all. During the 2009 financial crisis in the United States, the parent firm GM jettisoned several historic company brands during its bankruptcy reorganization. It got rid of Saturn, Pontiac, Saab and Hummer. But GM retained Chevrolet, GMC, and Cadillac, as well as Buick, largely because of its China sales. These days, more Buick—or *bie-ke*—vehicles today sell in mainland China than mainland America.

What's surprising is, my cousin does not consider his employer to be a foreign multinational company. "I think of it as a state-owned Chinese firm," he once told me. "Which makes my job more stable." He's half right. All foreign automakers in China must operate under a joint venture with a Chinese company. GM partners with the Shanghai city-owned Shanghai Automotive Industry Corporation, or SAIC. The Chinese partner's name always goes first, so on back of every Buick, there's the logo: SAIC-GM.

General Motors fought hard for this partnership. In the early '90s, both GM and its rival Ford wanted to enter China and courted SAIC as a partner. To up the ante and impress SAIC, GM offered to assemble luxury Cadillacs in China. Automotive industry analyst Michael Dunne tells the story in *American Wheels, Chinese Roads: The Story of General Motors in China.* He writes:

> No, SAIC said, Cadillac is too ostentatious, too over the top. The central government would kill the project if they were to see Cadillac on the cover page. Growing a little impatient, the SAIC team finally came out and named their target. What we really want, SAIC revealed, is Buick.

Buick has enjoyed a long and successful history in China. In case you've not been to China and you're laughing now, this is not a joke. The last emperor, Puyi, rode in a Buick, as did Shanghai urbanites during the Roaring '20s and '30s in China. Sun Yat-sen and Zhou Enlai, the legendary Communist-era premier and diplomat, were also fans.

Early on in my Shanghai assignment, I reported a piece on this alternative automotive universe of China—every business reporter does. In the story, I mentioned that Cathy and I were looking to lease a vehicle—with a driver—for our family in China. Like many expats, we chose to avoid driving ourselves. A friend referred us to a vehicle leasing agent, a middleman, who went by the English name Alex.

"I recommend a Buick, quite suitable for you," he said on tape. Alex claimed he dealt frequently with expats and wanted to do the interview in English. "If you buy a US van, you are quite a little bit high class," he said. Our problem was, the monthly rate for the Buick far exceeded our budget, so we went down-market and rented a Honda instead. For the story, I also interviewed a GM sales director, who highlighted a special designed-for-China Buick Century. It featured a longer wheelbase, to provide extra legroom for the executive in the second row.

"There's a very proud Buick hood ornament," the sales director said. "In China the consumer still really appreciates the jewelry." The notion of Buick bling struck me as odd. Every culture has its own rules of engagement for showing off. In China, you're frowned upon if you brag about how fast your kid runs, or how much money you make, and yet you can roll down Huaihai Road with a gangster-size Buick ornament on the hood of your car.

Buick was not the only foreign firm to successfully "localize" its product in early twentieth-century China. In 1902, British American Tobacco struggled at the outset, but then hired local Chinese artists to design ads promoting its Ruby Queen brand. By the 1930s, BAT was producing fifty-five billion smokes every year for Chinese men and women.

Any international journalist will tell you that the "fixer" is the unsung hero of the news business. The job of the fixer is a hard job to define, simply because there are so many dimensions to a good one: translating, arranging travel, booking interviews, monitoring local papers and social media. A good fixer has a good network for finding stories and people, and for avoiding confrontations. If we go to a certain place, will we get followed? Detained? Blocked? Beat up?

Some of my best moments in the world—as a reporter and as a person—have been with fixers. In Iraq in 2003, I worked with a Shi'a fixer named Fakher. He'd been part of the Shia resistance against Saddam Hussein's Sunni crackdown. After taking our team throughout Basra and Nasiriyah, he said goodbye with one last request: if I'd buy his children T-shirts with the US flag on the front. He truly thought the American "liberation" would bring better days. I went to Target and bought them before realizing the postal service did not deliver to Iraq. Fakher was murdered a few years later, working for the *New York Times*, his body found in a trunk.

At a Somali refugee camp in eastern Kenya, the biggest in the world, my fixer Paul warned me to stay on the edges of the camp. Al-Shabaab militants were active on the inside, he explained. In the car on the way back to Nairobi, he showed me how to send money via text message, texting continuously behind the wheel. In Venezuela, Yesman asked me to bring him a sack of Pampers for his baby girl, as the most basic goods were in short supply. Then he led me to the Colombian border, where grains in short supply were being smuggled out by the army. In Japan, Fumiyo led me through the tsunami-destroyed coast before offering to take me shopping for a toilet seat with the plug-in warmer my kids requested.

In China, fixers are hard to retain, and at the start I struggled to keep them. So many stay in the game for a few years and move on. As experienced English speakers, they are in high demand in the job market. One of mine was conflicted about doing stories that were embarrassing to China's image. Another was finishing up university and quit after graduating. A third was sweet and diplomatic, but like many Chinese did not have an ability to say no. The conversations went something like this.

Did you call person X yet?
—Let me come talk to you about that.
Is the expense report done?
—You asked me to do these other things first.
Is this a good story for us to chase?
—It's hard to say.

The most important job of the fixer—far more important than scheduling, translating, reading, and chasing interviews—is calibrating risk. For a story on electronic waste (old computers around the world recycled and shipped illegally to China), one fixer smartly suggested we visit a town in Zhejiang rather than Guangdong, where plain-clothed thugs had harassed and beaten up reporters in the past. In a smuggler city at the border with Burma, she lectured me for wandering out late at night for ice cream and a haircut. "It's not safe like Shanghai," she said.

On the mainland, the Chinese nationals who do this job face more risk and harassment and physical injury than their foreign reporter bosses making five or ten times more money. If I get into some incident, I can extricate myself, or try to, by calling the US consulate or embassy. That does nothing for a local fixer. One fixer for the *New York Times* was imprisoned for three years, on grounds of leaking state secrets.

Fixers also tend to be the journalists harassed by government minders. Cecilia Chen first started working at *Marketplace* in 2008 as an intern, and within a few months came on full-time as my fixer. One morning soon after starting at *Marketplace*, Cecilia's cellphone rang at dawn. The female caller did not identify herself as working for the Public Security Bureau, but simply said, "I think you know what this call is about." The caller recommended they meet in person, to "have tea."

"I was pretty sure they were monitoring me and knew I was home alone," Cecilia later tells me. She was given two choices of where to meet: the city's central police station, or a coffee shop on Wujiang Road near our office. She picked Wujiang Road. The woman on the phone showed up with two other men. None gave their names. The older man was clearly in charge. *What did you do abroad in Canada? Why did you come back? How does the bureau work? How are story topics chosen? What will you report on next? Why did you take this job? What do you do in your free time?*

Cecilia didn't give up much. "I was like: 'I have to make money. I need a job, just like everyone else. I'm no different from anyone else—I just watch cartoons for fun.'"

She laughs as she tells me this part. What she'd failed to tell the minders was what she was reading at the time: *Tombstone: The Great Chinese Famine, 1958–1962*, a book on the Great Leap Forward that was banned on the mainland.

Implicit in the conversation was that the Public Security Bureau wanted her to be their source on the inside of the bureau, to tell them what stories we were doing. "And I'm like, 'All right.' But inside I really told myself, 'I'm really not going to tell you any-thing.'" Before their meeting ended, the minders told Cecilia not to tell me about the meeting—at which point she went back and promptly told me.

After the first meeting, Cecilia was no longer nervous. The minders called less frequently, and when they did, they asked uninformed questions. They were bureaucrats ticking boxes. Cecilia started rolling her eyes when they called and began to ignore them. From the outside, Chinese censors and minders are often considered savvy operators, but not in Shanghai. I came to believe that the eavesdropping authorities are simply not very good at their jobs. Either they're lousy data collectors, or they don't have the expertise to connect the dots. Or perhaps the minders in Shanghai are second rate compared with those in Beijing. If they'd been paying attention, they'd have disrupted our reporting on slave labor. But we heard nothing then. Nor did anyone call Cecilia after our story on a sensitive factory strike outside Shanghai.

One assignment turned out particularly challenging for Cecilia. It had nothing to do with the actual story and everything to do with the dirty old man traveling with us. For a series on the thirtieth anniversary of the one-child policy, we traveled for two days with a noted demographer. He was somewhat famous for opposing the strict policy and advocating a less harsh, voluntary program. Our story focused on a secret family-planning experiment in northern Shanxi province, a bone-dry area of hills made from windblown loess silt. For twenty-five years, the city of Yicheng allowed rural couples to have two children instead of one—so long as they spaced out the births. It succeeded. Yicheng kept under its population target, but Beijing ignored the experiment for decades.

The demographer helped us schedule key interviews. He was in his sixties, and by tradition referred to us as Little Chen (Xiao Chenr) and Little Tong (Xiao Tong). On our first day in the Shanxi hotel, he and Cecilia were alone in the hotel elevator when it suddenly got stuck. The elevator was quite small. The respected demographer looked Cecilia up and down.

"Xiao Chenr . . ." he said slowly. "Does this . . . mean anything?" This sixty-something man assumed his academic stature entitled him to this moment. I wonder how often this kind of thing occurs in China. This is another occupational hazard for fixers: Cecilia needed his help, and he'd suggested civilization's oldest quid pro quo. Mercifully, the elevator restarted and nothing more happened.

But that wasn't all for Cecilia. On that same trip in that same hotel, I made the mistake of abandoning her during a dinner banquet. A group of local government officials hosted us—and the demographer—at the hotel restaurant. After the meal and a nasty shot of sorghum alcohol, I excused myself from the table. This early departure required a bit of diplomacy. "I'll drink for him," Cecilia said jokingly, even though she's allergic to alcohol. Nonetheless, they pressured her into drinking. The next morning I learned she drank two shots and threw up before leaving the table.

She recovered in time for the next morning. The demographer took us to a village where he seemed to know everyone. He complimented middle-aged village women on their appearances, and they laughed nervously. Then he led us to a local two-child policy enforcer; even a relaxed population policy requires muscle.

Her name was Che Yuelian, a solid, immovable woman in her sixties with ebony black hair. Che lived in a large house with a gate and a Chinese national flag in the front. It seems she'd been rewarded by the nation for a job well done. Che brought out an old, dusty binder, with a series of index cards, lined up one after the other. Each card was entitled "Childbearing woman fertility condition registration card."

The sections read:

Name:
Name of spouse:
Work unit:
Political status:
Age:
Male children:
Female children:
Date of most recent birth of child:
Date of sterilization:
Date of intrauterine device implantation:

Each card corresponded to a village woman of childbearing age.

"The campaign was hard at the start," she said. "Villagers teased me, but I wasn't ashamed. One year, I convinced seven women to get IUDs, six to have abortions. And once we needed five women to get sterilized. We did a great job. The best year was when every single woman gave birth to her second child after the age thirty. Yes, that was our best year."

One year, Che explained, she'd faced a personal dilemma. Her niece in the village had married and conceived at the age of twenty-two—too young for either marriage or conception. If she carried the pregnancy to term, not only would she be fined, but her aunt Che Yuelian would also have to pay a fine of about $15. Money was the key enforcement lever: if a local official prevents a birth, she gets awarded financially. If not, she personally pays. This was a more complex incentive structure than I'd realized. Perhaps it was easier to dole out financial carrots than enforce with sticks.

Che did not tell us what happened in the end, but said in general she'd avoided paying personal fines. That meant she, or her colleagues, had terminated many pregnancies. "If I couldn't convince them all to have abortions," she said, "I would have to pay all the fines from my own pocket."

Whenever I go out to eat with my cousin Tong Chengkan, he finds a way to pay. I never win, and for this I blame my father, whose own success rate is low. He once told me that historically, the most skilled operators used one hand to lunge for the check and the other to grab the opponent's right wrist. That way the opponent could not reach into the outside right pocket of his jacket and pull out his money (he says men back then kept their money in their outside right pockets). But there also charlatans: if a person grabbed another person's *left* wrist—a useless hand for wallet purposes— he was faking his intention to pay. I don't know where he got the story.

Tong Chengkan is quick on the draw one summer in 2014. He's off this weekday, and I visit him at a Taiwanese restaurant near his parents' apartment. I'm just back from the Delingha labor camp out in Qinghai. "I should pay," he says, slipping the waiter his debit card with a very quick reaction time. "You can pay next time." Sure.

Interestingly, he is a traditionalist seeking to preserve cultural tradition. And yet at the same time he is a great consumer of modern products and technology. He wants it both ways—the kind of East-West hybrid our great-grandfather from the Tong village might have appreciated. In a way, my cousin is asking a question Chinese reformers have been asking themselves for at least a century: how to be modern and Chinese all at the same time.

On this day, my cousin wants to take me somewhere and make a history point. In his *bie-ke* LaCrosse we ride a couple miles to an expansive, wide-open part of the city I've never seen. It's in the northwest part of Shanghai, a spot curiously devoid of traffic lights, apartments, and office buildings. The area stretches as broad and wide as the grounds of the Washington Monument. "Shanghai Sports College," he mumbles as we walk past a few tennis courts and a soccer field.

Then a majestic, imperial-era building rises up as we approach. Deep-blue shingles slope down from a gold roof line. Orange porcelain animals perch on the ridge line, atop a giant building held up by thick red pillars.

"It's from the *min guo* period," he says, the time when the Chiang Kai-shek's Nationalist Guomindang Party ran the country from 1927 to 1937. Here, the GMD had planned to design a new Chinese Shanghai, far north of the old foreign devils' concessions. A China for Chinese people. This is what he has brought me to see—something Chinese and not copied and pasted from an outside influence. "Why does everyone like everything Western?" he asks.

His griping strikes me as refreshing. In China's fast-forward dash for scarce resources—jobs, spouses, college spaces, affordable housing—the importance of something so vague and subjective as historical preservation generally cannot compete. Why keep up an old, decrepit building when you can knock it down and build seventy apartment units?

Once, Chengkan fumed when I told him my fixer could not recall the old folk story about the origins of sweet, sticky dumplings during mid-autumn festival. Even I knew this one: a government bureaucrat named Qu Yuan was so distraught about the emperor's military failings that he committed suicide in protest. Qu Yuan threw himself into a Hunan river. As the story goes, loyal members of the public jumped into boats and paddled madly to find his body (the origins of the Dragon Boat race). And people in boats threw rice into the water so the fish would eat the rice instead of Qu Yuan's remains. Ladies and gentlemen: the origins of sticky rice dumplings.

"What? She doesn't even know about Qu Yuan?" Tong Chengkan shakes his head. "We've forgotten our history."

The classically Chinese building was once the city hall of Shanghai, until war interrupted the story. The Japanese invaded Shanghai in 1932 and again in 1937. "If there weren't these wars, it would have been a lot better here," he says. My cousin has a certain independence that makes me wonder if he was born in the wrong era. Today's China seems to have no space for above-average sons who play clarinet, ride fancy road bikes, and think about history. These pursuits hold value in the States, but not so much here.

After returning home, I researched the old city hall. In 1927, the Guomindang made its return to national relevance. The blueprint for the nucleus was a cross-shaped intersection that resembles the Chinese character *zhong*, or "middle," for a proud Middle Kingdom. Four buildings were meant to anchor each corner of the main intersection: a city hall, a museum, a library, and a hospital. But there was a surprise. For all the Chinese symbolism, the city plan was drawn up by an Englishman named Ebenezer Howard, founder of a global garden-city movement (his ideas influenced the design of cities including Greenbelt, Maryland, near DC). In addition, the architect who designed the city hall, Dong Dayou, studied at the University of Minnesota. The city hall exuded Olde China on the outside, but inside there were Western features: the entrance and the reinforced concrete walls. Dong described this hybrid style as "Chinese Renaissance."

As Tong Chengkan suggested, the war derailed the whole plan. Japanese forces first attacked Shanghai in January 1932 and interrupted construction. The full-on invasion came five years later, damaging the buildings and the entire district of Yangpu in general. When the war ended in 1945, the GMD returned to Shanghai but abandoned the Ebenezer Howard plan. Instead it set up the city government in the old Shanghai municipal council building in the former International Settlement. Later, when the GMD itself was driven out in 1949, the Communists did not reinstate the plan either. Today, the grand imperial city council building belongs to the Shanghai Sports Academy. The architectural dream of a Chinese Shanghai flopped.

In 2009 Cecilia and I fly to western Hunan to look into a case of mass lead poisoning of village children. This is a follow-up trip to a previous story in the same place. The boss of a manganese smelting plant had been found guilty of using an illegal smokestack. It was too short, so concentrated pollutants belched upward and then fell to the ground, leaching into the soil and groundwater. "The smoke was black and thick, darker than a thunderstorm," one mother told us. More than a thousand children were diagnosed with lead poisoning. The local government pledged to pay for medicine and treatment, and now we are returning to update the story.

We try to enter quietly. For embarrassing industrial stories like this, local jurisdictions are known to send cops or thugs to intercept reporters. One way to track journalists' locations is by employing cell tower technology to geo-locate their phones. Our evasion strategy is to turn off our phones and to remove the batteries and SIM cards. Hours before we approach the village of Wenping, we buy brand-new SIM cards. And we hire a local cabbie on a friend's recommendation. We are feeling very smart.

Cecilia and I tape a few follow-up interviews with parents. As we suspect, after the public spotlight has dimmed, so has the government assistance. "The government gave us one hundred dollars, paid for one treatment, and that's it," says one mother, Hu Xianghong. Her son always seems to have a cold now, and he hardly eats. The US Centers for Disease Control and Prevention suggests lead poisoning can result in long-term damage to a child's attention span and IQ, but local officials have told the parents that lead has "been eliminated" from their children's systems. We want to interview these officials.

This is the kind of story many Chinese nationals hate to tell the outside world. They want to keep the ugliness inside the family, at a time when there are so many other positive stories to tell about China. But Cecilia has no compunction exposing the dark side. She is as critical as I am. But it's a lonely position. More than once, she's expressed disappointment about failing to contribute to Emerging China "from the inside." Instead, she's spent so many years on the outside, in Canada or working for foreign companies. Chinese nationals have a keen, instinctive sense of who the team players are and aren't.

On our way to the government building, we detour briefly to an adjacent apartment complex. Something has happened in this complex. A few weeks prior, Chinese news websites had reported that a midlevel government official had mysteriously died. The reports said he'd committed suicide by jumping off the roof, but his widow called reporters and denied he'd killed himself. Cecilia tracked this widow down, who said her late husband "had been suicided" because he held incriminating information about corrupt officials. The idea was, this man and his information were eliminated. But after a couple days, the widow stopped taking Cecilia's calls.

We approach the suicide spot. The complex is quiet. It's clear the apartment building in question is tall enough for a suicide jump— or push. But there is no blood on the ground, no sign of foul play, no police markings. No one answers when we knock on their doors. So Cecilia and I start to make our way back out.

Then a uniformed man rushes at us. He is very angry. "Who are you? What are you doing here? This is a private complex!" The man is very small and looks like he might be in his sixties. He is wearing a security guard uniform, with his name tag over the left pocket. He's quite rude, and by now I'm quite tired—of the Hunan heat, of evasion strategies, of alternate phone SIM cards. I throw his attitude right back at him.

"Private?" I shouted. "The gate is wide open."

"You can't be in here."

"Really? Why?"

"What's your name? I'm going to report you."

Fine. I pull out my notebook. "What is *your* name?"

Cecilia joins in. "Why are you so rude?"

"Tell me your name!" The man blocks us from getting by, and then gets up in our business and flings curses. We curse back, but there is a problem. Even though I've descended to his level, I'm not trash talking very clearly in my second language. "Who taught you to speak that way?" seems to lose something in the translation, as does "Go home, look at yourself in the mirror, and see who you really are."

Then he shocks us. "I'm going to call the police, and tell them the American journalists are here."

American journalists? Have we been followed? Monitored? How does this very small man know who we are?

Cecilia tries to call his bluff. "You don't know who we are."

I turn the conversation back to him and repeat: "What's your name? Is that it?" I point to the three words above his pocket and start writing them down. The problem is, I don't recognize one of the characters, and as I squint, the man whips his right palm over his heart to block his name tag.

And then the thugs come. Four young men in white T-shirts approach from out of nowhere and surround us. I'm scared, but only a little. They are the youngest, skinniest thugs I've ever seen, yet they still outnumber us.

"Is there anything wrong?" one thug kid asks.

I put away my notebook. The small security guard is emboldened, like a small dog who barks ferociously and then retreats behind his owner's leg, continuing to yap. Finally, another kid speaks up.

"It's best that you leave," he says. Cecilia and I look at each other, then walk out.

Our driver speaks up after we get back in. "When you got out of the car, someone immediately went to follow you. I saw him mention 'American journalists.'" We have no answers for what just happened. It's the only time in China I've knowingly been tracked on the road.

Fortunately, we escape unharmed and with a story. And we are on our way to the next meeting a few hours away: a visit with a convicted baby seller.

<table>
<tr><td>Chapter
Fifteen</td><td>DAUGHTERS
FOR SALE</td></tr>
</table>

I tried a few times to leave her on the street. But nobody wanted her. So I brought her back home.
—Duan Yueneng, convicted baby trafficker

"This is my daughter," the Hunan baby seller says. "Do you want her?"

Those are the first words out of the mouth of thirty-eight-year-old Duan Yueneng. He has just been released from jail, for the offense of trafficking babies—that is, selling them to Chinese orphanages that send infants to America via international adoption. It was a family operation for the Duans, and his wife and sister remain in prison for their roles. This man, busted for selling girls, is now apparently offering to unload his own.

Neither Cecilia nor I know if he's being serious, so we dodge the question and step into his house. We are cold and exhausted on this afternoon in February 2010. We've spent five rainy hours on the road—long-distance taxi, bus, pedicab—to arrive in the cheerless, rainy Hunan city of Changning. Duan motions us to a square, wooden table with an orange skirt on each side. He sticks his hands under the skirt, rubbing them together for warmth. A primitive charcoal heater burns beneath the table—the only source of heat in the house.

The daughter in question appears with tea and tangerines and a straight face. She keeps her head down throughout, her long bangs almost covering her eyes entirely. She is fifteen, the younger of two sisters, Duan explains, making her an over-quota child born illegally (this is before China's relaxation of the one-child policy).

"I wanted to get rid of her," Duan says matter-of-factly. "So I'd still have a chance to have a baby boy. We need boys. I tried a few times to leave her on the street. But nobody wanted her. My mother didn't want to abandon her, so I brought her back home."

The younger daughter presents two problems for him. First, she is a she, a liability in this backwater place, despite all the talk in today's China about boy-girl equality. There is a joke going around I've heard a few times: having a son turns you into the China Construction Bank: you have to build a new home for him and his wife. But a daughter makes you the China Investment Bank: you attract money—girls are profitable enterprises. I presume the joke had yet to arrive in Changning when the second daughter was born in the mid-'90s.

Strike two: she is Daughter 2. Many Chinese couples at the time were willing to conceive a second child, and even pay the fine, if that child turned out to be a desired boy. Duan and his wife took this chance and failed.

Duan's mother joins us at the table. I start the recorder, place the long shotgun microphone on a stand in front of them, and return my cold hands to the charcoal heater. And the Duans begin to talk about the underground adoption economy.

———————

When it comes to China's embrace of the global connected age, of modern science and technology and market forces, it is without question a remarkable economic and governance feat. In 1900, it was one of the poorest countries on earth; the late economic historian Angus Maddison estimates China's GDP per person was below India's, below the African continent's, and one-seventh that of the United States. Today China has achieved a level of poverty reduction that took centuries in Western Europe and North America. There are plenty of ways to measure this progress: per capita GDP, Olympic gold medals, cumulative train tracks, stock market capitalization, space exploration trips, calorie consumption, power generation. This is how dramatic "catch-up," in the words of development economists, can be.

Yet all this represents "the things you can see," to quote a driver I met in Wuhan. I've often heard this described as the empirical "hardware" of an economy. What's lacking is the software: Education. Transparency. Meritocracy. Innovation. Morality. Trust. And, notably, the rule of law. Show up in any Chinese city or village and tongues start wagging about corruption and public money disappearing, in some cases turning up at craps tables in Macau.

Mainlanders didn't invent corruption, but given the opportunity, they do it well. This is particularly the case when a lot of foreign money trickles in and gets spread around, with limited oversight. Case in point: international adoption. American couples, motivated by virtue or child-rearing desperation, arrive and plop down $3,000 for a child to bring home. This naturally draws profiteers out of the woodwork. Yet it's remarkable how China—which takes such a battering for rule bending in other areas—has long benefited from a clean image when it comes to baby girls. We don't trust the pet food or the quality of Dollar Store goods, but somehow believe in the integrity of the supply chain for baby girls.

Certainly my wife, Cathy, and I did in 2002, when we began our paperwork to adopt a daughter from Hunan named Guo Shanzhen (to provide her a modicum of privacy—so that this story does not define the next seventy years of her life—I will use her Chinese name from the orphanage rather than the English one we use at home). We were living in Alexandria, Virginia, with our son Evan, who had just turned two. Cathy and I had no fertility issues, yet chose to adopt largely because of her own family history. The daughter of two white social workers, she was born their biological child in Canton, Ohio. Eighteen months later, her parents adopted her brother from Akron, to provide for an infant in need. He is the mixed-race biological son of a black man and white woman. Then came her sister from Saigon, the product of a black American GI and Vietnamese woman from the Vietnam War. The youngest brother was also adopted from Akron, also part black.

Soon after Cathy and I married, we talked about adopting as well. A baby from China intrigued me, not simply because of my family heritage, but because of mainlanders' well-known abandonment of unwanted girls. I'd seen photos of babies in orphanages, left in trash cans to die overnight, and we both knew China's one-child rule led to infanticide and abandonment. The narrative pitted heroes against villains, and we chose a side. As an added benefit, a Chinese daughter would be an easier sell to my own parents.

The process began with what's called a home study performed by a social worker. Ours, named Vivian, asked us about our family situation, salaries, health, and reasons to adopt. When we brought up China, she described the process as if she were selling a Toyota: affordable, reliable, good quality. Chinese orphans tend not to come with fetal alcohol syndrome associated with babies from Russia and Eastern Europe. The waiting time for a Chinese kid was a predictable twelve to eighteen months—a two-term paperwork pregnancy. And the fees were competitive, relative to adopting domestically or from other countries: $20,000 ballpark included the home study, paperwork, fingerprints, fees, flights, hotel.

And the Chinese system was considered legally smooth: all cases run through the central government, so parents could avoid dealing with the small, local jurisdictions as found in some other countries. The image offered by Vivian—and virtually all the English-language websites we Googled—suggested an efficient, rules-based system. Bureaucracy, the good kind. Each Chinese girl comes with a paper trail. Her file lists where she was found and who found her. There is also an important step known as the "finding ad." When an orphanage takes in a new child, it buys an ad in the local newspaper notifying the public of the timing, place, and description of the found child. That way, if a baby is stolen rather than abandoned, her biological parents can pick her up. Here's a passage from the adoption organization Chinesechildren.org from the time:

> During your trip to China, you will receive a certificate of abandonment that proves the biological parents have relinquished their parental rights through abandonment. There is no legal avenue for the birth parents to reclaim custody.

The message: yes, you can trust China. And in 2002, we did.

The Hunan provincial court in 2006 convicted Duan Yuening and four other family members of trafficking. According to the verdict, they bought eighty-five babies from Guangdong and sold them to six orphanages in the province: Hengnan, Hengdong, Hengyang, Changning, Qidong, and Hengshan. "But in reality, we transported far more babies," he says. "More than a thousand." In addition to Duan, his two sisters, wife, and sister-in-law were convicted. He received the lightest sentence.

"The women did the long-distance traveling," he explains. They transported babies north by train to Hunan, where Duan drove them by car to local orphanages. He negotiated sales.

At this point, he backs up and starts from the beginning. I take a sip of tea, crack open a few watermelon seeds, and on his direction dump the shells on the table. He and his mother Chen Zhijin explain that they stumbled into the baby-selling business. In the mid-1990s, she took Duan's unwanted second daughter and moved to another Hunan city, Qidong, to hide the baby from local enforcers of the one-child policy. This was a common workaround; officials can't extract fines for over-quota babies they don't see. Chen took a job caring for babies in the local Qidong orphanage, for $2 a day.

Then, Chen says, she started finding abandoned infant girls around town and bringing them to the orphanage. "They were left on street corners to freeze." At the time, the technology of ultrasound was just arriving into rural townships, so parents rejecting daughters did not have the option of sex-selective abortion. Instead, they resorted to sex-selective abandonment.

Duan jumps in. "When I was in my twenties, I'd ride my bike and see abandoned babies, dead. They smelled terrible. No one would bury them. Ants crawled in babies' mouths, but no one cared for them. It was very cruel. Back then, only a fraction of the babies were adopted by foreign families."

I must look captivated by this, because his mother eyes me and chooses this moment to say something important. "Those babies I picked up in 1990s must be sixteen, seventeen years old by now.

Many are now in America. Will these well-off children hear your radio report, and then share some of their wealth with us?"

Aha. So this is why they have agreed to this interview: money. I should have thought of that. Convincing a Chinese person to speak in front of a microphone is a particular challenge in a low-trust place. In America, if I wave a mic at someone, she figures, *Why not?* In China, a person asks, *Why?* This is the reason.

Duan and his mom watch for my reaction. Could they cash in on this interview? In reality it's preposterous to think an American couple would see the Duan family as their daughter's savior. But I can't say that with my outside voice, so I mumble something vague about possible payment, which is enough for his mother to continue.

"If I found a baby and it later got adopted, the orphanage paid me ten *kuai* [renminbi] each time." About $1.20. This was described euphemistically as "travel reimbursement." Sometimes, the Qidong orphanage would pay a tad more for transportation costs if a baby came from farther away, or at night.

"Sometimes an orphanage made an arrangement with my mom late at night, when it was too late to take the bus," Duan says. "She'd get money to come by taxi. Or perhaps motorcycle taxi." I try to picture this grandmother, cradling a wrapped newborn, balancing sidesaddle on a motor scooter.

Around 2000, demand rose, and Chen's finding fees began to skyrocket. Word got out to local orphanages that this grandma was picking up abandoned babies. "Orphanages started asking for more babies," she says. "They started paying one thousand kuai [$120 US]. Then two thousand. Then four thousand." Orphanage workers came from miles away to pick up babies, very likely representing foreign demand for Chinese baby girls. Chinese local media reported workers in the Hengyang orphanage received bonuses for bringing in at least three babies a year. In 1991, 115 Chinese babies went overseas via adoption, according to official Chinese government records. The number ballooned to two thousand babies in 1995 and five thousand in 2000. The majority of those babies went to the United States. By the turn of the twenty-first century, the sight of a white parent with a Chinese kid in a suburban American mall had become less and less unusual.

For Cathy and me in 2002, the adoption paperwork was stifling, the equivalent of doing our taxes for six straight months. We submitted pay stubs, employer letters, recommendation letters, HIV test results, criminal background checks, and official fingerprints. We drafted wills. Every piece of paper had to be notarized, and then separately "authenticated" by the State Department. And then officially approved once again by Chinese authorities. It was all so proper. What could go wrong? Again, a passage from Chinese children.org:

> The Chinese government and local orphanages highly value their international image and have an effective reporting and processing system to maximize the reliability and accuracy of adoptive children's information provided to adoptive families. Our nearly 20 years of international adoption experience with China has shown us that China is doing a very commendable job!

Where our money would go was also complicated. Of the $20,000, a few thousand went to the home study, hundreds to airlines, hotels, official Washington, official Beijing. The more checks we wrote, the more we got lost in the details. Buried in the transactions was that $3,000 would go to the baby's orphanage. In 2002, that was nine months of income for the typical Chinese person. I never even paid attention to that, treating it simply as a cost of doing business rather than a whopping amount of money on the mainland. Instead we shopped for a crib, and a daycare for our son Evan. He was two at the time, and ended up at a daycare with three adopted Chinese girls. Evan informed us that all sisters came from China.

Cathy's parents supported us wholeheartedly, though my folks were underwhelmed. "Why do you need to adopt?" my father asked. "You have your own." He suggested that adoption brought new risks. We'd have no control over any inherited health problems, or even know about them. This was one of those rare moments when my folks advised me on how to live. I assumed adopting from China could buy them off emotionally. Not only were my parents both born on the mainland, but China offered the closest thing to a guaranteed girl in a family that had struggled to produce a single female. My parents had two sons, and so did my brother. Now, we were in pursuit of an unwanted baby girl from mainland China. Still, they were skeptical.

It took us about a year and a half to complete our paperwork. With the help of Vivian and the Holt International adoption agency in Eugene, Oregon, we shipped off our adoption paperwork, known as a dossier, to Beijing in August 2003. And we waited for a baby match.

———————————

Duan Yueneng places a big stack of handwritten receipts on the table. Each documented the sale of a baby to a Hunan orphanage. The receipt on top is dated July 7, 2003—one month before Cathy and I submitted our own dossier to Beijing.

"They gave us money, and it shows clearly here," Duan explains. He points to the receipt's memo section: "for baby foster-care fees." The payment amount: 4,200 yuan, or about $500. Another read 2,400 yuan, or $350. I'm stunned. In a country where so much of the economy is informal and undocumented, these black-market transactions were written down, as it was required for orphanage record keeping.

"All these deals all have receipts?" I ask.

"All have receipts," his mother says.

In other ways, the scheme required falsifying documents. By law, a Chinese orphanage can only accept babies from its local area. Hunan orphanages had to hide any evidence of babies delivered from provinces far away. Duan finds a case to illustrate. He shows a photo of a baby girl with a round face and thick eyebrows, looking out from the top-right corner of a Changning government document. She's identified as belonging to the Changning orphanage. Name: Ning Yucui. Date of birth: October 27, 2002. Date delivered to orphanage: November 3, 2002. Duan flips a page. A separate document from the police department lists the same girl and her finding person: Duan Zilin, younger sister of Duan Yueneng. The paper lists the place where the baby was found: the front entrance of the Changning Shengyuan Department Store, a place close to the orphanage.

That was the lie. Duan explains the false location is embedded in much of the paperwork, including the finding ads printed in local newspapers and documents shared with adopting parents overseas. Whenever a baby arrives in an orphanage, it has to be documented. It all starts with the orphanage log, tallying each new baby's arrival time, finding person, and finding location. He pulls out multiple logs from different orphanages—Qidong, Changning, Hengyang— all listing one of his sisters as the babies' finding persons. Going down the handwritten lists, we keep noticing the names Duan Mei-lin and Duan Zilin. All those babies in fact came from Guangdong province five hundred miles to the south, he explains.

Duan pulls up one last document, called an adoption agreement. There, Ning Yucui is pictured with an American couple from New York, what the adoption community calls her "forever family." For all the forever family knows, Ning Yucui was found at a local department store and delivered to a local orphanage

By 2003, Duan's family was selling babies at scale. As demand rose, so did prices. "There was an old woman in Guangdong who lived on picking up rubbish," Chen Zhijin says. "She also picked up babies. She brought babies back and took care of them." One of Duan's sisters lived and worked in the nearby industrial port city of Zhanjiang. Her husband worked on a chicken farm there, and he first met this old woman.

"She gave babies to whoever wanted them, not wanting them to die. She says it was good for us to take some babies, because she couldn't care for all of them. I asked her, 'You have this many babies, can I bring back some?'" In reality, things may not have been so simple. A local newspaper would later report the Duans once paid the old woman 720 renminbi for six babies, or roughly $15 each.

Each delivery required a five-hundred-mile, twelve-hour train ride. Chen Zhijin explains: "We put six babies in three big powdered-milk cardboard boxes. We boarded the train at Zhan-jiang station. My daughter was with me. In the middle of the trip, one box fell, but they weren't hurt. Then, I started feeding them, one after another. Each of us was holding one baby, and we had the other four babies in two boxes."

It must have created a scene. Six babies on a crowded train, ferried by two women. The typical ratio in China was a single child in a stroller, escorted by a mother, father, grandparent, and perhaps a nanny. I could only imagine the staring, in a place where gawking is an approved sport.

They ended up drawing the wrong kind of attention. A local policeman took the women off the train and questioned them. "The police wanted to know if we stole the babies," she says. "He looked into it, didn't find a problem, and released us. He says, 'What you're doing is not a bad thing. It's a good thing for these babies.'"

This is one of several times Duan and his mother declare themselves proud of what they did, that they'd taken abandoned baby girls and helped send them on to a better life abroad. In a market economy, the thinking goes, what's wrong with charging a fee? They imply that this is simply how a supply chain works: wholesalers find an item in demand, buy it at a low price, and sell it for higher. The item changes hands a couple times, and eventually finds a retail customer domestically or overseas. It works this way for T-shirts, socks, frozen tilapia, power drills, and iPhones. Why not abandoned girls? If an orphanage can buy a baby from the Duans for $500 and "flip" her for three thousand, the return on investment is 500 percent.

"Orphanages have relatively big profit-margin space," Duan Yueneng explains. "They wanted more babies. They kept asking us for more. They'd take our whole families out to dinner. Orphanage directors took my sister to the best restaurant in town. The director at the Qidong orphanage invited my whole family to a banquet. Hengnan County gave us rice wine every Chinese New Year."

"Mom, we got our referral."

Tears streamed down Cathy's face as she sat up in bed and called her mom on the phone. We'd waited about two years for this. Beijing bureaucrats had "matched" us to a then eight-month-old named Guo Shanzhen. It was April 9, 2004. The news came in a manila envelope that included three small photos. In one, a child is sitting up, propped up, in an orange T-shirt, maybe five months old. She is bald. Her big, dark, round eyes look straight at the camera. In the next one she lies on her belly on a mat, a few months older, thin black hair creeping in from the back. The third shows a baby with an outright comb-over, standing in front of a playground slide. The location: Hunan province, Zhuzhou city.

I looked up Zhuzhou. Population: three million. It serves as a railway hub, the intersection of a north-south trunk line and an east-west track. There is farming, mining, and steel in Zhuzhou, where several rivers come together. "It's the Pittsburgh of China," I said, and Cathy groaned on cue.

The accompanying paperwork included medical information:

Height: 65 cm
Sitting height: 38 cm
Spleen: Not palpable
Deformity: No
Heart rate: 110 beats/min

The packet also included a progress report: "Guo Shan Zhen, female, was born on March 22, 2003 (based on the note she carried). On March 28, 2003, she was picked up by Jianshe Police Station of Zhuzhou City at Collecting Station. She was then sent to our institution. Because her birth parents were not found, she is thought as a foundling." The next section was "Progressive Information": "Guo Shan Zhen looks like a boy with a round face, black and thick hair, bright eyes and a fairly [sic] complexion."

A separate "abandonment certificate" indicated Guo Shanzhen was six days old when she was found alone, on the doorstep of a public welfare building in an alley by the train station. The finding person was listed as Zou Guohua, a police officer. This was her origin story.

Two months later, we flew to China, joining twelve other families matched to babies from the same orphanage in Zhuzhou. They hailed from Georgia, California, Montana, New Jersey, Pennsylvania, Wisconsin, Minnesota. Our group included a pilot, a pastor, and a dentist. Two families brought biological children along for the trip, though we chose to leave then-four-year-old Evan in the States with Cathy's parents in Toledo. My parents flew to join us in China, from their home in Portland, Oregon.

The agency Holt International scheduled us all to meet first in Beijing, to do some orientation and sightseeing, before flying into Hunan's capital city, Changsha. Holt domestic staffer Matthew Xiao met us there, ushering us to an air-conditioned coach bus to take us to our hotel. Matthew spoke English and would be our main guide. There is a thing about tour buses in China. Every single one I've ridden in is prewired with speakers and a plug-in microphone, for karaoke singing and announcements. There is a time for silence, but this is not it. Matthew grabbed the mic and welcomed us visitors from America.

"You people are living my dream," he said—something my grandmother Mildred Zhao would have said ninety years ago at the Stephen L. Baldwin School for Girls in Nanchang. He had a wife, a grade school son, and a mountain bike he took on planes to ride all over China. Matthew aspired to own a single-family home in North America, with a car to drive and clean air to inhale. In a week and half, thirteen Chinese baby girls would get that life. Matthew explained he'd volunteered and worked at Chinese orphanages for more than a decade. He began in his hometown of Nanning in southwest China's Guangxi province, just north of the Vietnam border. It's one of the poorest corners of China.

"They used to put the weakest babies in the trash cans at night" in the '90s, he said, "still alive. Workers assumed they would die overnight. I saw one baby put in the trash can two nights in a row. But each time, she survived. She was strong. So the next time they put her in the trash can, one orphanage worker took the baby and cared for her at home." He said three hundred to five hundred babies were abandoned every year in Nanning.

In the decade that followed, China's economy took off in the great capitalist resumption, the era of reform and opening. The average person's income rose from one dollar a day to five by 2004. Still, many in our group from the United States sought to donate to the orphanage and asked Matthew how to give. Cash? Through a US intermediary? Give as a group?

"Do not give money," Matthew said pointedly. "You don't know where it's going to go." Orphanage workers might pocket the money. He suggested we instead ask the staff what supplies the babies needed—perhaps milk powder or clothes or toys—and buy those goods directly for donation. This was my first hint of fraud in the system, but at the time I totally missed it (my mother reminded me of Matthew's warning years later). It was June 7, 2004.

"Let's eat," Duan Yueneng, the baby-trafficking ex-con, says. He stands up and beckons us to a large square table for eight. Unwanted Second Daughter emerges from the kitchen, this time to set the table. Everything we eat—pork with tofu, green beans, cabbage—is mind-bendingly spicy here in the land of red peppers, which naturally prompts Duan to ask: "*Ni hui chi la ma?*" Can you eat spicy?

"Sort of."

A small boy arrives at the table, sits down, and commands attention the way an emperor does. It is Duan's six-year-old son. He demands soup, and it appears before him. He points chopsticks in the direction of what he wants. An image appears in my mind, of a victorious contestant on the *Wheel of Fortune* television game show shopping with her winnings and pointing with chopsticks at her choices: a mink coat, a cruise, a gift certificate, a spoonful of tofu. The boy's grandmother fetches what he desires; he eats, excuses himself, and runs off. The sister barely says a word.

I've seen his face before. This boy's photo has been posted on several walls in the Duan home, one of them some kind of kindergarten certificate. His grandmother explains he is the product of Duan Yueneng's second marriage. The woman in jail for her participation in the baby-selling scheme is not his first wife. Then comes the bombshell.

"The first wife committed suicide," she says. "After she gave birth to a second daughter, local family-planning officials found out. They came to our house and confiscated our valuables."

Often, one-child policy enforcers took things from poor families unable to pay fines. Officials seized sewing machines, appliances, bicycles, couches—anything to send a message—and in the process obtained something nice to personally enjoy or sell. In the Duans' case, enforcers also went to his relatives' homes nearby and took their items too.

"Everyone in the family blamed the first wife for this," Duan's mom says, "for another baby girl. So she killed herself." The first wife faced a lifetime of shame ahead of her, but instead chose an alternative way out. Duan's mother speaks with the characteristic Chinese detached matter-of-factness. She isn't telling me a tragic story; it is simply a story. *Everyone in China has a story like this. This is just mine.*

On the morning of June 8, 2004, Cathy, my parents, and I waited in our hotel room for the delivery of our Zhuzhou baby. On Matthew's suggestion, we left the door of our room open in the four-star Huatian Hotel in the Hunan provincial capital of Changsha. In the lobby below, guests and diners glided across the marble floor bisected by a stream filled with carp. An arched walking bridge led across.

The elevator dinged, followed by the sound of a baby field trip. Matthew's voice barked out directions; adult female voices complied. Tiny voices cooed and clucked, but there was no outright wailing. It sounded as if the workers brought all the babies into a central room, then distributed them one at a time. A woman staffer walked past our door with a baby girl in a yellow dress. Large, round eyes. Pigtails.

"Guo Shanzhen?" my dad asked. "Is that her?" The worker scurried past. No.

Moments later, we heard the shrieking before we saw her. Thirteen-month-old Guo Shanzhen was carried in, crying more desperately than any of the others. She wore a pale-yellow dress that matched the other girls. Her hair had grown out from the comb-over, and was gathered atop her head and tied up in a whale spout. Already her eyes were puffy. Around her neck dangled a cheap plastic yellow name tag. Guo Shanzhen directly translated means "country walk pearl."

Her skin color wasn't "fairly," as the paperwork suggested. Guo

Shanzhen's skin tone looked a shade or two darker than any of the photos, the color of my deepest summer tan. She smelled "sour," Cathy would later say, wondering when the baby was last bathed. "You should change her clothes now," the orphanage worker directed, explaining that Guo Shanzhen threw up on the bumpy one-and-a-half-hour bus ride from Zhuzhou. Before stepping out, the woman handed us a thin slip of torn-off paper with one hand-written line: "2003.3.22." Her presumed date of birth. March 22, 2003.

She bellowed for more than an hour. The Holt staff a few days prior had warned us not to anticipate a baby Hallmark moment. We each attempted to hold her, set her down, change her, bribe her with snacks. Nothing worked. Each time she would look at one of us, wind up, and pitch another fit. At the end of each cry she pursed her lips and made an *ooh* sound. My mother eventually came to the rescue—as if often the case—pulling out a set of stacking toy cups and distracting her new granddaughter. The wailing tapered. Perhaps Guo Shanzhen found the face of an adult Chinese woman most familiar. The immediate crisis ended, and our lives together began.

For the first two days, she seemed to remain in shock. Through those deep, bright eyes, Guo Shanzhen watched us and the other girls in the group, but did not smile or play. When eating or playing, she'd put one hand on one of us, as if to prevent us from leaving. Surprisingly, she was fully toilet trained. And on the third day, after a significant bowel event on the kid potty, she began to smile and visibly relax. It was as though she came to a realization that we might be permanent in her life.

We stayed in Changsha three days, always within earshot of Matthew on a tour bus microphone. We filled out provincial papers at the local government building and shopped for strollers at an overpriced specialty shop. At local restaurants, waitresses held our daughters as we dined. Guo Shanzhen ate with a certain desperation, as if competing for crackers, or spoonfuls of steamed egg. She stuffed in one bite after another without pausing to swallow. This should have been a clue to us about the orphanage, loaded with American parents' money yet apparently underfeeding its own babies. Where was the money actually going?

The next morning, we headed for Zhuzhou, the orphanage city. The bus ride offered sweeping views of rivers and rice paddies—this is one of China's breadbasket regions. Situated behind a gate and a guard, like all Chinese institutions, the orphanage campus featured a grassy courtyard with the playground in the center, surrounded by administrative and residential buildings. The female orphanage director welcomed us in a large hall, when Cathy discovered something.

On her way to the bathroom, she passed through the director's office. It was so upscale as to be out of character: air conditioner, carpet, high-end large desk. Clearly a fair bit of Foreigner Price money had gone to furnishing this CEO-type space. There was a striking contrast to the babies' spartan quarters across the compound, three floors up with no elevator. We walked over and found a dozen babies in matching green outfits in an empty playroom. They sat and rolled around on old gymnastics mats, but we saw no toys. Across the hall was a group bedroom where Guo Shanzhen and the other adopted twelve used to sleep. Sixteen rudimentary cribs were lashed together in rows of four. We laid Guo Shanzhen down in one, to see if she might remember it or find some comfort, but she screamed and demanded out.

The next stop: the spots where our babies had been found. Holding a list of addresses, Matthew directed the driver to the respective finding spots. One of the first was a gas station, the finding spot for baby Molly, at ten months old the tiniest of the group. Her new parents stepped off with her and Matthew to look around. It seemed the person dropping her—likely Molly's birth mother—came by car or truck, left the infant, and drove away. After a few minutes, her adoptive mother, a dentist from New Jersey with short brown hair and glasses, reboarded the bus, teary and emotional. Molly's adoptive father—round face; short, straight brown hair—followed, as we looked at them and the gas station.

"Whenever I fill up," he said. "I'll think of Molly."

Most of the finding sites were busy, public spots: a train station, a busy street corner, a supermarket entrance. When the bus stopped on a bridge over the train tracks, it was our turn. "We'll get off and walk down," Matthew said. The five of us plus Guo Shanzhen walked down metal steps to an alley parallel to the tracks, separated by a concrete wall. The alley was surprisingly quiet. Suddenly a man and woman emerged from a small lane to our right, gave a stare, and moved on. A third of a mile down, we turned right into a court-yard surrounded by dusty gray mid-rise apartments with laundry hanging above: white tank-top undershirts, gray pants, floral tops, boxer shorts. The finding spot.

To our right stood a drab government building, the local welfare benefits office where on March 8, 2003, police officer Zou Guohua found a six-day-old baby, according to our papers. No one else was in sight. Unless you walked this alley every day, you'd never know it existed. Why did someone abandon Guo Shanzhen here? She might not have been noticed for hours, in contrast to a busy train station. Did the drop-off person come by train? Or was she a local resident who knew the welfare office opened early in the morning? Lots of questions, no clear answers.

We spent maybe five minutes in the courtyard, gave Guo Shan-zhen a few extra squeezes, snapped a couple photos, and started back toward the bus. I pulled out my video camera and started roll-ing and narrating in the alley, until a middle-aged woman walked into the frame from the left. She spat—not at us, but just some-thing she needed to do. The moment was over, and we got on the karaoke bus. A week later, we flew home with our new daughter to Detroit Metropolitan Airport, where her four-year-old brother and Ohio grandparents and cousins met her for the first time. It was mid-June 2004.

The first members of the Duan family ring got caught on a Friday in 2005.

Previously, the baby-selling family members had had a num-ber of close calls but managed to emerge unscathed. They'd been stopped and questioned by authorities in Changning, and in Zhu-zhou, the city of Guo Shanzhen's orphanage. Chinese newspapers reported that the Duans sold three babies to Zhuzhou for a total of 6,900 renminbi, just under a thousand dollars. Police detained the women briefly and then let them go. But not in November. Two women in the Duan family operation emerged from the Hengyang train station and delivered three babies into a black car with two orphanage workers inside. The police pounced. The guilty verdicts came three months later.

Why were they busted this time? During and after reporting the story for *Marketplace*, I came across a few theories. By then, the local news media had reported on baby-selling rumors, so perhaps party leaders figured it was time to crack down on a story already out. Perhaps junior-level orphanage managers smelled an opportunity to nail their bosses and get promoted, so they started talking to authorities. Or maybe local police officers sought hush money from orphanage directors who refused to give it, so the cops turned on them.

After his conviction, an angry Duan stewed in the Qidong city prison, where he found the food inedible. Stir-fried dishes contained bugs. The rice was boiled excessively, so the grains broke down into an unrecognizable mush. He assumed, as many do in China, that the well-connected big fish escaped justice even as his group of low-level crooks paid a price. In this case, orphanage directors in the baby supply chain stood to profit the most, yet only one of six identified orphanages was convicted and sentenced. The others somehow got off, he said.

"What about the Zhuzhou director?" I ask during the 2010 interview at his house. "Why wasn't she named in the trial?"

"We sold babies to so many orphanages across Hunan," Duan says. "The trial just made examples of a few people, but not everyone involved." The logic made sense, but Cecilia and I struggled to confirm this. Duan received a sentence of six years but was released early after four to care for his elderly mother. He emerged a bitter man and started talking to reporters.

———

After lunch at Duan's house, Cecilia and I record another hour's worth of interviews, take a number of photos, and prepare to return home to Shanghai. In a Chinese meeting, this is always when the key question comes.

"Can you take my bank account information?" Duan asks. "If you come across any Americans who want to donate money, they can send it there."

I jot it all down, wondering to myself why Americans would send anything to this convicted baby seller. He knows what I'm thinking. "Because I helped them. I helped them get to America."

In the small world of Chinese adoption, Brian Stuy of Utah is a lightning rod. The adoptive father of three Chinese girls, he investigates Chinese adoptees and their origins. Stuy also writes a controversial blog, arguing the system is fundamentally flawed; he assumes that given the economic incentives, baby buying and selling by mainland orphanages is widespread.

"There's the potential for tremendous dark-side activity," he said in an interview, part of which airs on the 2010 *Marketplace* story. "People kidnapping kids to bring them to the orphanages, people having babies simply to give them to the orphanages. If the international adoption program was not there, these children probably would not have ended up in the orphanage to begin with."

Stuy explained he'd just investigated twenty babies adopted from one particular orphanage. In more than half the cases, "the information as it relates to their finding was fabricated. Everything about the origin of the child was fiction."

For our story on Duan and the baby selling, Cecilia and I contacted the national adoption authorities in Beijing, the China Center of Adoption Affairs; they declined an interview. In the States, the US adoption industry downplayed any notion of fraud. Chuck Johnson at the National Council for Adoption in Washington agreed to be interviewed by phone. The council's vision, according to its website, "is a world in which all children everywhere have nurturing, permanent families."

"China is considered one of the premier intercountry adoption programs," Johnson told me. "They have a very strong system of laws and an extremely involved, authoritative central authority." He added that China's adoption ministry, the CCAA, investigated the Hunan scandal and found that "none of the children were adopted by American families."

I told him this conflicted with the court documents we saw, indicating at least one child was. Johnson said, "I'm not going to comment on that because I have not seen the documents. And also, we've had to rely on the investigation completed by the CCAA."

The Duan case was an exception, he said. The narrative of a one-time, local case served the interests of the US adoption industry as well as Chinese authorities. The problem is, it did not fit the evidence—or the economic incentives. When an American adoptive couple brings $3,000 (the orphanage payment has since grown to $5,000) into a local economy, that demand creates a market. It's like walking into a shopping mall offering $40,000 for a smartphone: people will respond.

The phenomenon of baby abductions is frequently reported on by local media on the mainland. Cecilia and I tallied eighty-eight domestic baby-trafficking convictions between the 2006 verdict and the 2010 airing of our story. She even called one orphanage director in Jiangxi province, who offered the equivalent of $150 for a healthy baby girl to be dropped off, no questions asked.

The Duan family story faced an extra amount of scrutiny inside *Marketplace*. Many public radio journalists have adopted from overseas, and I assume some of my colleagues found the idea of adoption fraud distressing. The radio script was put through several rounds of edits. Yet even as many in the States were shocked, I polled ten American expats in Shanghai who'd adopted babies in China. None were surprised by the story, having lived in a still-developing country with a certain level of everyday rule bending.

One US expat, Kentuckian Kathy Sue Smith, an international school teacher, shared her own suspicions of the system. She'd adopted two girls from Hunan. One, from the capital Changsha, turns out to have a twin sister, also adopted and living in the United States. This was based on a DNA match with 99 percent certainty. But here's the twist: the twin sister was adopted from a different orphanage, in Guangdong province hundreds of miles south of Hunan. It dawned on me that these presumed twins were adopted at each end of the Duan family baby-smuggling route.

No one I talked to for the story suggested that there could be an independent investigation into Chinese adoption fraud. Too many

interests—on the mainland and abroad—were aligned in support
the current system. One adoption executive in Holland, Ina Hut,
told me she'd tried to pursue an independent inquiry after hearing
from mainland colleagues that baby selling was widespread. But
the Dutch government warned her to back off. "They threatened to
take away our adoption license if I did," she said in a Skype interview. Her government did not want to "upset trade relations with
Beijing."

———————————

Ever since we learned of the China adoption scandal, Cathy and I
faced an obvious set of nagging personal questions: Was Guo Shanzhen caught in the baby-trafficking economy, sold to her orphanage
before we adopted her? Was her paperwork faked? Could she have
been transported to Zhuzhou by a Duan family sister, perhaps by
milk box on a train? Duan Yueneng said in 2010 this was a possibility, but there was no way he could really know. There was no way he
could identity her from a baby-photo lineup, and his baby-selling
receipts and orphanage logs did not represent every transaction.
We'll likely never know for sure.

Still, there was one lead to pursue: the police officer who supposedly found our daughter. A few months after interviewing Duan,
our family flies down to the Zhuzhou orphanage. My Shanghai
assignment for *Marketplace* is about to end, so this is one last chance
to visit before repatriating. By now, Guo Shanzhen is seven—her
brothers are ten and five—and her large, bright eyes now see the
world through pink spectacles.

She wants to own this return trip. Normally a child who stays
close to us in public, Guo Shanzhen now strides several paces ahead
of the family through the Hunan airport. At the orphanage, the
woman director greets us in the same ceremonial greeting room
from six years prior. On this hot day, I'm reminded of her fancy
office with air conditioning.

The orphanage is a shadow of its former self, now run down and
bereft of clucking baby sounds. None of the Tong children show
interest in the playground, which is now full of holes and broken
equipment. It's the scene of an old backyard swing set of a family

whose kids have long grown up and left. The courtyard is full of weeds. When we visit the orphanage children's room, we see only special-needs children and not a single healthy child. It's as if the supply of healthy girls desired by most Americans has run out, as has the Foreigner Price revenue.

This comes as no surprise. Our sources and friends in the mainland adoption world have observed the same scarcity. They offer a few possible explanations: Perhaps domestic adoptions are surging, which I doubt; never in my time in China did I run into a domestic family that adopted a child outside its extended family. Or maybe parents are abandoning girls less often and keeping them instead; I also find this hard to believe, given the continued preference for boys in the countryside. These patterns don't reverse overnight.

Most likely: healthy girls are no longer born in the first place. By now, ultrasound and abortion are widely available to terminate a pregnancy in the case of an unwanted female. Abortion in China is not a fraught religious and moral debate, the way it is in the States. Sex-selective abandonment has given way to sex-selective abortion.

On our second day in Zhuzhou we seek out police officer Zou Guohua, the man listed as the person who found Guo Shanzhen seven years prior. She and I arrive early at the local station, and within half an hour Zou walks in with a flat-top haircut and middle-aged paunch. He's very tall. And he lacks the cautious hesitation of many mainland men.

"I remember that evening clearly," he says, delving straight into his memory bank. "It was a spring night, very chilly. I got a call and found a baby in this courtyard. It was so cold." So far, everything is accurate. Zou grabs my notebook and draws a diagram of the exact location by the train tracks. If for some reason he's lying, he is very good at it.

"Is this the girl?" The officer smiles and shakes hands with my daughter, and we snap a couple of pictures before saying goodbye. The story seems to check out, though it's impossible to know. One mainland-born reporter cautioned me against overtrusting this encounter. "You don't know," she said. "What if he always had this fake story prepared in his head, for this exact conversation?"

This question can make me crazy, and for a while it does. Like our biological boys, Guo Shanzhen asks frequently about her origin story. *How much did I weigh at birth? How many inches long? How small was my hand? What was my favorite first toy?* We have no good answers, except to cite the Zhuzhou documents as if they are reliable and accurate.

Someday I will sit down with her and try to explain what we know. By then she'll be old enough and certain that I don't have all the answers, which will be helpful. First I'll tell her how we cannot imagine life without her. And then I'll start to detail this complicated tale: of people and money, of Americans and Chinese acting in their own self-interest. Who was looking out for the babies' interests? I don't know. I'll tell her how naive and trusting Cathy and I were as we entered the process, and how cynical we emerged after it. What kind of person buys babies and flips them like houses? What kind of orphanage director traffics in human beings and can still sleep at night?

At some point she will ask straight up if she was sold as a baby, at which point I will go with my gut—and that is to believe Mr. Zou, the policeman. He is the closest person to her origin story. That day in the police station, I looked him in the eye as he told the story, and I trusted him. Certainly I could be wrong, though my line of work requires a reasonable BS detector. In the end, we need stories to tell ourselves, and this is ours. And finally, if she's still listening, I'll mention the mysterious and powerful forces of globalization— forces that brought my ancestors out of China to America, and then delivered me back to the mainland to become her father.

My friend Kathy Sue Smith from Shanghai has prepared very well for this same conversation with her adopted daughters. She tells them: *Your origin story isn't the whole story, and in fact it isn't even the main story. It's just the story of where you began.*

And the rest of your story after that is with me.

Seven years after we first met, I look up Matthew Xiao again in 2011. He has left the adoption industry and moved back to his hometown of Nanning in Guangxi province. Matthew says he was fired from Holt after attempting to be a corruption whistleblower in the organization. Now outside the system, Matthew speaks much more directly.

During the heyday of Chinese adoption, he suspected Hunan orphanages like Zhuzhou profited as part of a broader supply chain. These orphanages were approved to send babies overseas, so he suspected other orphanages around China delivered baby girls to them. The upshot: more orphanages sent more babies overseas, and they split the profits. Zhuzhou was effectively one of several store-fronts for these operations. "I always assumed this was the case," he says.

There is no anger or moral judgment in his voice. The way he describes this, it's a matter of simple economics. But I have to ask him: What does he make of this whole system? Is it structurally flawed? Don't all the actors in this system deserve to know what it's really about? Doesn't he want to know the truth?

Matthew takes a breath. "You cannot say the system is all good or all bad," he begins. I've heard this line many times. The typical mainlander is better equipped than the average American to hold two opposing ideas at the same time. A system that is opaque, flawed, and even corrupt has also managed to deliver benefits to baby girls who would have been abandoned and discarded not long ago, he says.

But his takeaway is bigger than that. He sees a modern China that is starting to give a message to girls they are finally valued—at school, at work, and in the home. I begin to think about my grand-mother Mildred Zhao, her American Methodist teachers, and their aspirations for China more than a century ago. "You cannot believe what the situation was for abandoned girls in the 1980s and '90s," he says, shaking his head. "Every day, life for Chinese girls gets a little better than before."

Epilogue

One of the few terrifying moments from my childhood was the time I was locked with my mother inside a gas station for hours. At least, it seemed that way. We'd stopped at a lonely filling station in New York's Hudson Valley, "around 1973," she recalls. On that day I was still in preschool, yet I still have a faint recollection of the bad memory—likely because we've replayed it a few times since then. According to my mother's recollection, we walked around the back side of the station to enter the bathroom. There was nothing else there. As we tried to get out, the lock somehow failed, and we were trapped. I looked to my mother's face for calm assurance, but that's when she screamed out loud for help, and I melted down into a four-year-old panic attack.

"I don't remember anyone freeing us," my mother says, trying to replay the moment. She somehow found a way to liberate us, but doesn't recall how.

We became trapped in the first place because she was working to help her mother pay off debt. Grandmother Mildred in Hong Kong owed a family friend $1,000, and my parents in the States had offered to pay it off. So as my father worked at IBM, my mother concocted a gig to sell coffee machines to area filling stations. In our pale-yellow Ford Gran Torino wagon, she drove from one station to another, hawking machines and refills. In the end, "it was not a good business investment," my mother wrote in one e-mail. "We ended up bringing all the machines to the dump." Yet somehow she zeroed out her mother's debt.

Borrowing is an act of faith in yourself and your ability to pay it off. This faith can be reasonable or misplaced, but Mildred had a lot of it from early on. When she was forced to drop out of Ginling Women's College at the age of nineteen after a mental health "brokedown," she asked her former teacher Anna Graves to locate American friends willing to lend money for Mildred's tuition in the States, in case she ever got there. "My father still wants me to get a scholarship to go abroad at the time," Mildred wrote. "I don't know whether you would like to help me in this way or not." Two decades later—after losing her parents and being washed out of Wuhan by the deadliest flood in recorded history—she started over in Shanghai, by borrowing. She took on debt to build the Light of the Sea private grade school, then again to secure funds to apply to Colorado State University, and then once more as a refugee mother in Hong Kong in the 1950s. Since most banks would have turned her away, she joined informal lending clubs, or *hui*. In a *hui* each borrower puts x dollars into the pot on a monthly basis. One member of the pool withdraws the full pot for a month, after winning an interest-rate bidding contest (highest bidder wins). Then, in month two, another member takes the money, and so on. It is a common immigrant financing scheme. Mildred scraped and owed her entire life, borrowing against a future she imagined in the United States.

She of course never made it to America. I don't know if she actively gave up on her dream, or whether the fatigue of supporting three children as a widow simply caught up with her. It's clear from her letters that she measured her own worth against the achievements of her peers. In the end, "I think she lost her dignity," my mother observed.

As is often the case, the payoff came a generation later. My mother, Anna, graduated from Hong Kong's Diocesan Girls' School, the same sort of English-based, Christian education Mildred received five decades prior. After that, Anna sailed for San Francisco and eventually studied home economics at Augsburg College in Minneapolis. She worked the grill at the Big Ten Restaurant by the campus of the University of Minnesota and married an engineer from Taiwan, and their American lives began. Like many scholar families from the days of imperial China, my parents' families survived or escaped the reprisals of the Communist state and sent their children offshore to study. "We just knew we had to go out," my mother said of leaving Hong Kong to study in the States. What Mildred really passed on was the promise of what she called the light of the sea. "Magic water" is what my older son, Evan, as a toddler called the shimmering Potomac in DC. His great-grandmother saw it the same way. She died of an aneurism in April 1976. In the end, Mildred had the privilege and curse of having a window seat to an outside world she never got to visit.

Her fate was not unique. Many pioneering women saw their promises and contributions swept away in Mao's tidying up of history. I think of the five women from her era profiled in historian Wang Zheng's *Women in the Chinese Enlightenment*. Each chose not to join the Communist Party (or left it early on), and as a result had her story excluded from the party canon. The stories rhyme in certain ways with Mildred's. One woman attended a missionary school, studied in the States, and returned to China a political activist. Things got worse from there. Her husband was executed for aiding the Japanese occupation in World War II. She herself was arrested during the score settling of the Cultural Revolution, accused of working for the CIA as a secret agent. She died in a Shanghai prison, which refused to send her ashes to her family. In a symbolic gesture, relatives buried her comb in a tomb. Another disguised herself as a boy to enter school, studied economics in Japan, and founded a school emphasizing physical education—to literally strengthen Chinese women. When the Communists nationalized the school, authorities found photos of her with Guomindang officials. They fired her. She went on to open a knitting shop on Nanjing Road. "If I were a man, I would not be in this shape," she told Wang Zheng.

Another woman stubbornly refused to get married. She disdained as "flower vases" women employed by companies as decorations to attract male clients. She also opened a school, but in the Maoist era ripped up a poster of the Great Helmsman, inviting the inevitable persecution. Here is her money quote: "If a woman marries a chicken, she has to follow the chicken; if she marries a dog, she has to follow the dog."

"My friends have all passed away," one eighty-eight-year-old interviewee told Wang. "I won't be able to die with my eyes closed if I do not tell the stories of these sisters." She designed her own tombstone, etching on it the names of several female peers. She herself died three months after that.

In an e-mail, I asked Wang Zheng to place my own grandmother's life in some perspective. She replied: "Your grandma was implicated by politics of her time, which led to many tragedies in her life. However, the spirit to be independent was a shared value for all the educated women who were shaped by May Fourth feminism, regardless of their political orientations."

Wang argues that these May Fourth women won a "breakthrough in the long process of Chinese women's liberation." Today, a girl born in China has a 95 percent chance of knowing how to read, and will live to be seventy-seven, on average. She'll join a workforce with more female participation than Japan or the United States. She inhabits an empirically driven, science- and GDP-focused China (if anything, overly so). And if she lives in Shanghai, she won't even have to carry her own purse, a duty now outsourced to her subordinate male partner.

To be sure, there's more to do. Women's salaries are falling off, relative to those of men. Many of today's Material Girls obsess about marrying Material Boys with property. The top party bosses remain male. And yet, when my third cousin's teen granddaughter in the inconsequential Tong village greets me with a forceful jab in the chest, I pick myself off the floor and thank the early, big-footed Cinderella's Sisters who ended up on the wrong side of history.

It's now been six years since my family and I left Shanghai and returned to suburban Virginia. Our China memories fade by the day. Sure, a painting of the Bund waterfront circa 1920 hangs over our mantel (it was produced beautifully by a migrant artist for the Foreigner Price of $30). We often cook our nanny Ayi's Subei wings and sweet garlic broccoli. But the kids' Mandarin has pretty much gone out the window; Cathy has returned to her primary care medicine job unavailable to her in Shanghai; the boys play travel soccer, engaging us fully in the parenting arms race, American flavor. I find myself sighing over our day-to-day "issues." A breakdown in the air-conditioned subway. A leaking valve cover gasket (whatever that is). A prescription delivered late. Dog pee in the basement. Mutual-fund fees. We take these lives pretty much for granted, except on the occasion I find myself in Houston.

My reporting job at *Marketplace* now focuses on environment and energy issues, and periodically this work takes me to the energy capital. The oil business is of course a boom/bust sector for unabashed risk takers, so it's fitting that Grandmother Mildred lies at rest there. For decades, her ashes lived in a crowded Hong Kong cemetery, but when Aunt Lily moved to Texas in the early 1980s, she brought the urn with her. On a late autumn day in 2016, about a dozen of my family members and friends gather before her tombstone at the Forest Park Cemetery on Westheimer Road. At my behest, we have come to remember someone else: her late husband, Carleton Sun, my maternal grandfather, six decades after his passing. For the first time, there is a place in the world where he can be remembered.

My parents and older brother have flown in from the West Coast. Also joining us is a distant cousin of mine from California, whose grandfather was Carleton's brother. When this brother died in his early twenties, Carleton took care of his widow and his brother's three daughters, bringing them out of the Hubei village to live in Shanghai. At this ceremony we have no remains to bury, though I've brought the soil I scooped up from the mass grave site at the Delingha prison labor camp. Since then, I've waited three years to bury my grandfather, symbolically, on the advice of the woman bureaucrat in the Qinghai provincial prison department.

My Houston-based cousin Marjorie says a prayer, and then I'm given five minutes to summarize everything I've learned about Carleton Sun, which is impossible. So I race through a timeline of his life, interspersing quotes here and there from family letters: his birth into a merchant family in the dying days of imperial China;

his meeting the daughter of his father's work colleague ("we two were small friends"); confiscation of his family's land ("his family property was occupied by the Communists for nearly seven years"); his participation in college student protests against foreign imperialism. My attempt to lighten things up by mentioning his mediocre college grades falls flat. No chuckles.

I take a breath. Then I mention his fateful decision to work for the Japanese occupation of China during World War II. A couple of nods. This is when I mount his criminal defense, which may matter only to me. Looking back, I say, we know the victors from that period—the Communists, the Guomindang—got to write the history we read today. I cite the argument of convicted collaborator Chen Bijun, who won a courtroom ovation for arguing it was actually the collaborators who fed the local people. They were the ones who traded land for peace and halted the killings. They were the true patriots, Chen's argument goes, not the other parties who retreated like cowards.

A couple of heads nod again, but mostly the audience remains stoic. That is the Chinese way, but it also tells me it's time to move on. In framing his story on the right or the wrong side of history, I am playing the Chinese Communist Party's game—on their turf. In challenging the party's historiography about who the true patriots and enemies are, I am viewing the past through their lens. The older generation here has long moved beyond this fight. It's me who has come late to understanding my grandfather's life on his terms, not anyone else's.

My five minutes are up. I close briefly with what I learned about his arrest, sentence, and imprisonment, and end with this anecdote: he rewarded his children for taking cod liver oil with ten peanuts. But don't eat the nubby seed of the nut, he warned, "or else peanuts will grow out the top of your head."

It's now Aunt Lily's turn to speak about her father. She ends up speaking directly to him. She leans forward in her chair and faces a large, grainy photo of Carleton Sun we've blown up from his 1950 passport picture. She says: "I am going to speak *jiali hua*." Family dialect. What she spoke at home to her parents is a jumbled mix of Mandarin, Hubei, and Nanjing dialect that is remarkably easy for me to understand. "In 1950 you dropped us off at the train station," she begins. "We went to Hong Kong and you stayed behind. Then we heard you were locked up, and we were so worried. You took such good care of us."

Then she proceeds to update him on the last six decades, as if it's a family Christmas letter to catch him up. "The three of us children are still around. Anna and I live in the United States; right now we are in Houston. Brother Eddie is in Hong Kong. I saw him last year. Anna will likely go visit him next year. You don't have to worry about us any more—we are all doing very well. Every day I write ink-brush characters, but not as good as you." It is odd to hear an eighty-something aunt speak this way, even though she is speaking to a father she last saw at the age of seventeen.

She says that because of the information I have found, "we finally can have an understanding of your life. This is the burial ground of your wife. And my husband. And for me. Before long we can see each other again, and I can call you 'Father' one more time. Thank you that you married a woman who could take care of us all these years." Then Aunt Lily yields to my mother, who stands and reads from her iPad.

My mother speaks with a quiet anguish that makes me wonder if she'll make it through. "After I came back from my trip with Scott from China, I was incredibly saddened," she says. "I was saddened for my parents for their hard lives, and the unthinkable torture my dad had to endure while he was in prison. So to this dark place I rarely dared to venture." The wound from her childhood never really healed. So many Chinese people of a certain age walk around with these same wounds just beneath the surface. In my mother's case, her reckoning began with therapy, convincing her "to stop feeling so guilty" and to focus on her parents' essential hope: for their children to have better lives than theirs. "To remember them and thank them." It's a cliché in America that a parent wants his or her child to have a better life, but in the early 1950s China, it was hard to imagine what that might have looked like.

My mother concludes by holding up his passport from 1950, with a blue cover and visas stamped inside for Argentina, Chile, and the United States. In the end, he never left China. "Even though it never materialized, this is the passport. And after sixty years, he is here. So my wish for my mom and dad is to finally rest in peace together, in a place they didn't get to come when they were alive." Her words bring to mind an image: when she and her siblings left Shanghai during the war, they set out with a heavy trunk full of family photos and heirlooms. But on the long journey south, they had to get rid of the chest—perhaps to keep moving. In the same way, my mother has had to slough off this heavy burden of guilt in order to continue forward.

After the last speaker, a four-person Chinese choir sings the Mandarin version of my mother's favorite hymn:

When peace, like a river, attendeth my way,
When sorrows like sea billows roll;
Whatever my lot, Thou hast taught me to say,
It is well, it is well with my soul.

At the end, we each place a yellow Texas rose at the base of my grandmother's tomb stone and then sprinkle a handful of Qinghai graveyard soil on top. It's the closest we can come to burying him, at least for now (I will continue looking for any records of his life and death). At some point Carleton Sun's name will be etched on the same stone. We have spoken his name aloud so many times this day, and I wonder when the last time was that my mother and aunt did that. His name for so many years had only been whispered in shame.

———————

For me, discovering Carleton and Mildred has opened up something bigger. I now locate their hopes and hurts in a broader picture of China—and its long, interrupted opening up to the outside world. At the start of this project, I sought to step back and try to refocus my own lens and challenge my assumptions about the Deng Xiaoping reboot and China's supposed instant rise. To be sure, there is no definitive take on any history. "You can't *prove* history" the way you write out a math proof in high school, one Beijing historian lectured me early on. Each of us lives through a series of events and then packages them in a particular way. How it affects you dictates how you frame the picture. Still, there is a framing that makes most sense to me. If you've endured reading up to this point, it's probably obvious to you by now. But just to restate my view—borrowed from intellectual historians—it goes something like this:

Mildred and Carleton were born children of the Chinese enlightenment, its Great Opening to the early twentieth-century connected age. They worked in the cultural import business, bringing ashore the isms from overseas: Darwinism, feminism, Marxism, empiricism, Adam Smithism. *I am asked to play in chapel, Glee Club, and YWCA meetings sometimes.*

These cultural transactions had counter-parties, Westerners who found their way into the treaty ports, including Welthy Honsinger Fisher of Rome, New York. *Firm of chin, large of mouth, deep bosomed, and straight backed, and was sure I cut a figure that did not suggest the Methodist missionary-teacher on her way to the Chinese interior.*

Much has been written and alleged about the outsiders, who traded and shot their way in, who were arrogant, who built hospitals, who brought opium and civilization all at once. But equally important are the Chinese nationals they influenced, who adopted the leading ideas and transplanted them onto local soil. Some mainlanders found their way abroad, in search of revolution and science. They sought to turn the page for themselves and for a weak China. Great-Grandfather Tong Zhenyong was one of these first movers.

For all the promise, this golden age did not lift up the Chinese masses. The impact was limited mostly to treaty ports. Into these beachheads of modernity came steamships and sewers, protests and political pushback, gaslights and Glee Clubs, nationalism and natural feet for girls. It also didn't last. The Great Opening yielded to a Great Interruption, a series of events that closed the window to the outside and turned China inward: Floods. Nationalism. Infighting. Invasion. Mao. *In 1949 I was in the prime of my life . . . but my life has been wasted since then.*

Out went the nefarious foreign influences and what the regime called the Four Olds: old customs, old culture, old habits, old ideas. Those with overseas relations were persecuted, exiled to farms, and kicked to the back of the line. Uncle Tong Bao lived this story. Some were fortunate to get out (including maternal grandmother Mildred Zhao) even as the political net ensnared those left behind. Mildred's husband, Carleton Sun, was imprisoned. Tong Bao was left behind. Into this age of scapegoating and rationing came the next generation of only children: cousin Tong Chengkan and Cecilia Chen. *The price was forty kilograms' worth of grain ration coupons. My parents went home that night and thought about whether to buy me a brother. But by the next morning, he was already sold.*

They were also born into a Great Resumption, an age that tapped into the golden age of the bourgeoisie of the pre-Mao period. Many capitalists never went out of business during this time. Education never went out of style. Tong Bao's generation of children of the intellectual elite lived before and after the Maoist trials, returning to universities when they reopened in the late 1970s. Other intellectuals and bankers who fled during the 1949 Communist liberation returned from places like Singapore, Hong Kong, and Taiwan (with their technology, contacts, money, and ideas). The economic historian Thomas Rawski calls education in China a historic "embedded institution" that never went away, along with what he calls "market thinking." These are the old and deep roots. "A lot of people who write about China now think it started in 1949 or even 1976," he told me. "It just in my view doesn't work that way."

Rawski doesn't discount the role of the Communist Party. In fact he credits it for doing what the predecessor GMD could not: put the power and finance of a centralized state behind market reforms—to scale them, to let people move around to where they could make the most things and the most money, to build the infrastructure to connect people and ideas and investors, to let small companies form and thrive and fail. And of course the party allowed in technology and investment from overseas Chinese and foreigners on the outside. The larger point, though, is that today's China is far more than a simple (or nefarious, if you're so inclined) Communist Party story. It is also a story of long delayed modernization, what economists call "catch up," finally happening for hundreds of millions of people.

My great fortune has been to learn this story through my own family. In a way, that makes the long China story my own. But there is also great misfortune here: many ancestors were doomed to have front-row seats to history. Actually, no: like so many, they were in fact thrust onto the stage to play the villains in the show. Across several generations of the Tongs and the Suns, most gambled on the opportunity of going out of China. Of those who placed their bets at exactly the wrong time, I see in my head the weary, shaking head of Tong Daren, my late third cousin in the Tong family village who got the worst plot of land because of his "overseas relations." I see the winter icicle water torture dripped upon Tong Bao's mother for the same political crime. And I hear Uncle Tong Bao's simple explanation for all this: "It was because of Dad."

And I think of Grandmother Mildred, who at a young age read what was then a scandalous commentary on the role of women: Henrik Ibsen's *A Doll's House*. You may recall the ending: the main character Nora is trapped in a hopeless marriage to a narcissistic man who calls her "lark" and "featherbrain." In the final scene, she challenges the male-dominant world, and her status as her father's "doll-child" and her husband's "doll-wife." Nora states: "I must try and educate myself—you are not the man to help me in that. I must do that for myself. And that is why I am going to leave you now." She walks out the door and slams it, and the play ends. We don't know how it turns out for Nora, but Grandmother Mildred yearned for the same opportunity to venture out.

China's reopening provided fruits to Uncle Tong Bao and his son, cousin Tong Chengkan. At the same time, the money flows coming in also invited corruption, of officials lining their own pockets in orphanages delivering baby girls to America. Those girls may have included my own daughter.

Looking back on this incredibly broad sweep of time, it's as if I've hiked up a punishing mountain of history with my intergenerational team. It has been a privilege to take this trip. Not long ago, Cathy, the kids, and I trekked up Old Rag Mountain in Shenandoah National Park, a place with many boulders and not enough water.

Only when we crested the peak could we turn around and take in the terrain we'd covered. When I look out on the winding switch-back trail of the Tongs and the Suns, I see many attributes and qualities I'd use to describe the Chinese people in general: Resilient. Pragmatic. Opportunistic. Exploring. Thin-skinned. Gritty. Weary.

Much of this I knew, though one takeaway came as a surprise. I met so many regular people—on roadsides and inside third-rate government offices—willing to help me chase this story. This is unusual. As a foreign correspondent in China, I reliably got nowhere asking strangers for help: they walked away, hung up, and uttered *bu tai qing chu*, it's not so clear. There was nothing in it for them. For this project, there were no quid pro quos for the people who reopened their memories, connecting me with others, flipped through prison records and offered a bed for the night.

For those relatives still alive, surely it was not easy to speak openly of their victories and failings. In China, it's one thing to spill your guts at the dinner table in private, and quite another to speak information that might be published overseas. Cousin Chengkan shared hours of his time, patiently answering my questions and not knowing what I might write, and for this I am indebted to him. He also taught me that for all the opportunities globalization has brought to China, there is also a cost. Chinese cultural history is being forgotten by the day.

Will this opening continue? Or will China—as in regular Chinese people—turn away from the outside world and inward? I am not so sure. Certainly, there is a movement afoot in the world today to pull back and raise drawbridges. Beijing has taken more measures to favor domestic state-owned companies at the expense of foreign multinationals. Chinese President Xi Jinping has played up nation-alism and xenophobia, and state newspapers warn of "hostile for-eign forces." The Chinese military with regard to disputed islands has taken on a distinctly muscular posture. In the end, though, it's my view that the Chinese people know they need the out-side world.

Mainland students are flocking to American universities in num-bers not seen before; during my fellowship year at the University of Michigan, by far the second language I heard most on campus was

Mandarin. Any game-changing innovation that can scale globally will likely come from outside China. Mainlanders of certain means are still snatching up Starbucks lattes and Samsungs and iPhones. Conversely, they're not sure whether to invest in a domestic Chinese economy that is slowing down. The real estate market remains notorious for booms and busts. "Every one of my friends has sent her money overseas," my old landlord from Shanghai told me during a 2014 trip there. "And their kids." She subsequently moved her family, including two children, to London.

When I've reported in other countries, the Chinese footprint has been unmistakable. When I reported in Kenya's capital of Nairobi, a Chinese infrastructure company was building a freeway overpass, to the delight of my taxi driver there. "The Chinese are so fast, and they don't come in and tell us what to do," he said. "Just business." In Addis Ababa in Ethiopia, just outside my hotel, there was a car dealership for the mainland brand Lifan. In Venezuela, my third cousin Tong Daren's son-in-law recently completed a two-year construction stint for a Chinese state-owned firm partnering with the Venezuelan oil producer PDVSA. In São Paulo, much of Brazil's slowdown has been blamed on sagging exports of soybeans and other commodities to China. Oil drillers in West Texas are trying to assess Chinese demand to get a sense of whether the global price of crude will rise.

The world is clearly a part of China's present and future. But the point here is that this has been the case for China's past as well. Some of the key supporting actors have been Chinese cultural middlemen who ventured out in the first place. But theirs is a quiet chapter in history, given the xenophobic, anti-foreign campaigns that followed.

––––––––––

On that day in Houston when we symbolically buried my grandfather, I realized that in the end, much of my pursuit of his life did not succeed. To this day, we do not know where he died, exactly when (the year 1957 is often suggested), or how. My mother and Aunt Lily do not seem much to care at this point, but this reporter will keep chasing the story. As best we know, he died in the gulag around the time of the great famine, in his midforties—the age I am now.

But for his children, they prefer to remember him as the father who said goodbye to them at the Shanghai train station in 1950. He dropped them off on the 4:30 train bound, eventually, for Hong Kong. Then he returned home to the Light of the Sea School and wrote his seven-year-old daughter:

> My heart always follows you. I hope you can go to school. You left your playing cards behind. I hope you can find something else to play.

December 2016, Houston, Texas

Sources

For Chinese characters, I have used the system of romanization used on the mainland known as *hanyu pinyin*. There are a few exceptions, for alternative spellings that are familiar to many Americans—for instance, Chiang Kai-shek, Sun Yat-sen, and Taipei. My grandmother Mildred Zhao went by other surnames in her letters, including Djao and Chao.

I have quoted each person of significance by given name, with three exceptions. Uncle Tong Bao actually uses his mother's surname. He does not live in a world of oversharing Americans and has told me several times he's uncomfortable making public his "private affairs." The same applies to my cousin Tong Chengkan. My daughter in this manuscript goes by her orphanage name, Guo Shanzhen, rather than the English name she uses today. She deserves to shape her own identity rather than one set by her father. In these three cases, my editor agrees that identifying them by their current names would not add any benefit to the reader but bring real costs to them.

I have described historical events as accurately as possible, based on written and oral sources. In cases of fuzzy or conflicting recollections, or based solely on one person's oral memory, I have sought to identify that uncertainty. The main research for this manuscript took place during visits to China after my 2006–10

Shanghai assignment for *Marketplace* public radio. I returned in the summers of 2011, 2013, and 2014. I'm particularly indebted to Uncle Tong Bao, his wife, Qi Menglan, and their son, cousin Tong Chengkan, for spending countless hours sharing their life experiences with me. More than anyone else, they inform my understanding of today's China and how it has come of age. Special thanks also to Tong Daren's daughters, Tong Yuqin and Tong Yuhua, for hosting me every trip to the Tong family village.

Many China academics provided me hours of explanation and analysis. They include Shanghai economic historian and commentator Ye Tan, economic historian Thomas Rawski of the University of Pittsburgh (author of the paper "From Divergence to Convergence: Reevaluating the History Behind China's Economic Boom"), historian Clayton Dube of the University of Southern California, MIT economics and management professor Yasheng Huang (his book is *Capitalism with Chinese Characteristics*), University of Hong Kong historian Frank Dikötter (*The Age of Openness, Mao's Great Famine*) and historian Odd Arne Westad of the London School of Economics (*Restless Empire: China and the World Since 1750*).

My grandmother's letters to her American teachers are housed in two places: the special collection of Welthy Honsinger Fisher at Boston University's Howard Gotlieb Archival Research Center, and Anna Melissa Graves's collection at Swarthmore College's Peace Collection. The archive of Ginling Women's College at its sister school, Smith College in Massachusetts, also provided valuable archival documents and photos.

I began this project expecting little to no help from government archives and officers in China. My time as a reporter in China led me to assume public offices were xenophobic, corrupt, or useless—or all three. How wrong I was. I'm thankful to the Tilanqiao prison guard who guided me through the document process there, and to the neighborhood police officer near the Light of the Sea School who turned up a dusty yellow household registration book from 1950. In Hubei, the Hanchuan foreign affairs office led us to the Zhao family village and one of two valuable genealogies on my mother's side of the family. A special shout-out goes to (1) the officer at the Shanghai municipal police headquarters who bent a couple rules to find Grandfather Carleton Sun's official sentence and conviction date; (2) Mr. Jin, the retired Qinghai prison department official (now an Amway salesman) who snuck me past the building guard and into the prisoner file room; and (3) the retired worker from the Delingha labor camp who would not speak for the record but poured out his memories out of a "responsibility to history."

At the outset of this project, I told myself I could really use a couple of semesters at a major university with a serious China studies department. That's where the University of Michigan came in. The university's Knight-Wallace journalism fellows program admitted me to their 2013/14 class, providing me the college do-over I never thought I'd get. Historian Pär Cassel let me audit his course on treaty ports ("islands of modernity," in his words) and continued conversations over lunch in Ann Arbor to help me frame this narrative. University of Bristol historian Robert Bickers (*The Scramble for China: Foreign Devils in the Qing Empire, 1832–1914*) met with me the morning before his guest lecture to Cassel's class. Linda Lim of Michigan's Ross School of Business discussed how Chinese people over time have dealt with their own "cultural hybridity," a term that aptly describes many of my ancestors, particularly my grandmother Mildred Zhao. How typical was she? *Women in the Chinese Enlightenment: Oral and Textual Histories*, by mainland-born Wang Zheng in the gender and women's studies institute at Michigan, provided instances of similar women in similar times. Wang Zheng spoke with me and tried to situate my grandmother in that time. Many thanks also to University of Michigan historians Charles Bright, for allowing me to audit his course on globalization history, and Juan Cole, for his historical insights.

My time at Michigan offered me the chance to delve into a host of recommended books. On general history: *China: A New History* (John King Fairbank); *The Search for Modern China* (Jonathan Spence); *The Chinese Economy: Transitions and Growth* (Barry Naughton); *Deng Xiaoping and the Transformation of China* (Ezra Vogel); *Historical Perspective on Contemporary Asia* (Merle Goldman); *Forgotten Ally: China's World War II, 1937–1945* (Rana Mitter); *Rural Development in China* (Dwight Perkins, Shahid Yusuf); *China on the Eve of the*

Communist Takeover (Doak Barnett); *Wuhan, 1938: War, Refugees, and the Making of Modern China* (Stephen McKinnon); *From the Ruins of Empire: The Intellectuals Who Remade Asia* (Pankaj Mishra); *Diamond Hill: Memories of Growing Up in a Hong Kong Squatter Village* (Feng Chi-shun).

On treaty ports: *Shanghai: China's Gate to Modernity* (Marie-Claire Bergère); *In Search of Old Shanghai* (Lynn Pan); *Shanghai Splendor* (Lynn Pan); *Global Shanghai, 1850–2010* (Jeffrey Wasserstrom).

On prison labor camps: *Grass Soup* (Zhang Xianliang); *Prisoner of Mao* (Bao Ruo-Wang, Rudolph Chelminski); *New Ghosts, Old Ghosts: Prisons and Labor Reform Camps in China* (James Seymour, Richard Anderson); *Great Wall of Confinement: The Chinese Prison Camp through Contemporary Fiction and Reportage* (Philip Williams, Yenna Wu).

On wartime collaboration: *Collaboration* (Timothy Brook); *Chinese Collaboration with Japan, 1932–1945: The Limits of Accommodation* (David Barrett, Larry Shyu, editors); *In the Shadow of the Rising Sun: Shanghai under Japanese Occupation* (Christian Henriot, Wen-hsin Yeh, editors); *Wang Jingwei: A Political Biography* (Tang Leang Li).

On women in Chinese history: *Gender and Education in China* (Paul Bailey); *Writing Women in Modern China: An Anthology of Women's Literature from the Early Twentieth Century* (Amy Dooling, Kristina Torgeson); *To Light a Candle* (Welthy Honsinger Fisher).

On adoption: *Sold Into Adoption: The Hunan Baby Trafficking Scandal Exposes Vulnerabilities in Chinese Adoptions to the United States* (Patricia Meier, Xiaole Zhang); *The Missing Girls of China: Population, Policy, Culture, Gender, Abortion, Abandonment, and Adoption in East-Asian Perspective* (David Smolin).

This book project was shepherded by many. Carole Sargent in the scholarly publications office at Georgetown University advised me on the book proposal and contract. Pietra Rivoli, business professor and author at Georgetown, encouraged me to insert myself into the narrative. Travis Holland in the creative writing department at the University of Michigan provided constructive suggestions throughout the process. I am in the debt of editor Priya Nelson at the University of Chicago Press for her initial interest in this project, and for providing much-needed narrative focus to an unwieldy first draft. The keen eye of copyeditor Johanna Rosen-bohm saved me from myself countless times throughout this man-uscript; any errors are mine alone.

I thank all the colleagues who read draft sections and provided insightful suggestions: Clayton Dube, Laura Starecheski, Cynthia Rodriguez, Travis Holland, Don Lee, Linda Lim, Pär Cassel, Curt Nickisch, Tony Wan, Mei Fong, Adam Allington, Peter Clowney, and Paul Orzulak. And of course my parents, Anna and Alvin Tong—who spent countless hours reading drafts but, more important, let me share these illuminating, shameful, painful, and noble stories with you the reader—and my wife, Cathy Tong. They made this entire journey with me, and this book is for them.

AVON PUBLIC LIBRARY
BOX 977 / 200 BENCHMARK RD.
AVON, CO 81620